THE LIBRARY OF LIBERAL ARTS

Oskar Piest, *Founder*

THE ODYSSEY

THE
ODYSSEY
OF HOMER

Translated by
Ennis Rees

Macmillan Publishing Company
NEW YORK

Collier Macmillan Canada
TORONTO

Maxwell Macmillan International
NEW YORK OXFORD SINGAPORE SYDNEY

Macmillan Publishing Company
866 Third Avenue, New York, New York 10022

Collier Macmillan Canada, Inc.
1200 Eglinton Avenue East
Suite 200
Don Mills, Ontario M3C 3N1

Library of Congress Cataloging-in-Publication Data

Homer.
   [Odyssey.   English]
   The odyssey of Homer / translated by Ennis Rees.
      p.   cm.—(Library of liberal arts)
   Translation of Odyssey
   Includes bibliographical references and index
   ISBN 0-02-399141-0
   1. Odysseus (Greek mythology)   I. Rees, Ennis,   II. Title.
III. Series: Library of liberal arts (Macmillan Publishing Company)
PA4025.A5R4   1991
883'.01—dc20   90-49756
                      CIP

Printing: 1 2 3 4 5 6 7   Year: 1 2 3 4 5 6 7

TO JEFFREY,
AMY, AND
ANDREW

About the Translator

Ennis Rees attended the College of William and Mary and
Harvard University, then taught at Duke University and
Princeton University before coming to the University of
South Carolina, where he is an emeritus professor of English.
In addition to his translations of Homer and Aesop, he is the
author of a book of selected poems and a number of books of
verse for children.

The Greek text of the *Odyssey*, used in making this translation, was edited by David B. Monro and Thomas W. Allen
and published by the Oxford University Press in 1908.

CONTENTS

CONTENTS

INTRODUCTION

I. It is at least probable that the *Iliad* and the *Odyssey* are largely the work of one great poet, or perhaps two, who flourished over twenty-five hundred years ago. Both poems are consciously and elaborately organized, and the convincing and subtle characterization is remarkably consistent from one to the other. Myths, the rich language of epic formulae, and many of the technical devices the poet used were doubtless part of his heritage as a bard, and it seems certain that the art of poetry in the Aegean area was a very old art long before Homer put hand to lyre. We may also be sure that he greatly enriched the language and tradition in which he worked, for to his material he brought verbal and structural powers of the first order. At any rate, the two Homeric poems became the primary and most important educational influence on Greek culture and one of the most powerful forces that worked to form the mind of Europe and the modern world. To our literary and cultural tradition Homer is central. His poems have informed our liberal education for centuries and continue to be an influence of great fertility, as, with special reference to the *Odyssey*, the names of Joyce and Kazantzakis are enough to indicate.

Why are the poems of Homer so universal in significance and perennial in appeal? First, he tells a good story and tells it well. What Sidney says of the poet is true of him: "with a tale forsooth he cometh unto you, with a tale which holdeth children from play, and old men from the chimney corner." But however literally Homer may or may not have taken his poems, we are naturally conscious of their symbolic import. And for us, Homer, like other poets, deals in metaphor, in what Robert Frost calls "the pleasure of ulteriority," or "saying one thing in terms of another." If his fables were not essentially and obviously metaphorical—saying life is a battle, life is a journey—one is at liberty to doubt if they would have lasted so well or attracted such a various audience. In both poems we see heroes go from a state of alienation to one of reconciliation, thus symbolizing, dramatically and beautifully, the deepest and most enduring concerns of people everywhere. Then too, the poet's sense of humor is both subtle and large. No wonder children are enthralled by the action or that more mature readers have found aesthetic, ethical, and religious satisfaction in the poetic myths of Homer. After all, the myth of death and rebirth, the journey from sin to redemption—in short, the return, is surely one of the most central and universal images in the human soul.

We may also do well to remember that the long narrative of Odysseus to the Phaeacians, of the Cyclops, Circe, and so forth (Bks. IX-XII), may be more consciously metaphorical than has been generally thought. The poet means it to contrast with the idealized life and institutions in Phaeacia, and Odysseus tells it well. But he seldom tells strangers anything literally. He prefers to fabricate, to speak in metaphor and say precisely what his experience has been like. These stories and fabulous tales, he says in effect, are *like* what I have been through, and thousands have agreed that they are also like what they have been through. But whatever the attitude of Odysseus himself toward his tales, for us he speaks as a poet who takes considerable satisfaction in finding and expressing symbolic action that tells his listener not what literally happened but what his experience amounted to in moral and spiritual, that is to say, poetic, terms. Immediately, of course, his fabrications serve the surface functions of deception, entertainment, and so forth.

From ancient times to the present, many readers have appreciated the poems ethically and allegorically. Homer himself consciously allegorizes at times and is without doubt aware of the ethical import of his action, and possibly he would not have objected too strenuously to efforts of Renaissance readers to make this element central in his work. In the early seventeenth century, George Chapman studied the story of Odysseus, the gifted man who massacres the Cicones and is harassed by the sea god Poseidon for blinding the only eye of his son the Cyclops, Odysseus the patient man whom Athena, goddess of wisdom, helps, and who goes from a state of homeless alienation to one of peace and security at home again—Chapman read, and with the help of earlier commentaries concluded that "the information or fashion of an absolute man, and necessary (or fatal) passage through many afflictions (according with the most sacred Letter) to his natural haven and country, is the whole argument and scope of this inimitable and miraculous poem." In other words, it could be read as an effective Christian allegory. Nor is it very difficult to see how earlier readers found religious meaning in the old poem. The situation of the family in Ithaca and the return of their savior Odysseus, as well as the spiritual progress of Odysseus himself, do very well in the realm of symbolic representation to suggest "that religion" which, says Pascal, "has always existed on earth, which consists in believing that man has fallen from a state of glory and of communion with God into a state of sorrow, penitence, and estrangement from God, but that after this life we shall be restored by a Messiah who should have come. All things have passed away, and this has endured, for which all things are." So the *Odyssey* remained a vital book through centuries of Christian-humanistic education, and its poetry continued to convey not only aesthetic delight but the nature and significance of decay and regeneration, of sin and redemption.

In more modern times the poem has provided spiritual nourishment of a not dissimilar kind. Chapman and Professor Jaeger agree that, whatever else it may be, the *Odyssey* is essentially a religious poem where, as in the *Iliad*, the world of men and the world of gods are inseparable. Denton Snider, in one of the most stimulating commentaries we have on the *Odyssey*, offers a reading of the poem which is very much in line with this view and centuries of interpretation. "The theme," he says, "deals with the wise man, who, through his intelligence, was able to take Troy, but who has now another and greater problem—the return out of the grand estrangement caused by the Trojan expedition. Spiritual restoration is the key-note of

this *Odyssey,* as it is that of all the great Books of Literature."
And recently Bruno Snell, commenting on Homer, has given
us more in much the same vein: "the reflections which the
myths are designed to assist usually produce a greater sense of
humility; the majority of the paradigms teach men to realize
their status as men, the limitations upon their freedom, the
conditional nature of their existence. They encourage self-
knowledge in the spirit of the Delphic motto: 'Know thyself,'
and thus they extol measure, order, and moderation."

Still we may, indeed must, read the poems primarily for
the story, for a whole new world of exciting experience pre-
sented with art, insight, and gusto, including but transcending
any merely ethical significance. The "descriptions and simili-
tudes" of Homer, says Goethe, "seem poetic to us; yet they are
of an inexpressible naturalness, though delineated, of course,
with a purity and intimacy never equaled. Even the strangest
and most fantastic of the described occurrences have an in-
evitable naturalness. . . . the ancients represent life itself; we
commonly describe its effects." And as Dio of Prusa said in the
first century A.D., "Homer praised almost everything—animals
and plants, water and earth, armor and horses. In fact, he
passed over nothing without somehow honoring and glorifying
it." Such a statement reminds us that Homer and Walt Whit-
man, for instance, have a good deal in common, and that both
are part of one long and great poetic and cultural tradition.

Finally, every good poet must be not only interesting and
exciting but significant as well, and Homer measures up. His
poems, the one of war, the other of return, his symbolic stories
of Achilles and Odysseus, have to do with spiritual loss and
recovery in the individual and society, and hence are never
likely to lack a responsive audience.

II. In the following paragraphs I have assembled further
information which a reader of Homer might like to know or be
reminded of.

The poet speaks of a time several centuries before his own,

a heroic era that he regards in a way not too unlike that in which some of our writers regard the Civil War years. But often his epic similes give us vivid glimpses into his own world and time, and greatly enlarge the scope and interest of the poems. He never calls his people Greeks, but always Achaeans, Danaans, or Argives. His language consists to a large extent of epic formulae, traditional expressions like "swift-footed Achilles" and "noble, long-suffering Odysseus" which are part of the bard's standard equipment as an oral composer and reciter of poems and which he thinks nothing of repeating whenever his mood, material, and especially his meter will allow. Homer not infrequently repeats passages of considerable length several times in a poem. Scholars have shown that fairly long and elaborate poems may be orally composed and rather accurately remembered for many generations, but they have also made it clear that Homer very probably had the assistance of writing. The division of the poems into books, however, is thought to have been made in the third century B.C. by scholars at Alexandria, especially Zenodotus of Ephesus, head of the library.

The Achaeans have been sieging the city of Troy for more than nine years when the *Iliad* opens. Paris, son of Priam, the King of Troy, had started the war by abducting Helen, the beautiful wife of his host, Menelaus of Sparta. Agamemnon, brother of Menelaus and commander-in-chief of the Achaean expeditionary forces, performs a similar act at Troy by willfully taking the girl Briseis from her lover, the mighty Achilles. Thus the *Iliad* deals with the wrath of Achilles, who withdraws from the fighting and refuses to return until finally the death of his best friend Patroclus at the hands of Hector, son of Priam and mainstay of Troy, forces him into reconciliation with Agamemnon and battle again. He wins in a fight with Hector, and the *Iliad* ends with the return and burning of Hector's body. After the war, which Achilles does not survive, the various heroes are faced with all the problems of return and rehabilitation that have resulted from a decade of camp life and warfare. The *Odyssey* deals with the return of Odysseus, with how he gets home and what he does when he gets there. It also tells us something of other returns, especially that of Agamemnon, whom his wife Clytemnestra and her lover Aegisthus murdered shortly after his arrival in Argos.

Throughout both poems the power of the gods is constantly present. As the invocation of the *Iliad* says, "the will of Zeus was done." In that poem the gods are divided in two factions supporting the earthly factions of Achaean and Trojan warriors. Zeus, the almighty "Father of gods and men," helps both sides. His wife Hera, Athena, and Poseidon, plus Hephaestus, god of fire and famous artificer, Hermes, messenger of the gods, and Achilles' immortal mother, the sea nymph Thetis, all support the Achaeans, while the Trojan side is helped by Apollo, archer god of pestilence as well as the lyre, and his sister Artemis, goddess of the chase and of sudden fatal illness in women, by the love goddess Aphrodite and her lover Ares, god of war. In the *Odyssey* Poseidon puts many obstacles between Odysseus and home, but Athena gives her favorite more or less constant aid and zealously works for his return and the re-establishment of his authority in a peaceful and plentiful Ithaca. The will of Zeus is all-powerful, but he explains at the beginning of the *Odyssey* that men can, through their own willfulness and folly, bring many more sorrows upon themselves than fate had in store for them. On the other hand, Odysseus is a good example of the man who indulges in his share of folly but who wins through successfully by faith in the gods and the employment of as much self-control and intelligence as he can command. In Homer the meaning of earthly events is frequently deepened, enriched, and clarified by analogous action on the part of the gods. The inner impulses of people are, as a rule, either aroused or responded to by deity.

It may be noted with regard to the complex but unified structure of both poems that early in each work Homer has his hero absent from the scene—Achilles withdrawn at Troy, Odysseus away from home—absences which cause the complication to grow more complicated until a climax is reached with the return of the hero—Achilles to battle, Odysseus to his own identity in Ithaca again—after which the resolution is effected.

Eight books lead up to Achilles' rejection of Agamemnon's efforts to make amends in Book IX, six more to the death of Patroclus and the battle for his body in XVI and XVII and Achilles' decision in XVIII to return to the fight, and three more to the death of Hector in XXII. Odysseus gets to Phaeacia at the end of Book V and in IX through XII gives his flash-back account of what he has done since leaving Troy. He reaches Ithaca in XIII, but the interest continues to mount till the beginning of XXII when he leaps upon the threshold with bow and arrows in hand and reveals himself to the terrified wooers. The remaining action in each poem is resolved in the final two books.

III. For most people the more and better a myth is translated into their own language the more effective it is likely to be, and needless to say the translation of poetry is effective only insofar as it approaches re-creation. This is a truth of which early translators of Homer such as Chapman and Pope were well aware but which, since the eighteenth century, has been sadly neglected, in practice if not in theory and frequently in both. The Greek text of this version is, with few exceptions, that most generally accepted by modern editors, and I have tried to be faithful to the sentiments, ideas, and images of the original and to include whatever is necessary to the literal sense of the Greek poem. But I have also done what I could to make a readable English poem, since something of the quality of Homer's poetry would seem to be the most essential quality for a translator to convey. In diction I have aimed at effective expression in the large area between the stilted and the vulgar and always with regard to dramatic context. In meter the line I have found best suited for rendering the original dactylic hex-ameters is a loose measure of five major stresses plus a varying number of relatively unaccented syllables. The poem should, of course, be read with the natural and idiomatic stress that best interprets the sense.

ENNIS REES

THE
ODYSSEY
OF
HOMER

BOOK

I

ATHENA AND TELEMACHUS

Of that versatile man, O Muse, tell me the story,
How he wandered both long and far after sacking
The city of holy Troy. Many were the towns
He saw and many the men whose minds he knew,
And many were the woes his stout heart suffered at sea
As he fought to return alive with living comrades.
Them he could not save, though much he longed to,
For through their own thoughtless greed they died—blind fools
Who slaughtered the Sun's own cattle, Hyperion's herd,
For food, and so by him were kept from returning.
Of all these things, O Goddess, daughter of Zeus,
Beginning wherever you wish, tell even us.

Now all the others who had managed to escape destruction
Were safe at home, untroubled by war or the sea.
Odysseus alone, full of longing for wife and friends,
Was kept from returning by that beautiful nymph Calypso,
The powerful goddess who hoped to make him her husband.
Even in the year of his predestined return,
At home among his own people, his toils were many.
And for his suffering all the gods pitied him

Except Poseidon, who continued to rage against
That godlike man till at last he reached his own country.
    It happened that Poseidon had gone to receive a hecatomb
Of rams and bulls from the far-off Ethiopians, remotest
Of men—some live where Hyperion sets, some
Where he rises—and there he was, enjoying himself
At the feast. But the other gods were gathered in the palace
Of Olympian Zeus. And he was the first to speak,
For lately he had been thinking of handsome Aegisthus,
Whom Agamemnon's son, the renowned Orestes,
Had slain. And thus he spoke among the immortals:
    "Ah, how quick men are to blame the gods!
From us, they say, all their evils come,
When they themselves, by their own ridiculous pride,
Bring horrors on far beyond anything fate
Would ever have done. Consider, for instance, Aegisthus,
Who far outrunning fate, not only took
For himself the absent Agamemnon's wife, but killed
The King himself when he returned from the war.
Yet all the time he was without doubt aware
Of his self-destruction, since he had been forewarned
By Hermes, the keen-eyed slayer of Argus, that he
Should neither murder the man nor woo the wife,
Lest vengeance come from Orestes, who as a man
Would naturally covet the kingdom that is rightfully his.
So spoke well-meaning Hermes to heedless Aegisthus,
Who already has paid in full for all he did."
    Then the bright-eyed goddess Athena answered him thus:
"Our Father, son of Cronos, ruling high
Above all other rulers, surely that man
Got what he deserved and what anyone else
Deserves who does such horrible things. But my heart
Bleeds for the living, for that luckless but clever man
Odysseus, who far from his friends, on a lonely island

At the great sea's very navel, has long been miserable.
It's an island of beautiful trees, the home of a goddess,
The daughter of irritable Atlas, who knows how deep
Is every sea and upholds the monstrous pillars
That keep the sky from falling. His daughter is she
Who holds as her beloved prisoner that hapless
And mournful man, forever enchanting him
With soft, seductive words, that he may forget
His home. But Odysseus would give his life for a single
Glimpse of smoke from the fires of rocky Ithaca.
Yet, Olympian Father, your heart is heedless.
But is not this forgotten Odysseus he who sacrificed
To you so generously beside the Argive ships
In the wide land of Troy? Why then are you so angry,
And why has Odysseus become so odious to you?"

  Then cloud-gathering Zeus answered the goddess:
"My child, what words are these that you let pass
The barrier of your teeth! Forget indeed!
How could I forget godlike Odysseus, who is
In mental power beyond all other mortals,
And who to us has sacrificed most generously.
But Poseidon, who embraces the earth, is full of wrath
Because Odysseus blinded the only eye
Of powerful Polyphemus, mightiest of all the Cyclopes
And Poseidon's own son, borne by the nymph Thoösa,
Who lay with the god in the hollow caves, Thoösa
The daughter of Phorcys, who commands the desolate sea.
Ever since that day, earth-shaking Poseidon, instead
Of killing Odysseus outright, makes him a wanderer
And homeless. But come, let us all consider how he
May return to Ithaca, for Poseidon will not be able
To hold out alone and sustain his wrath against
The will and wisdom of all the other gods."

  Then the blue-eyed goddess Athena made this reply:

5

"O Father, king of kings and son of Cronos,
If indeed the blessed gods look now with favor
On the return of wise Odysseus, let us dispatch
Immediately Hermes our messenger to the island Ogygia,
That he may tell that nymph with the beautiful braids
What we have decided: that Odysseus, now so wretched,
Be allowed to leave for Ithaca. And I will go there
Now, that I may better encourage Telemachus,
His son, to call a meeting of the long-haired Achaeans
And tell the wooers exactly what he thinks
Of them, who continue to kill his milling sheep
And long-horned shuffling cattle. And I will go with him
To sandy Pylos for news of his dear father,
That such a son all men may admire."

    She finished, and quickly put on her lovely sandals
Of magic immortal gold, which bear her always
Swift as the wind over boundless earth and the sea.
And she took in her hand her mighty spear, with which
In wrath she conquers with ease whole armies of men.
Then down she went darting from the topmost peaks
      of Olympus
And stood in Ithaca at the outer gates of Odysseus
Looking in on the court, and still in her hand she held
The great bronze spear, but in looks she appeared as a stranger,
As Mentes, the Taphian leader. There she found
The insolent wooers, sitting on the hides of oxen
They had taken and slaughtered themselves, playing at draughts,
And nimble attendants were busy mixing for them
Bowls of wine and water, while others were sponging
And setting the tables, and others still served up
A large supply of dressed, delicious meats.

    The godlike Telemachus was far the first to see her,
For he had need of her as sadly he sat
Among the wooers, dreaming of his noble father,

6

How if only he might suddenly appear from nowhere
To scatter the insolent wooers throughout the palace
And resume his rightful sway in his own house.
The Prince got up at once and went to meet her,
For he thought it wrong to keep a stranger standing
At the gates. He went up to her and gave his right hand
And from her he took the spear of bronze. Then he spoke
These winged words to the goddess:
     "You are welcome, stranger,
And here within you shall find a hospitable home,
And after you have eaten you will tell us, I hope,
Of anything you need."
     With this he led the way,
And Pallas Athena followed him into the high house,
Where he placed her heavy spear in a gleaming rack
Against a tall pillar among many other spears,
The splendid weapons of patient Odysseus himself.
He spread a cover on a lovely, daedalian chair
With a footrest below and seated the goddess, and beside it
He placed another richly wrought chair for himself,
Apart from the wooers for fear their manners should spoil
The appetite of his guest, who would surely regard them
       as arrogant,
And besides he wanted to ask about his father.
Then a maid brought water in a beautiful golden pitcher
And poured it out above a silver basin, that they
Might wash their hands, and she drew up in front of them
A polished table, whereon the respected housekeeper
Put bread and other good things to eat, freely
Giving them plenty of all she had. And before them
A carver placed platters of selected meats and beside them
Goblets of gold, which a herald kept filling with wine.
     Then the insolent wooers came in and sat down,
       and heralds

Poured water over their hands while serving girls
Put bread in baskets and young men filled the bowls
Brimful of wine. Thus the wooers fell to feasting,
But when they had eaten and drunk their fill they called
For song and dance to crown the meal, whereupon
A herald handed a lovely lyre to Phemius,
Who was forced to entertain the wooers. So he struck a chord
Or two and began to sing his beautiful song.
        But Telemachus turned to Athena, leaning close to her
Bright eyes, and spoke, not wishing the others to hear:
"Friend, I hope what I have to say won't offend you,
But these men you see can call for song and the lyre
Quite carelessly, since they are wasting the goods and stealing
The music of another, a man whose bones may lie
Somewhere on the mainland, white and rotting in the rain,
Or perhaps they wash in the waves of the sea. Were he
To walk in that door at this moment they would all much rather
Be fast on their feet than rich in garments and gold!
But now he has come to an evil end, and here
We have no hope at all that he will return,
Regardless of what man says so. But come, won't you tell me
Who you are and where you're from? What kind
Of ship did you come in, and who were the sailors
                who brought you
To Ithaca? For I'm sure you didn't walk. And also
Please tell me if you were ever a guest of my father,
For he loved entertaining and visited often himself."
        Then Athena, her blue eyes blazing, answered him thus:
"To you I will frankly tell all, and nothing but the truth.
My name is Mentes, the son of keen Anchialus,
And I am King of the sea-loving Taphians. Now
With ship and crew I've put in here while sailing
The wine-dark sea on my way to foreign Temese
For bronze in exchange for a load of gleaming iron.

8

My ship lies out by the fields a good way from the city
In Rheithron bay under shady Mount Neion. You
And I must be friends even as our fathers were friends,
Of which, if you will, go ask the old hero Laertes,
Who, I hear, comes to the city no more
But suffers his woes far out in the country alone
Save one old woman who serves his food and drink
After he has exhausted himself by creeping about
His vineyard on the hill. I came, in fact, because
Men said your father had returned, but now
It seems that the gods are against him, though I don't for a
        moment
Believe that godlike Odysseus is dead. He's probably
On some island in the open sea, a most
Unwilling guest of cruel and savage men.
Though I cannot tell fortunes or explicate omens, in this
I speak with prophetic voice for the immortal gods:
Though now he lie in chains, Odysseus will soon
Return to his darling country! That resourceful man
Will surely think of a way. But come, tell me truly,
Tall fellow, are you really the son of Odysseus?
Your head and beautiful eyes, your face and features
Are very like his as I remember him
Before he sailed for Troy along with the best
Of the Argives in the hollow ships. Since that day
The great Odysseus and I have never met."

    Then brooding Telemachus answered her thus: "To you,
My friend, I'll speak with perfect frankness. My mother
Says I am his child, but personally, of course,
I cannot say: it's a wise child that knows his own parents.
Would I were the son of a man more blessed,
Of one who grew old at home and died at home.
But since you ask, they do say I am the son
Of that man, that most unlucky man of all."

Athena's blue eyes blazed as she answered him:
"Since you're surely Penelope's son, we can take it on trust,
I think, that the gods have given to you a great father.
But tell me, what feast is this? Why all the carousing
At your expense? For clearly this is no picnic
To which each brings his own. Who are these men
Who brawl so shamelessly, with so little regard for your home?
Their behavior is enough to disgust any man with good sense!"
    Then Telemachus answered: "Stranger, since I believe
That you really want to know, there was a time
When our house seemed destined to prosper, back when that man
We speak of was still among us, but now the gods
Have contrived much evil against him, for never have they
Hidden a man in darkness more deep than his.
Had he been killed among comrades in the land of the Trojans,
Or died in the arms of a friend when he had wound up
His career in the war, his death would not trouble me so.
Then all the Achaeans would have made him a tomb, and his story
In days to come would have won great glory for both him
And me. But now some fiendish storm has swept him
Ingloriously away, completely out of sight, out of hearing,
And I am left with a heritage of worry and weeping.
Nor is the loss of my father the only cause
That the gods have given me for grief and lamenting.
These men are island lords, from Dulichium and Samos,
From shady Zacynthus and rocky Ithaca, and all
Of them are out to make my mother marry,
And meanwhile in feasting they're wasting all I have,
For she neither refuses their loathsome offers completely
Nor can she make up her mind and end them. Meanwhile,
They're carousing and laying waste my home,
And soon, at this rate, they'll destroy me altogether!"
    Then spoke Pallas Athena, her wrath aroused:
"O shameless! you do indeed have need of lost

10

Odysseus, that he might take some action against
These insolent men. O what wouldn't I give
To see him standing now in yonder door,
Complete with helmet and shield and a couple of spears!
And still such a man as he was when I first saw him,
Drinking and enjoying himself in our house, where he
Had stopped on his way from Ephyre, from a visit to Ilus,
Son of Mermerus. For there had Odysseus gone,
Swiftly by ship, in search of a deadly drug
With which to smear his swift bronze-headed arrows.
Nor would Ilus give it to him, he being afraid
Of what the immortal gods would do, but my father,
Who thought a great deal of Odysseus, gave it to him.
I would, I say, give much to see him come in
And take his stand among the wooers with form and strength
Such as used to be his. Then, I assure you, they would
Indeed die young, finding their wooing woeful!
But his return to exact full payment from those
Who desecrate this house depends on the gods. Meanwhile,
It is my wish that you begin thinking how to rid
Your halls of these men.

      "Now listen closely to me.
Tomorrow call a meeting of all the Achaean lords
And have your say with the gods as your witnesses. Tell
The wooers to take their separate ways home. As for
Your mother, if she really wishes to marry again,
Let her return to the house of her powerful father,
And there they'll prepare a feast and wonderful gifts
For the bride, all such things as a dearly loved daughter
Should have. And now, if you will, I have wise counsel
For you. Man your best ship with twenty oarsmen
And go see what you can learn of your missing father
For perhaps some mortal can tell you of him, or you
May hear the very voice of God, which most often

Informs the hearts of men. Go first to Pylos
And put your questions to Nestor, the god-fearing King,
Then on to Sparta and tawny-haired King Menelaus,
For he was the last to come home of the bronze-clad Achaeans.
If you should happen to hear that your father lives
And will return, then surely, though sorely beset,
You can endure for another year. But if
You should hear that he's dead, go back to your own dear country,
Make a monumental grave for him, perform
The many due rites, and find a husband for your mother.
Then give your heart and mind to devising death
For the wooers within your halls, by force or fraud,
For you are no longer a child. Haven't you heard
What renown the noble Orestes won when he killed
The man, that scheming Aegisthus, who murdered his famous
Father? And you, my friend, so tall and so manly,
Be valiant! that many as yet unborn may speak well
Of you. Now I must go down to my swift ship
And comrades who may have grown weary of waiting. Finally,
Remember and value rightly what I have said."

    Then thoughtful Telemachus answered her thus: "Friend,
You surely speak as a man of great good will,
As a father would speak to his son, and I'll never forget
What you have said. But come now, though you are anxious
To go, stay at least long enough to bathe
And refresh yourself, that you may go back to your ship
In the best of spirits and with you some very lovely gift
Such as one friend would like to give another."

    Then blue-eyed Athena replied: "Keep me no longer
Here, since I am so eager to go, but your gift
I will gladly accept when I see you again, even here
On my way home. So select that very lovely gift,
Young man. It will bring you equal value in return."

    So spoke the bright-eyed goddess, then like a bird

Took flight and vanished. And she left him astonished there
With confidence and courage in his heart and thinking
More than ever of his father. He sat amazed,
Thinking that she was a god, then joined the wooers,
Godlike himself.

They sat in silence listening
To the famous bard sing the Achaeans' return,
The hard return from Troy that Pallas Athena
Imposed upon them. Meanwhile, upstairs in her room,
The daughter of Icarius, thoughtful Penelope, heard
The marvelous song and descended, with two of her maids,
The long stairway that led to the hall below.
There she stood, lovely by one of the pillars
Of the massive roof, her face partly hid by a shining
Veil, and confronted the wooers, with a trusted maid
On either side. Then weeping she spoke to the bard,
The sacred maker of songs:

"Phemius, surely
You know many other songs just as enchanting,
Deeds both mortal and divine which poets make memorable.
Sit here and sing one of those while your listeners drink
Their wine in silence, but do not renew that song
Of woe that never fails to rend my heart,
For already most unforgettable is the grief I have.
So dear a man I always recall with yearning,
My husband, known far and wide throughout all Hellas
And Argos."

Then gravely Telemachus answered her thus:
"Mother, why do you forbid this beloved poet
To entertain in the way his own mind moves him to?
Poets are not to blame, but Zeus much rather,
Who to toiling men doles out their separate lots.
No one can blame this man for singing the grievous
Fate of the Danaans: new songs are always praised

13

More highly than old. As for you, strengthen your heart
And soul to hear him, for Odysseus wasn't the only
Man who died at Troy. They were many!
Go, then, upstairs to your room and keep yourself busy
With the loom and spindle, and see that your maids are busy.
Leave public speaking to men—men in general,
But most of all to me, since I am now head
Of this house."

  Then back to her room she went, amazed,
And took to heart the spirited wise words of her son.
There with her maids she wept for her dear Odysseus
Until from blue-eyed Athena the sweet sleep came.

  But tumultuous talk broke out among the wooers
As they sat in the shadowy halls, and each of them lusted
To lie with the lady. Then bold Telemachus spoke out
Among them: "Wooers of my mother, lewd and insolent
You are, but for once let us have a pleasant meal
Without the brawling, that we may hear this splendid
Poet sing, this man whose voice is like
The voice of a god. But in the morning I'll address you
Seated in assembly, and there will officially command you
To leave these halls. Go feast in other houses
And devour your own goods, or if what you are doing now
Seems to you braver and more profitable, that one man's
Everything should be destroyed and destroyed completely
Without recompense, go right ahead and destroy.
But I will pray to the immortal gods and ask
That Zeus recompense you all, in which event
You all will surely die within these halls!"

  At this they bit their lips, amazed at his courage.
Then Antinous, son of Eupeithes, made this reply:
"Telemachus, truly the gods are teaching your tongue
To vaunt and be bold. May the son of Cronos never

Make you king here in sea-circled Ithaca, though king
You were born to be!"

    Then thoughtful Telemachus: "Antinous,
You won't like what I'm going to say, but this too
I should gladly accept if such be the will of Zeus.
Do you really think so ill of the lot of kings?
It is not that bad. One's house grows quickly rich
And as king one is held in greater esteem. But here
In sea-circled Ithaca are many potential kings
Both young and old. It's possible that one of these
Will replace the great Odysseus, now that he's dead,
But I will still be head of this house and the servants
That my great father won me."

    Then Eurymachus, son
Of Polybus: "Who shall be king in this rocky island
Is a matter in the lap of the gods, but of course, Telemachus,
You will keep your belongings and rule your own house. May that
      man
Never appear in this civilized island who will take
By force your possessions from you. But I, bold sir,
Would like to ask about the stranger just here
And where he is from. Who are his people and where
Do they live? Does he bring any news of your father, or did
He come to further some cause of his own? How quickly
He arose and disappeared, not waiting to be introduced.
Yet surely he seemed to be a man of parts."

    Then cautious Telemachus made this reply: "Eurymachus
Surely my father will never return, nor do
I have any use for news, no matter who brings it,
Nor do I care at all for foolish prophecies
Such as my mother hears when she has invited
Some seer to the palace. This stranger that you just saw

15

Was a friend of my father's. He calls himself Mentes, the son
Of keen Anchialus, and he hails from Taphos where he
Is King of the sea-loving Taphians."

       So Telemachus said,
But in his heart he knew the immortal goddess.

         Now the wooers struck up a song and began to dance
And carouse, and continued so till the dark evening came.
Then each of them went home and to bed. Telemachus
Climbed to his chamber high in the beautiful court
With a mind full of problems, and with him went the discreet
Eurycleia, daughter of Ops, the son of Peisenor.
Long ago, when she was just a girl,
Laertes bought her for the worth of twenty oxen,
And in his house he honored her as much
As his faithful wife, but he never went to bed with her,
Since he wished to avoid the wrath of a certain woman.
Now Eurycleia bore the blazing torches
And lit the way to bed for Telemachus, for she,
Of all the servants, loved him most and had been
His nurse when he was a child. He opened the doors
Of the well-made, thick-walled room and sat down on the bed,
Removed his soft tunic and gave it to the careful old woman.
She smoothed and folded the tunic and hung it on a peg
Beside the corded bed, and then withdrew,
Closing the door by its lovely silver handle
And pulling the bolt into place by the leather thong.
Then there all night, wrapped in a warm wool blanket,
He pondered the journey Athena had advised.

BOOK

II

THE ASSEMBLY
IN ITHACA

As soon as early Dawn, that rosy sweet lass,
Appeared, the dear son of Odysseus got up from his bed
And put on his clothes. He slung his keen blade from his shoulder
And on his shining feet bound beautiful sandals.
Then, like a god in appearance, he went out of his chamber
And with no delay at all gave orders to the heralds
That they might employ their powerful voices to call
A meeting of the long-haired Achaeans, and very quickly
The Achaeans came. After they had assembled,
Telemachus appeared, holding a spear of bronze
And accompanied by a brace of flashing-swift hounds. The grace
Athena gave shone wonderfully bright about him,
And the people gazed in admiration as he made his way
Through the yielding elders to sit in the seat of his father.
　　First to speak was the stooped and gnarled old hero
Aegyptius, a man of truly great wisdom, and he spoke
Because of brave Antiphus, his own dear soldier son,
Who had gone with gallant Odysseus in the hollow ships
To Ilium, famed as the home of fine horses, but he

Was already dead, for the barbarous Cyclops had made
His last meal of him in the monstrous cave. The old man
Had three other sons, Eurynomus, one of the wooers,
And two who had always worked in their father's fields.
Even so, he could not forget nor cease to mourn
For the boy who had not come home, and with eyes brimming over
For him he addressed the assembly:
    "Hear me now,
O men of Ithaca. Since godly Odysseus left
In the hollow ships, this is our first assembly.
Naturally, then, we wonder what man, young or old,
Has called us together here, and why. Can it be
That someone has news of our soldiers' returning, or does one
Of you wish to speak on some other matter concerning
Us all? Whoever it is, I assume he's a man
Of courage and good will, and I pray that Zeus
Will grant him whatever good his heart desires."
      These words greatly encouraged the son of Odysseus
And he arose in the midst of those assembled,
Eager to speak. When he had received the staff
From the judicious herald Peisenor, he addressed these words
To old Aegyptius:
    "That man, O aged one,
Is not far to seek. Who else but me, for whose
Afflictions can compare with mine? I have no news
Of our soldiers' returning, nor do I wish to speak
On any other matter of general concern. The problem
Involves my house alone, upon which a double woe
Has fallen. As you know, I have lost my noble father,
Who once was King and father to you all,
But now has come an even greater evil,
Which very soon will cause my house to crumble
Into ruins with all I own. Your own sons—

And I'm speaking to the best men here—have
            presumptuously come
To woo my mother, completely against her will.
They shrink from presenting themselves at the house of her father
Icarius, where he might plainly say what gifts
Befitted such a bride and choose for her the most
Impressive man. Instead, day after day,
Our house is full of them, killing our cattle,
Our sheep and our goats, reveling and riotously feasting,
And drinking reckless drafts of the flaming wine,
Completely wasting whatever they touch. For there's no one
To stop them, no man like Odysseus to keep our house
From ruin. Certainly I am no such man.
I'd surely make a dismal mess of things
And prove myself a weakling if not a coward.
Truly, if I could defend myself, I would,
For unendurable deeds have already been done
And my house already sunk alarmingly low.
You had better consider what it is you're doing, and how
Your neighbors will regard it. You had better, I say,
Fear the wrath of heaven, lest the gods themselves
Turn against you in anger at your incredible evil.
In the name of Olympian Zeus and of Themis, who gathers
And dismisses such meetings as this, I beseech those of you
Who call yourselves my friends to forbear, and leave me
Alone with bitterness and sorrow, that I may wear
My life away with just myself and these
For company—unless my noble father did
Some spiteful wrong to the well-greaved Achaeans, for which
You're spitefully punishing me by encouraging the wooers.
I would much rather that you, my friends, would waste
My livestock and my gold, for recompense from you
Would surely come, since we would never cease pestering
And dunning you, going up and down the city

From door to door, till all that we had lost
Was reimbursed. But quite paralyzing is the misery you're causing
Me now!"
　　　　Angrily he threw the speaker's staff
To the ground, his eyes burning with tears, and of all
The men there, only Antinous had the heart
To answer him with bitter words: "Telemachus,
What cheek, what brass, what unrestrained nonsense is this,
Your putting the blame on us? You must be mad!
I'll tell you who is really at fault: not the wooers,
But your own crafty mother—yes, the craftiest mother
A boy ever had. For three years have passed, and the fourth
Will soon be gone, since she began her deceitful
Game with Achaean hearts. She holds out hope
To all, sending each of us messages, promises—completely
Insincere. But talk of guile, hear this! At the palace
She had a great loom set up and began to weave yards
Of very fine cloth, explaining herself this way:

" 'My ardent young suitors, gallant Odysseus is dead,
And you can't wait for me to marry again,
But you, my wooers, must try to be patient until
I finish this shroud for lord Laertes, for him
When the painful fate of leveling and grievous death
Arrives. Naturally, I would not have my labor
Go to waste, nor any Achaean woman
Speak ill of me for not providing a shroud
For one who has amassed so great a fortune.'

"Such was her request, nor could our proud hearts
Deny it. There daily she wove at that great web,
But at night she unraveled her work by the light of torches.
Thus for three wily years she beguiled the Achaeans,
But when the fourth arrived and winter gave way
To spring, one of her women, who knew whereof
She spoke, told us all, and we surprised her

20

Unraveling that marvelous fabric. She finished it then,
Believe me! unwilling though she was. So now
This answer the wooers make to you, that you
And all the Achaeans may know just where we stand:
Send your mother away, and bid her marry
The man that her father chooses and she prefers.
For your mother knows that Athena has given to her
More skill and understanding than most women have,
Has indeed given her a bag of tricks such as we
Have never heard of before, not even among
The fair-haired Achaean women of old—women
Like Tyro and Alcmene and Mycene of the beautiful crown—
Not one of those was as shrewd as your mother Penelope!
But if she persists in willfully tormenting the sons
Of Achaeans, she will not be acting wisely, for all
Her famous shrewdness. For just as long as she
Continues to obey what the gods now put in her heart,
Even so long shall we continue to devour
And destroy your precious belongings. O yes, she's making
A great reputation for herself, but not,
I believe, without some small cost to you. As for us,
No fields and farms for us, no anywhere else
But at home with you, until she finally marries
One of the Achaeans, the one that she likes best."
     Then thoughtful Telemachus made this grave reply:
"Antinous, from my house I could never drive
The woman who bore and raised me. As you know,
My father is away, in another country,
But whether alive or dead no man knows.
Nor could I pay the tremendous price to Icarius
That I would have to pay if of my own
Free will I sent my mother back. From him,
Her father, I should certainly suffer, and from the gods
As much or more, for as she leaves the house

My mother will surely cry out to the hateful Furies.
Finally, all men would put harsh blame upon me.
I'll never, then, give any such command.
If you and your friends have any decency left,
Leave my house. Go visit each other and consume
What belongs to you. But if you think it better
To ruin one man's living, with no returns
At all, then go ahead. But I will call out
On the everlasting gods, call out to Zeus himself
For vengeance. Then truly with no returns at all
Each one of you will die within my palace!"
    Now, by way of a sign, far-seeing Zeus
Sent a pair of eagles from off a lofty peak,
And side by side for a while they soared on high,
Swift as the blasting wind. But as soon as they
Were directly above the rumor-riddled assembly,
They began to circle, wildly flapping their wings,
And from their eyes death glared on the men below.
Then with their talons they tore at each other until
Their heads and necks were raw, and sped away
To the right above the houses of those now met
In assembly. They wondered greatly as they watched the birds
And pondered within themselves the things that were
To be. The first to speak was the old hero
Halitherses, son of Mastor, for of all men
Then alive his was the greatest knowledge
Of birds and ominous skill. That day as a man
Of great good will he spoke to those assembled:
    "Hear now these words of mine, O men of Ithaca,
And for you wooers especially is what I have to say,
For surely a great calamity is rolling upon you!
No longer is Odysseus far from his friends. Even now
I feel his presence and know that he is sowing
The fateful seeds of death for all of you,

And many more of us in sunny Ithaca
Will have to suffer. But long before these things
Can be, let us find some way of ending this evil—
Better still, you wooers, know what is good for you
And end it yourselves. I do not prophesy naively,
But only of what I am sure of. And now I say,
Concerning Odysseus, that all those things are coming
To pass whereof I spoke when the Argives and he,
Resourceful as ever, set sail for Troy. I said
That he would come home unknown to all in the twentieth
Year, having suffered his way through a multitude of evils
With the loss of all his comrades. And most of this
Has now already happened!"
      Eurymachus, son
Of Polybus, replied: "Go home, old man, and prophesy
To your children, for perhaps something dreadful is about
        to happen
To them. Of matters here, I am far more fit
To prophesy than you. Many are the fowls that frolic
In the rays of the sun, and all are by no means ominous.
Odysseus is dead—he died very far from home,
And I heartily wish that you were likewise there.
Then surely you wouldn't be babbling so much of omens
Or unleashing more wrath in an already wrathful Telemachus,
Always hoping for some rich gift from him.
Now I will tell you what is surely going to happen.
If you with your worn-out wisdom urge this younger man
On to more rage, it will doubtless be the worse for him,
Since he can do nothing at all against so many,
And as for you, old man, we will make you pay
A fine great enough to wring your sorrowful soul!
And here in the midst of all I give this advice
To Telemachus. Send your mother back to the house
Of her father, where they will prepare a wedding feast

And many gifts—as many as should go
With a beloved daughter. For I do not think that we
Will end this costly wooing until you do.
We fear no man, certainly not spouting Telemachus,
Nor do we care a straw for any idle jabber
That you, old dotard, are pleased to call prophetic.
You'll just make us despise you even more,
And we'll go right on devouring what belongs
To your hapless protégé, with no repayment at all,
So long as his mother continues postponing her marriage
And wasting our very lives. For her great merit
Makes rivals of all of us here, and so we go on
Waiting day after day, while other women
That any of us might reasonably expect to marry
Must go uncourted."

      Then thoughtful Telemachus: "Eurymachus,
Regarding these things I make no further plea
To you and your illustrious friends, for now
The gods and all the Achaeans know how things are.
But come, let me have a swift ship and twenty oarsmen,
For I shall journey to Sparta and sandy Pylos
To learn what I may of my long-lost father's return,
Hoping to hear some word from mortal men,
Or, what is more likely, from Zeus himself.
If I hear that my father lives and will return,
I might hold out, despite these gross afflictions,
For another year. But if I hear that he's dead,
That he's gone forever, then I will return
To my own dear country and build a barrow for him
And perform above it all due funeral rites.
Then will I give my mother to another man."

      When he had taken his seat, Mentor, a friend
Of noble Odysseus, arose. On the day Odysseus
Departed with the ships, he had left this trusted comrade

In charge of his household, bidding them all obey
The old man and him to be steadfast in his authority.
Now, as a man who meant well, he addressed the assembly:
    "Hear me, Ithacans, hear what I have to say.
May no sceptered king ever again be generous,
Gentle, and kind, nor let his heart be filled
With righteousness. May they all henceforth be cruel and unjust,
Since you do not remember sacred Odysseus,
You, of all people, whose kind and fatherly King
He was. I am not now concerned with the deeds
Of these proud and malicious wooers, for in violently devouring
The house of Odysseus, who they say will never return,
They put their very lives at stake. But I
Have blame enough for all the rest of you
Who sit in silence, though greatly outnumbering the wooers,
And offer no word of rebuke to end their folly."
    Then Leiocritus, son of Euenor, answered him thus:
"Mentor, you trouble-maker! you must be out of your mind,
Telling these men to interfere with us. It would,
I think, be exceedingly hard on them to fight
About a feast with us, and we should see just who
Outnumbers who! Why if Ithacan Odysseus himself
Should come with a heart most eager to drive from his palace
These feasting lordly wooers, you can be sure
That his longing wife would hardly be glad to see him,
For right there would he die a mean and ignoble death,
Since I'm very certain that *he* would be outnumbered!
All in all, Mentor, you haven't the feeblest
Idea what you are talking about. But come,
Let each man go back to his house. Mentor and Halitherses
Will help this boy get ready for his journey,
Since they're such dear old friends of his father's house.
But I have a notion he'll wait for his news right here

In Ithaca and never make this trip at all."

    The meeting broke up and many men headed for home,
But the wooers went to the house of godly Odysseus.

    Telemachus alone went down to the shore of the sea.
There he washed his hands in the salty gray wave
And prayed to Athena: "You who came as a god
To our house yesterday and bade me go in a ship
Over the misty deep in search of what I can learn
Of my long-lost father's return, hear me. For in all this
The Achaeans thwart me, and the proud and evil wooers
Most of all."

    Athena heard his prayer,
And in the likeness of Mentor, with his form and voice,
She approached and spoke these winged words to him:
"Telemachus, if you have received anything at all
Of your father's worth, such a man of his word was he,
You will not be a mean or stupid man,
Nor will this journey of yours be unsuccessful. Now if
You were not his and Penelope's son, I would have
No reason to think that you will ever do
What you desire. Even so, not many sons
Are like their fathers. Most are worse, though a few
Are actually better. But surely we know that you
Will never be a mean or stupid man,
Nor are you without a true son's proper share
Of a wise father's wisdom. Hence there are very good reasons
For thinking that you will succeed in this undertaking.
From now on, Telemachus, pay no attention at all
To what the wooers wish and say, for they
Are completely unjust and foolhardy men, who have
No knowledge of death or dark fate, which even now
Is hovering very near them, who do not know
That on a single day they all shall die!
The journey you long for shall not be delayed much longer,

For your father stands in such great favor with me
That I will make a swift ship ready for you
And go with you myself. Now you must go
To your palace, where the wooers continue to swarm, and there
Get all your provisions ready, putting the wine
In jars and the nourishing barley meal in bags
Of durable leather. Meanwhile, I will go
Throughout the town and round up a willing crew,
And from the many ships, both new and old,
In sea-girt Ithaca, I'll pick the very best
For you, and then, having fully equipped her, we'll launch her
At once upon the broad sea."
    So spoke the daughter
Of Zeus, and Telemachus, now that he had heard
Athena's voice, returned to the palace, his heart
Still full of sorrow. There he found those insolent
Men, some within his halls while others
Were in the courtyard skinning goats and singeing
The succulent swine. Laughing, Antinous rushed up
To him, took hold of his hand, and spoke as one
Who was willing to let bygones be:
    "Well, if it isn't
Telemachus, a big man at a meeting, the bravest of the brave—
But come, forget this grudge you bear. Sit down
And eat and drink with us as before. The Achaeans
Will surely furnish all you require in the way
Of a ship and hand-picked crew, that you may go
With all speed to holy Pylos, seeking some news
Of your most illustrious father."
    And spirited Telemachus
Made this reply: "Antinous, it is quite impossible
For me to relax and enjoy myself at a feast
With insolent men like yourself. Can't you be satisfied
With the many fine things of mine that you and your arrogant

27

Friends destroyed in the years of my helpless childhood?
I am now a man and can learn just what you have done
From those about me, and, just as sure as my spirit
Grows great within me, I will send disastrous fates
On all of you, whether I go to Pylos
Or not! But to Pylos I will surely go, nor will
I go in vain, though you have seen to it, since my loss
Is your gain, that I have no ship and crew of my own."

    As he coldly withdrew his hand from the hand of Antinous,
The wooers, greedily feasting throughout the hall,
Began to taunt and tease him. Thus an insolent
Young bully would say: "Alas, I fear that Telemachus
Is plotting to murder us all. He'll get help
From sandy Pylos, or even from Sparta, so terribly
Determined a man is he. Or for all I know
He's planning to visit the opulent land of Ephyre
And bring back lethal potions with which to poison
The wine-bowl and end us all!"

    And another, equally
Young and insolent, would say: "Who knows what
Will happen if Telemachus goes wandering far from his friends
In a hollow ship? He might very well die as Odysseus
Did. Just think of all the additional trouble
He would thereby cause us, for then we should have to divide
All that he owns among ourselves, though his house,
I feel sure, we would give to his mother for her very own—
That is, to his mother and the man who marries her!"

    Thus they jested, but Telemachus descended to the wide,
High-vaulted chamber where his father's treasure was kept,
Gold and bronze in heaps upon the floor,
Chests of fine clothing, and a rich abundance of fragrant
Olive oil, while along the wall were standing
Huge urns of unmixed, marvelous wine, old

And sweet, against the time, if ever, Odysseus
Should return, having toiled through many griefs.
The double doors were locked securely, and all things
There were in the keeping of shrewd Eurycleia,
Daughter of Ops, the son of Peisenor. Now,
Having called her to this rich room, Telemachus spoke:
      "Good nurse, come fill some flagons for me with wine,
Sweet wine from the best we have, not counting that superlative
Vintage you keep in memory of my unlucky father,
God-sprung Odysseus, who may yet escape death and the fates
And return from we know not where. Fill twelve great flagons
In all and fit them with covers, and into sacks
Of well-sewn leather pour barley meal for me,
Full twenty measures of mill-ground barley meal.
Keep what I tell you strictly to yourself, but get all
Of these things together and this evening, when my mother
          goes up
To bed, I'll come for them. For I am going
To Sparta and sandy Pylos, seeking some word
Of my dear father's return."
    Then Eurycleia,
His beloved nurse, cried out in grief, and weeping
She spoke to him these words so winged with sorrow:
"Dear child, how did you ever let any such notion
As this possess you? How could an only son
So dearly loved wish to go wandering away
In this wide world? God-sprung Odysseus is dead,
And he died in a strange and distant land. And you
Will no sooner be gone than these men here will plot
Your death, some treacherous trick whereby you'll die
And they be allowed to divide among themselves
All that you own. Don't go, my child. Stay here
Where you belong and in charge of your belongings.
There is no need for you to suffer such ills

As you must if you go wandering on the desolate sea."
    And Telemachus replied: "Good nurse, you must have
        courage,
For what I am going to do is the will of a god.
But swear to say nothing of this to my dear mother,
No, not until the eleventh or twelfth day,
Or until she misses me herself or hears
That I am gone, for it is not my wish
That tears should stain the flesh of her lovely face."
    So the old woman swore by the gods a great oath of silence,
Then drew the flagons of wine for him and poured
The barley meal into sacks of well-sewn leather.
Telemachus went back to the hall and mixed with the wooers.
    Meanwhile, bright-eyed Athena was also busy.
In the form of Telemachus she went throughout the town
And bade the men of her choice to meet that evening
Beside the swift ship—which she asked Noëmon for,
Noëmon, the brilliant and well-known son of Phronius,
And he, without hesitation, told her to take it.
    Thus, when the sun went down and the streets were all
Full of shadows, she launched the swift ship in the briny surf
And within it put all the equipment that well-decked ships
Have aboard. Then she tied up at the head of the harbor,
And about that swift ship the good crew gathered, all cheered
And encouraged by the goddess herself. Then bright-eyed Athena
Went elsewhere about her business—this time to the house
Of godly Odysseus, where she befuddled the wits
Of the drinking, drowsy wooers and struck the goblets
From their hands. So they loitered no longer, but got up
        and took
Their heavy eyes home and to bed. And the blue-eyed goddess,
In the likeness of Mentor, called the Prince out of the palace,
And spoke to him thus:
    "Telemachus, your well-greaved companions

Sit at their oars awaiting the word from you.
Come, let us join them, and delay their journey no longer."
     Quickly he followed the steps of Pallas Athena
Down to the ship and the sea, and there on the beach
They found the long-haired crew. Right then Telemachus,
Respected and strong, took charge: "Let us go, my friends,
And bring our supplies from the palace, for all our provisions
Are ready and waiting there, though my mother and her maids
Know nothing at all of this. I spoke of what
We shall need to one person only."
     They followed him then
To the palace, and obeying the dear son of Odysseus they brought
The supplies to the well-decked ship and stowed them away.
Then Telemachus stepped aboard, but just before him
Went Pallas Athena. He and the goddess sat close
Together in the stern of the ship, while the crew loosed
The stern moorings, came on board themselves, and took
Their seats on the benches. And now bright-eyed Athena
Made a wonderful wind spring up, the strong West Wind
That shrilly whistled and sang above the wine-dark sea,
And the men turned to the tackling as Telemachus bade.
They raised the fir mast, set it securely in place,
And made it fast with halyards. Then, with ropes
Of braided ox-hide, they hauled the white sail up.
The sail soon bellied before that wind, and the dark waves
Moaned and hissed about the bow, as the ship
Cut swiftly through them ever closer to her destination.
Now, in the swift black ship, having rigged and trimmed her
Well, they set out bowls brimming with wine
And poured libations to the immortal gods, and especially
To the bright-eyed daughter of Zeus. Thus all through the night
And into the dawn the ship went cleaving her way.

BOOK

III

TELEMACHUS
AND NESTOR

Now when the sun had gone up from the gorgeous sea
And into the burnished bronze sky, giving light to the deathless
Gods and to mortal men on the grain-giving earth,
They came to Pylos, the populous city of Neleus.
Here on the shore of the sea the people were offering
A sacrifice of solid-black bulls to mighty Poseidon,
The blue-haired master of earthquakes. They sat in nine groups
Of five hundred apiece, and in each of the companies there
Nine bulls were held ready for slaughter. By the time
                they had eaten
Of the inner parts and were burning the thighs as a gift
To the god, the men at sea put in to shore,
Hauled up and made fast the sail of their graceful ship,
Moored her securely, and then stepped out on the beach.
Telemachus too stepped out of the ship, but before him
Went Pallas Athena, the goddess with the blazing blue eyes,
Who lost no time at all in speaking to him:

"Telemachus, you no longer have the slightest cause
For shame, now that you've sailed the deep sea to learn

Of your father—of what earth covers him and what fate
Laid him so low. But come now, go straight to Nestor,
Breaker of horses, that we may learn what wisdom
Lies hid in his heart, and I want you to do
The talking. Don't hesitate to ask him for the truth itself,
For he is truly wise and will not lie."

But thoughtful Telemachus replied: "Mentor, how can
I go and greet him that way? I have no particular
Skill in speech, and besides, it makes a young man
Uneasy to question an elder."

Then the bright-eyed goddess:
"Telemachus, part of what you will need your own mind
Will supply, and heaven will give you the rest. For I
Do not think that you of all people came into this world
And grew up to manhood without the will and favor
Of the gods."

So spoke Pallas Athena, and quickly
Led the way to where the men of Pylos
Were gathered in companies, and there sat Nestor with his sons,
While around him his people were busy preparing the feast,
Putting meat on spits and roasting it. But no sooner
Did they see the strangers than they all came crowding
          about them,
Shaking their hands and urging them to sit down.
Then Nestor's son, the noble Peisistratus, came up
And taking their hands in his he seated them there
By the sea upon soft fleeces spread out on the sand
Beside his father and Thrasymedes his brother. He gave them
Helpings of bull's heart, liver, and lungs and poured
A golden goblet full of wine. Having drunk
To the goddess, he spoke these words to her, Athena,
The daughter of aegis-bearing Zeus:

"Pray now, O stranger,
To lordly Poseidon, for the feast you find yourself at

Is his. And when you have poured libations and prayed
In accord with your custom, then give the goblet of honey-sweet
Wine to your friend, that he may pour, for he too,
I think, is a man of prayer. All men have need
Of the gods. But he is younger than you—of about
My own age, I believe—so first to you I give
This golden goblet."
    With this he handed her
The cup of sweet wine, and Pallas Athena was pleased
At the man's good manners, so truly inspired, in giving
First to her the golden chalice. Then thus
To lordly Poseidon she prayed this earnest prayer:
    "O earth-encircling god, hear me now,
And willingly grant what I shall ask of you.
First of all, to Nestor and his sons give honor
And renown, and to all the other men of Pylos
Be gracious in your requital for this splendid hecatomb.
Grant also the safe return of Telemachus and myself
When we have done what we in our swift black ship
Came here to do."
    Such was the prayer she prayed,
She who was herself fulfilling all.
Then to Telemachus she handed the two-handled cup
And even as the goddess had done the dear son of Odysseus
Prayed. Now, having roasted the meat, they drew it
Off the spits, and dividing it up in ample portions
They feasted one and all in glorious celebration.
When they had eaten and drunk as much as they wished,
Horse-driving Gerenian Nestor was the first to speak:
    "Now truly the time is more fitting to ask of our guests
Who they are, since both of them now have feasted well.
Who are you, my friends, and where are you from? Is it
On business that you sail the ocean paths, or do you
Wander recklessly over the sea as buccaneers,

Risking your own lives and damaging those of others?"
> Then thoughtful Telemachus found an answer in
> his heart,
For Athena herself put courage there, that he
Might ask about his missing father and thus
Have good report among his fellow men:
"O Nestor, Neleus' son, so greatly glorious
Among the Achaeans, you ask where we are from
And very willing am I to tell you. Our home
Is in Ithaca below Mount Neion, and we have come
To you on business, private rather than public.
This I speak of concerns my famous father,
And I have come to learn what I can of him—
If indeed I should be so lucky—to learn what I can
Of gallant Odysseus, that man of patient heart,
Who once, they say, fought side by side with you
And sacked the city of Troy. For of all the others
Who fought the Trojans and are now no longer with us,
We know where each man miserably died, but the son
Of Cronos has completely obscured even the death
Of Odysseus, for no man can truly say where he died—
Whether he fell beneath foes on the mainland, or at sea
Among the waves of Amphitrite. So I have come
To your knees, hoping that you will be willing to tell me
How he so miserably died, since perhaps you witnessed
His death yourself or have heard his woeful story
From some other wanderer. For beyond all other men
He was born to suffer. Do not soften your words
Out of pity or compassion for me, but tell me exactly
How you happened to be there and how my father
Died. If ever Odysseus kept a promise to you
Of word or deed in the land of the Trojans, I beseech you
To remember it now and tell me his story unaltered."
> Then horse-driving Gerenian Nestor made this reply:

"Ah, my friend, many and sad are the memories
I now recall of the sorrows we suffered there,
And of all that we endured on the foggy deep
As we wandered in the wake of Achilles in search of plunder,
And of all the battles we fought about the great city
Of Priam. There so many of our best men
Were slain. There lies battling Ajax as well as
Achilles. There lies Patroclus, as weighty in wisdom
As the gods, and there lies my own dear son Antilochus,
Whom no one equaled in strength and speed and skill
As a warrior. Nor are these all the ills we suffered.
But what mere man could possibly tell them all?
Five or six years would not be long enough
To answer your questions of the horrors that we Achaeans
Endured there, and long before the tale was ended
You would have grown terribly bored and returned to
              your homeland.
We spent nine years busily plotting their downfall
With countless wily devices, but with little real help
From Zeus. But speaking of strategy, no man there
Could plot it half so well as godly Odysseus—
He that you say is your father, and indeed I am
Amazed at the way your speech resembles his,
And you a younger man at that. Not once
While we were there in the land of the Trojans did he
And I have an argument in assembly or in council.
But always we were of one mind in advising the Argives,
Shrewdly and with wisdom, as to the best course of action.

        "But when we had leveled King Priam's lofty city
And set out in our ships and been scattered abroad by a god,
Right then it was that Zeus decreed in his heart
A baneful return for the Argives, all of whom
Were not by any means thoughtful men and good.
Hence the furious blue-eyed daughter of the Father almighty

Let fall on many of them an evil doom,
For between the two sons of Atreus she stirred up strife.
One day toward sundown these two called an assembly
Of all the Achaeans, but called it without consideration
And the due formalities. The sons of Achaeans came,
Heavy with wine, and were told why they had been called.
Menelaus urged us to think of our return
On the sea's broad back, thereby much displeasing
Agamemnon, who was anxious to keep us all there and sacrifice
Holy hecatombs that he might appease the terrible
Wrath of Athena, thoughtless fool that he was
Not to realize that she would be unappeasable.
For the mind of everlasting deity is not easily changed.
So there the two men stood in angry disagreement
While the well-greaved Achaeans sprang up in noisy
    confusion
To ally themselves with one side or the other.
That night we rested, but in two opposing factions,
Harboring hard thoughts each against the other,
For Zeus was about to bring great misery upon us.
In the morning we launched our ships in the shining surf
And on board we put our belongings and the low-girdled
    women.
Full half as many, however, stayed where they were
With our commander-in-chief Agamemnon, son
Of Atreus, but the rest of us boarded our ships and pulled out
From shore. Then swiftly we sailed, for a god had made
The engulfing deep just calm enough, but at Tenedos
We stopped for sacrifice to the gods, so anxious were we
To reach our homes, but as yet Zeus had no intention
That we should return, unappeasable God, who now
A second time roused miserable strife among us.
Part of our number turned their curved ships back
To rejoin Agamemnon, and among them went King Odysseus,

That wise and wily man. But I, with the ships
That followed me, fled on, for I knew that God
Intended no good. The warrior son of Tydeus
Also fled, urging on his men, and late
In our wake came tawny Menelaus. He overtook us
In Lesbos where we were debating the weary voyage
Ahead, whether we should sail seaward of craggy Chios
Toward Psyria, keeping that island on our left,
Or to landward of Chios past windy Mimas. Then
We prayed to God for a sign and he gave us one,
Bidding us cleave the open sea straight across
To Euboea as surely the quickest way out of our trouble.
A whistling wind sprang up and swiftly the ships
Sailed on through the fish-infested sea, until at night
We reached Geraestus, and many were the bull thighs we burnt
On Poseidon's altar there, so thankful were we
To have safely crossed the wide water. On the fourth day
            the comrades
Of horse-taming Diomedes, son of Tydeus, beached
Their graceful ships in Argos, but I sailed on
Toward Pylos and home, and the god-sent wind never failed us
From the time it first started to blow.
      "Thus I came home,
Dear child, with no sure knowledge of loss or salvation
Among the Achaeans, but what I have heard from others
Here in these halls I shall certainly not keep from you.
Safely, they say, the spear-wielding Myrmidons got home,
Led by the glorious son of courageous Achilles,
And safely too Philoctetes, the noble son
Of Poias. Idomeneus made it back to Crete
With all his men who survived the war. He lost
No one at sea. But as for King Agamemnon,
You in your distant homes have heard how he
Returned and how Aegisthus successfully plotted

His murder, for which he has already paid
The terrible price, so good a thing it is
For a dying man to leave a son behind him.
That son took vengeance in full on the man who murdered
His famous father, even on scheming Aegisthus.
And you, my friend, so tall and so manly, be valiant!
That many as yet unborn may speak well of you."

  Then thoughtful Telemachus replied: "O Nestor, great son
Of Neleus and truly magnificent among the Achaeans,
That son took vengeance indeed, and surely the Achaeans
Will carry his story with them wherever they go.
Many men yet to be born will surely hear it.
O that the gods would grant such strength to me
That I might exact due payment from all the wooers
For the wanton and grievous crimes they commit against me!
But the gods have spun no such good fortune for me,
Nor for my father. I have but to suffer it all."

  Then horse-driving Gerenian Nestor answered him thus:
"Friend, now that you broach the subject yourself,
They do say that your home is swarming with insolent men,
Wooers for the hand of your mother. But tell me, do you
Willingly suffer these things, or is it the will
Of some god that all of your people should hate you? Who knows,
Odysseus may yet return and revenge himself
On them for all their violence, either he alone,
Or perhaps a whole host of Achaeans banded together!
I only wish that blue-eyed Athena would be
As solicitous of you as she was most lovingly so
Of famous Odysseus in the land of the Trojans, where we
Achaeans suffered so much. Never have I seen
The gods so openly loving as Pallas Athena
Was there, standing out in full view by your father's side.
If it were her will to give you a similar place
In her heart, then you may be sure that many a wooer

Would completely forget that he even thought about marriage!"

    Then thoughtful Telemachus answered: "O ancient one,
I don't think what you suggest can ever happen.
Such would be too great a thing by far,
The merest mention of which leaves me all but breathless
With awe. Nor have I any hope that this
Can ever be, though the gods themselves should will it."

    And now blue-eyed Athena spoke to him:
"Telemachus, what nonsense is this that you let pass
The barrier of your teeth! It is, of course,
Quite easy for a god who wills it so to bring
A man safely home from any distance at all.
I had rather, however, much rather, stay longer away
And suffer any number of woes than to return
And be slain at my own hearth as King Agamemnon
Was most brutally slain by the hateful guile
Of Aegisthus and his own wife. But all men must die—
That we know, and the gods themselves cannot
Prevent it when the ruthless fate of leveling death
Arrives to strike down a man they dearly love."

    Then thoughtful Telemachus answered her: "Mentor,
Let us no longer speak of these things you mention,
Grieved though we are. My father can never return.
Death by decree of the gods has been dark doom
For him already. But now there is something else
About which I would like to ask Nestor, since his wisdom
                and judgment
Are better than any we are likely to find elsewhere.
For they say that he has been King through three generations,
And very like an immortal he appears to me.
O Nestor, son of Neleus, answer me truly:
How died Agamemnon, the wide-ruling son of Atreus?
Where was Menelaus? How did treacherous Aegisthus
Manage to kill such a King, a man superior

To him in every way? Can it be that Menelaus
Was not in Achaean Argos but abroad at the time
And that thus was Aegisthus encouraged to kill as he did?"
      Horse-driving Gerenian Nestor made this reply:
"Surely to you, my child, I will tell the whole truth.
You yourself can imagine what would have happened
If tawny Menelaus, the son of Atreus, had returned
From Troy and found Aegisthus alive in his palace.
There would have been no funeral mound for him.
His body would have been left in an open field,
Somewhere far from the city, for the dogs and birds
To tear. Nor would any Achaean woman have wept
For him, since monstrous indeed was the crime he committed.
While we were at Troy, laboring in the toils of war,
He was leisurely living in the heart of Argos,
Where horses graze and grow fat, and doing his best
To talk Agamemnon's wife into being unfaithful.
At first she refused him, for lovely Clytemnestra knew sin
When she saw it, since she wasn't by any means stupid,
           and besides
A bard was there with her whom Agamemnon, in departing
For Troy, had given strict orders to watch over his wife.
But when the gods had decreed her fall and she fell,
Then Aegisthus took the bard to a desolate island
And left him there for the birds to feast upon.
Her he took home with him, nor was she any
Less willing than he. And the thighs of many bulls
He burnt on the holy altars and hung up many offerings
Of cloth and gold, for things had gone his way
Far beyond anything his heart had hoped for.
      "Meanwhile, as my friend Menelaus and I were sailing
Home from Troy, we came to sacred Sunium,
The Athenian cape, and there Phoebus Apollo
Assailed with his painless arrows the helmsman of Menelaus

41

And slew him as he held with both hands to the steering-oar
Of the speeding ship. So died Phrontis, the son
Of Onetor, whose equal at the helm when the big squall breaks
No nation could produce. And Menelaus, though anxious
To be on his way, put in to shore, that he
Might bury his friend with all due funeral rites.
But when his ships again were swiftly coursing
Through the wine-dark water, he reached the craggy steep cape
Of Malea, and then far-thundering Zeus decreed
A most miserable journey for him. For there Zeus hurled
The shrill and blasting winds upon him, and the waves
Were mountain high. His fleet was split in two,
And some of the scattered ships were driven to Crete,
Where the Cydonians live by the streams of Iardanus.
There they were blown toward the foggy coast of Gortyn,
Where the rocks that face the sea are tall and smooth,
For there on the left toward Phaestus the Southwest Wind
Makes the great waves crash, and seemingly small stone resistance
Holds back a great weight of water. Here their ships
Broke up on the rocks, the men just barely escaping,
But five of the blue-bowed vessels the wind and the wave
Bore on to Egypt. There Menelaus wandered
In the midst of alien men, and there he gathered
Much gold and many goods. Meanwhile, at home
Aegisthus was carrying out his miserable plans.
For seven years in golden Mycenae he lorded it
Over the people. But the eighth brought his bane in the person
Of noble Orestes, who returned from Athens and killed
The scheming Aegisthus, who had murdered his famous father.
Then for the Argives he gave a funeral feast
Over his despicable mother and the coward Aegisthus,
And on that very day arrived none other
Than battle-roaring Menelaus, bringing with him a weight

Of treasure as great as his ships could keep afloat.
   "And so, my friend, do not wander too long
And too far from your home, since there your treasure lies
In the midst of arrogant men who may indeed
Divide and devour all that you own, thus making
Your journey vain. But still I bid you go
To King Menelaus, for he has but lately returned
From another country, from men who live far over
A sea so great that one driven there by storms
Could scarcely have hope of returning, far over a sea
So awesomely great that the very birds fly not
So far in a full year's time. Go, now, to him
With your ship and your comrades, or if you would rather go
By land, I'll gladly provide the chariot and horses
For you, and my own sons will show you the way
To lovely Lacedaemon, the home of tawny Menelaus.
Ask him yourself for the whole truth, nor will he
Lie to you, since he is truly wise."

   Then, as the sun went down and darkness came on,
The bright-eyed goddess Athena spoke thus among them:
"Old man, you tell your story well. But come,
Let us cut out the tongues and mix the wine,
That we may pour libations to Poseidon and the other
Immortals and then get some rest, for already it is time
To retire. Day dims in the west, and we should not sit
Too long at a feast of the gods, but go when the time comes."

   Thus the daughter of Zeus, and everyone seemed
To agree. The heralds poured water over the hands of all
And young men filled the bowls brimful of wine,
And then the goblets, first pouring libation drops
In the goblets of all. Then, they threw the tongues
Into the fire, and standing up they poured
Drink-offerings on them. When they had made libations
And drunk as much as they wished, Athena and godlike

Telemachus started to take their leave and go back
To the hollow ship. But Nestor restrained them, saying:
    "May Zeus and the other immortal gods forbid
That you should go from me to your swift ship
As you would from some poor man without a rag
To his name—without, I say, a profusion of spreads
And blankets sufficient to sleep in all comfort both him
And his guests. Such are the spreads and such are the beautiful
Blankets in my house, and never while I am alive
Shall the dear son of that man Odysseus, and a guest
Of mine, make his bed on the deck of a ship. Nor shall it
Be so when I'm gone, so long as my children remain
In my halls to entertain strangers, regardless of who
He may be that comes to my house."
    Then the blue-eyed goddess:
"You say well, old friend, and it will be much better
For Telemachus to do as you say, to go home with you
And spend the night. But I will return to the black ship
To cheer my comrades with news of where we have been.
For among them I am the oldest man by far.
All of them have come out of friendship for Telemachus
And are of about the same age as this gallant young man.
There I will sleep by the hollow black ship tonight,
But at dawn I must depart for the bold Cauconians,
Who owe me a debt both large and of long standing.
But you see to it that Telemachus, a guest in your house,
Is sent on his way with a chariot and one of your sons,
And give him the fastest and strongest horses you have."
    So saying, the bright-eyed goddess Athena took off
In the form of a sea-hawk, leaving everyone gasping at the sight
Of her going. The old man, marveling at what he had seen,
Took Telemachus by the hand and spoke to him thus:
    "My friend, there seems to be little danger that you
Will ever be an evil or cowardly man,

If even when you are so young the gods themselves
Are your guides. For surely, of those who live on Olympus,
This was none other than the very daughter of Zeus,
The surpassingly glorious Athena Tritogeneia,
Who likewise honored your brave and noble father
Among the Argives. But now, divine maid, be gracious,
And grant me good repute, to me and my sons
And to my faithful wife, and to you in return
I will offer a yearling heifer, broad-browed and unbroken,
Never yet in any man's yoke. So sleek a beast,
With horns all wrapped in gold, will I sacrifice to you."
     Thus he prayed, and Pallas Athena heard him.
Then horse-driving Gerenian Nestor led his sons
And sons-in-law to his beautiful palace, and when
They arrived at the greatly glorious royal palace
They all sat down in chairs, both reclining and straight,
And the old man mixed for them a bowl of sweet wine
From a jar which now, after ten full years, the housekeeper
Opened. From this the old man mixed a bowl,
And as he poured libations he earnestly prayed
To Athena, the glorious daughter of aegis-great Zeus.
When they had poured libations and drunk as much
As they wanted, they went to their rooms for the night,
       but the King,
Horse-driving Gerenian Nestor, arranged for Telemachus,
The own dear son of godly Odysseus, to sleep
There in the echoing portico on a corded bed
And beside him Prince Peisistratus, a leader of men
And wielder of the good ashen spear, who alone in the palace
Among the sons of Nestor was still unmarried.
But the King himself went to bed in the innermost chamber
Of the lofty mansion, and beside him lay the lady
His wife, who prepared and shared the royal bed.
     At the first light touch of young Dawn's rosy fingers,

45

Horse-riding Gerenian Nestor got up from his bed,
Went out and sat down on the polished and glistening
         white stones
Before his high doors. On these in days gone by
Sat Neleus, divinely wise, who had long since
Yielded to fate and made the journey to Hades.
Now on those stones in his turn sat Gerenian Nestor,
A bulwark of the Achaeans, his scepter in his hands.
His sons came from their chambers and gathered around him,
Princely Echephron and Stratius, Perseus, Aretus,
And noble Thrasymedes. The warrior, brave Peisistratus,
Came last, making six in all. Then they brought godlike
Telemachus in and gave him a seat beside them.
Horse-driving Gerenian Nestor was the first to speak:
     "Quickly, dear children, go do for me these things
I desire, for to the goddess Athena first,
Of all the immortal deities, I wish to make
A pleasing sacrifice, for she it surely was
Who appeared to me so clearly at the bountiful feast
Of the god. One of you go right away to the fields
And have the herdsman drive, without delay,
A heifer here to us. Let another go
To the black ship of our valiant guest Telemachus,
And bring back all but two of his comrades. Still another
Go fetch Laerces the goldsmith, that he may gild
The heifer's horns. The rest of you stay here
And see that the maids inside prepare a feast
Throughout these glorious halls. Bid them bring chairs,
Plenty of wood for the altar, and clear fresh water."
     He gave the orders, and quickly they all got busy.
In haste the heifer was driven up from the fields,
And from the swift well-balanced ship came the comrades
Of the great-hearted young man Telemachus. The smith appeared,
Bearing the tools of his art—bronze anvil and hammer

46

And sturdy tongs—with which he worked the gold.
And Athena came to accept the sacred offering.
Then Nestor, the ancient charioteer, gave gold,
And the smith, having worked it, covered the horns of the heifer,
That the goddess Athena might see and be pleased with
      the sacrifice.
Stratius and noble Echephron led the heifer up
By the horns, and Aretus came from the storeroom, bearing
The lustral water in a basin engraved with flowers,
And in the other hand a basket of barley grains.
Steadfast Thrasymedes stood ready with a double-edged ax
To cut the heifer down, and Perseus held
The bowl in which to catch the sacrificial blood.
Then Nestor, the ancient driver of chariots, opened
The rites with a washing of hands and sprinkling with grains
Of barley, and fervently he prayed to Pallas Athena
As he began the sacrifice by cutting a lock
From the heifer's forehead and casting it into the fire.

      When they had prayed and sprinkled the grains of barley,
High-hearted, staunch Thrasymedes drew near and struck.
The ax divided the tendons of the neck, and the heifer
Collapsed. Then the women raised the sacred wail,
The daughters and daughters-in-law and the loyal wife
Of Nestor, Eurydice, the oldest among the daughters
Of Clymenus, and the men raised the heifer's head
From the much-traveled earth and held it while Peisistratus, leader
Of men, cut the throat. Now when the dark blood had gushed out
And no life at all was left in the heifer's bones,
They quickly cut up the body and sliced out the thigh-pieces
According to custom. These they wrapped in thick layers
Of fat and on them laid still more raw meat.
All this the old King burned on the flaming wood,
And over the meat he sprinkled the sparkling wine,
While around him the young men held their forks of five tines.

Now when the thigh-pieces were wholly consumed and all
Had tasted of the vital parts, they cut up the rest
And roasted it on the forks which they held in their hands.
    Meanwhile, the lovely Polycasta, youngest among
The daughters of Nestor, son of Neleus, was bathing
Telemachus, and when she had bathed him and rubbed him
        with oil,
She helped him into a tunic, and about his shoulders
She put a beautiful mantle. Then he came from the bath
Looking like one of the immortal gods, and making
His way to Nestor, the shepherd of the people, he sat down
Beside him.
    When the meat was done they drew it off the spits
And sitting down they feasted, with excellent men
To wait on them and keep their golden goblets
Filled with wine. But when they had eaten and drunk
As much as they wanted, horse-driving Gerenian Nestor
Spoke thus among them:
    "My sons, go harness horses
Of truly magnificent mane to one of our chariots,
That Telemachus may continue his journey."
    So he spoke,
And they, in willing obedience, were quick to harness
Fine fast horses to one of the chariots, and therein
The housekeeper put bread and wine and many other
Good things to eat, food such as Zeus-fed kings
Are accustomed to. Then Telemachus stepped into the beautiful
Chariot and beside him the masterful son of Nestor,
The leader Peisistratus, who caught up the reins and cracked
The lash. The horses, not at all unwilling, took off
For the plain at a gallop, leaving the tall towers of Pylos
Behind, and all that day they shook the yoke
On their shoulders as onward they went.
    Then, as the sun

Was setting and all the roads growing dark, they came
To Pherae and the house of Diocles, son of Ortilochus,
The son of Alpheus. There they stayed all night,
And he entertained them in a manner befitting strangers.
      But as soon as young Dawn touched the sky with her
          rosy fingers,
They harnessed the horses and mounted the colorful car.
Then out through the gate and loud colonnade they drove.
Peisistratus cracked the lash and the horses sped on.
Thus they came to the wheat-bearing plain, and so well
Did those fine fast horses perform, that now they approached
The end of their journey to King Menelaus, just
As the sun was setting and all the roads growing dark.

BOOK
IV

MENELAUS AND HELEN

Thus they came to the land of many ravines,
The rolling country of Lacedaemon, and immediately
Drove to the palace of the famous King Menelaus.
They found him at home in the midst of kin and retainers
At a marriage feast that he was giving in honor
Of his noble son and the Princess his daughter. She
Was soon to marry the son of rank-smashing Achilles,
For long ago at Troy he had sworn to give her,
And now the gods were seeing the marriage through.
He was sending her with horses and chariots to the marvelous
City of the Myrmidons, whose King was the man she was going
To marry. For his son he was bringing a bride from Sparta,
Alector's daughter, whom he had chosen for the powerful
Young man Megapenthes, his own dear son, born
Of a slave, for the gods gave no more children to Helen
Once she had borne that lovely child Hermione,
Who grew to be as beautiful as golden Aphrodite.
So the friends and kinsfolk of glorious Menelaus were feasting
Beneath the high roof of the King's great hall with mirth
And good entertainment, for among them there was a poet,
Divinely gifted, and as he began to strum

The lyre and sing, a pair of performers turned cartwheels
Gaily in and out among the guests.
        Meanwhile, Prince Telemachus and the gifted son
Of Nestor pulled up in front of the palace gate,
And one of renowned Menelaus's men, the zealous
Warrior Eteoneus, came out and saw them. Back
Through the palace he went to tell his King, the shepherd
Of the people, and to him he spoke these winged words:
        "O Zeus-fed King Menelaus, two strangers stand
Before your gate, in appearance themselves like the children
Of almighty Zeus. But tell me, shall we unharness
Their fine fast horses for them, or send them on
For some other host to welcome and entertain?"
        Then tawny Menelaus, injured and angry, replied:
"A fool is something you never used to be,
Eteoneus, son of Boëthous, but now surely
You are babbling like a baby. Think of all the kind
And generous entertainment that we two so much enjoyed
At the homes of hospitable men before we reached
Our own and could rest in the hope that Zeus would spare us
Further misery. Unharness their horses indeed!
And as for the strangers, bring them into the palace,
That they may share in our feast."
        So spoke the King,
And Eteoneus quickly took off through the hall, calling
His nimble comrades to come along. They took
The sweating horses from under the yoke and led them
Into the stable. There they tied them in stalls
And before them threw down a mixture of wheat and white
                barley.
The chariot they tilted against the bright wall by the gates
And into the royal halls they led the strangers,
Who marveled at what they saw as they passed through the palace
Of the Zeus-nurtured King. For a luster, as of the sun

Or moon, shone throughout the high-roofed house
Of illustrious Menelaus. When they had sufficiently feasted
Their eyes, they entered the gleaming baths, and after
The maids had bathed them, rubbed them with oil,
       and dressed them
In splendid tunics and mantles, they sat down in chairs
By the side of Menelaus, son of Atreus. Then a maid
Brought lustral water in a beautiful golden pitcher
And poured it out above a silver basin, that they
Might wash their hands, and she drew up in front of them
A polished table, whereon the respected housekeeper
Put bread and other good things to eat, freely
Giving them plenty of all she had. And before them
A carver placed platters of selected meats and beside them
Goblets of gold. Then, with a friendly gesture,
Tawny Menelaus himself greeted his guests
And spoke to them thus:
    "Eat and enjoy yourselves.
Then will be time enough for you to tell us
Who you are. For it's obvious that you're both men of family,
From a race of sceptered kings sustained by Zeus.
No meaner men could father such sons as you."
    As he spoke he took the rich roast of sirloin, the choice cut
Given to him as a mark of honor, and set it
Before them, and they helped themselves to the wonderful meal
Spread out on the table. When they had eaten and drunk
As much as they wanted, Telemachus leaned over and whispered
To the son of Nestor, that no one else might hear:
    "Peisistratus, good friend, just look around you
       at the flashing
Bronze and silver and gold, at the gleaming amber
And ivory throughout these echoing halls. Surely
The palace of Olympian Zeus must be like this
Inside, so indescribably great are the treasures here.

I look and amazement holds me!"
    Tawny Menelaus
Overheard what he said, and spoke these winged words:
"No mortal man, dear children, can compete with Zeus,
For his are everlasting halls and his treasures are forever.
My wealth, however, may very well bear comparison
With that of other men, as well it should.
For I wandered the world for seven long years and suffered
Countless misfortunes before I got home, with my ships
Riding low in the water from the weight of wealth they carried.
I have seen Cyprus, Phoenicia, and Egypt, and wandered
Among Ethiopians, Sidonians, Erembi. So too
I have been to Libya, where the lambs are born with horns
Already sprouting, and their mothers bear young three times
In one full year. No one in that land, from shepherd
To king, ever wants for cheese, meat, or sweet milk,
For the ewes never fail at a milking the whole year through.
But while I was wandering abroad amassing great wealth,
A cunning and stealthy man murdered my brother,
Who suspected nothing, and this crime he committed
            with the help—
The most treacherous help—of my brother's wretched wife.
Thus, you see, I take no joy now
In these possessions, for as you may have heard from your fathers,
Whoever they are, my sorrows have surely been many
And great, and I have already seen the decay
Of one rich and stately house. What peace would be mine
In these halls, with even a third of the wealth I have,
If only those men were alive who died long ago
In the broad land of Troy so far from horse-pasturing Argos!
Many times I have sat in these halls and found some relief
In weeping and mourning for all of those men, though never
For long at a time—one soon gets enough of cold crying—
Yet, though my grief is great for all who died there,

I mourn not so much for that lost army of comrades
As I do for one man only, of whom just to think
Makes eating and sleeping hateful, for of all the Achaeans
No one toiled and took on himself so much
As Odysseus—no one suffered as he did! And now
It seems that all his toils came to nothing for him
But still more suffering, and I am left with sorrow
For that long absence of his, and whether he's living
Or dead we have no idea, though I suppose
He has long been mourned as missing by old Laertes
And constant Penelope, by Telemachus too, who had just
Been born when Odysseus had to leave home for the war."

    When Telemachus heard his father's name, his eyes
Filled with tears that rolled down his cheeks and fell
        on the ground,
And with both hands he held up his purple cloak
In front of his face. Menelaus knew that he wept,
And in his mind and heart the King was undecided
Whether he should wait till the young man spoke of his father
Himself, or whether he should probe and question him further.
    While he debated thus with himself, down
From her fragrant and high-vaulted chamber came Helen,
        like Artemis
Of the golden bow, and her handmaids with her. Adraste
Drew up a beautiful chair for her, and on it
Alcippe arranged a robe of the softest wool.
Phylo carried a silver work-basket, which Alcandre
Had given to Helen in wealthy Egyptian Thebes,
Where she lived with her husband Polybus. He gave to Menelaus
Two silver baths, two three-legged cauldrons,
And a great weight of gold, full ten talents in all.
In addition, his wife gave exquisite things to Helen—
Among them a golden distaff and a basket on wheels,
A silver basket with ribs and rim of gold.

54

This lovely gift, now full of finely spun yarn,
The handmaid Phylo brought and placed beside her,
And across it lay the golden distaff, charged
With wool of deep violet. Helen sat down in the chair
With its footrest below, and with no hesitation at all
She asked her husband the things she wanted to know:

      "Have we learned, god-kept Menelaus, who our guests are?
But why should I go on pretending? Let me say
What my heart says I should, for I cannot look without marveling
At this young man. Never have I seen anyone,
Either man or woman, who so much resembled another
As this man resembles great-hearted Odysseus. Surely
He must be Telemachus, who was only a baby when his father
Had to leave for Troy and the war you Achaeans fought
So bravely, so fiercely for the sake of my worthless self."

      Tawny Menelaus replied: "I too, my lady,
See the resemblance, now that you point it out.
Such were his hands and feet and the way he looked
At people, such his hair and the shape of his head.
And just a moment ago when I spoke of Odysseus
And all the miserable toil he suffered for my sake,
This young man was moved to bitter tears
And held up his purple cloak in front of his face."

      Then Nestor's son Peisistratus spoke to the King:
"Zeus-nurtured Menelaus, son of Atreus and first
Among your people, what you say is true.
He is indeed the son of Odysseus, discreet
And with so much respect for you that he hesitates
To interrupt, fearing to seem overbold on this
His first visit here, for we both take most delight
In listening to you, whose voice is like that of a god.
Horse-driving Gerenian Nestor bade me go with him
And be his guide, for he was eager to see you,
That you might help him decide what action to take.

Many and great are the woes of a son whose father
Is no longer at home and who has no other helpers,
And so it is now with Telemachus. His father is gone
And he has no other friends to ward off injustice
And ruin."
    Then tawny Menelaus answered him thus:
"I can hardly believe it, that here in my own house
Sits the son of that man so dear to me, who suffered
So much for my sake in the bloody toils of war.
I had always thought that upon his return I would welcome
And honor him above all the other Argives, and so
I would have, if only far-seeing Olympian Zeus
Had willed that we both should return in our swift ships
From across the sea. I would have brought him from Ithaca
With his son, his people, and all he owned, then given him
A city in Argos and built him a palace to live in.
For him I would indeed have emptied a city,
One close by, that often we might have been
With each other and lived in mutual love and delight
Till death's dark cloud enclosed us. But of such bliss
Even God must have been jealous, for only to that
Unlucky man he granted no return."
    These words left them all in a mood of tearful lamenting.
The daughter of Zeus, Argive Helen, wept,
As did Telemachus and Menelaus, son of Atreus,
Nor did the son of Nestor remain dry-eyed,
For in his heart he was thinking of matchless Antilochus,
Whom Memnon, the bright Dawn's radiant son, had slain.
With him in mind he spoke these winged words:
    "Son of Atreus, whenever at home we talked
And asked about you, the ancient Nestor would always
Say that you were the wisest of mortals. And now,
If your grief will allow it, let me persuade you to listen,
For I take little delight in weeping and dining

Together, and besides, early Dawn will soon be here.
Of course I don't think it is wrong to weep for those
Who are now with the fated dead. What else can we do
For those miserable mortals but cut a lock of hair
And shed our tears? As for me, I have a dead brother,
Who of the Argives was far from being least able,
And surely you must have known him, though I never did.
I have heard men say, however, that Antilochus was hardly
To be surpassed as a warrior or in a foot race."

    Then tawny Menelaus replied: "Good friend, you speak
As a wise man should, nor could a much older man
Have done any better, so fine a thing it is
To have a father such as yours. It's easy to tell
The son of a man whom Cronos' son has favored
In his birth and marriage, as surely he has always favored
King Nestor, who now enjoys a comfortable old age
At home, having seen his sons mature in wisdom
And valor. But now we will stop this lamenting. Let us
Have water poured over our hands and again pay attention
To the meal before us. In the morning Telemachus and I
Can tell each other our stories through to the end."

    So spoke the King, and Asphalion, a zealous retainer
Of illustrious Menelaus, poured water over their hands,
And they helped themselves to the good things spread out
        before them.

    But Helen, daughter of Zeus, had other ideas,
And as soon as she could she put a powerful drug
In the wine they were drinking, a sweet and soothing nepenthe
To make one forget all pain of body and mind.
Whoever drank of a bowl in which this was mingled
Could not for one whole day shed a single tear,
Not even if his mother and father lay dead before him,
Nor if he should see his brother or own dear son
Put to the sword. Such soothing and subtle drugs

57

Had been given to the daughter of Zeus by the wife of Thon,
Polydamna of Egypt, for there the grain-giving earth
Is most fruitful of herbs that are used in the mixing of drugs,
Many quite helpful and healing, many quite deadly.
There all are versed in medical lore far beyond
What other men know, for they all claim descent from Paeëon,
The gods' own physician. Now, having drugged the wine
And made sure that everyone's goblet was filled, Helen
Once again spoke to her husband:
                    "Son of Atreus,
God-kept Menelaus, and you other sons of worthiest
Men, Zeus, in whose power all things are,
Gives good and ill to us as he sees fit,
And now surely is the time to sit in these halls
And feast and enjoy the telling of tales. Already
I think of a story that fits the moment well.
It's true I cannot begin to tell all the toils
And achievements of enduring Odysseus, but what a deed
That strong man did at Troy, where you Achaeans
Suffered so much, when he with disfiguring blows
Marred his own flesh, clothed himself in rags
Too vile for a slave, and walked through the hostile city,
Up and down the wide streets, disguised as a beggar, a far cry
From what he really was among his own people
At the ships of the Achaeans! So dressed he entered the city,
And not one of the Trojans knew him. Only I saw through
The disguise. But when I questioned him, he cunningly
Tried to evade me, till finally, having bathed him and rubbed him
With oil, having dressed him and sworn a great oath that I
                    would not
Reveal his name to the Trojans until he got back
To the huts and swift ships of the Argives—only then
                    would he tell me

In any detail what the Achaeans were planning.
Then, after slaying many Trojans with his long bronze blade,
He made his way back to the Argives loaded with information
And left a city full of wailing women.
But I was glad, for already my heart was longing
To go back home, and I groaned for the stupid infatuation
Aphrodite gave when she caused me to leave my own
Dear country, my child, my marriage chamber, my husband,
A man with far more than his share of good looks and good sense."
          Then tawny Menelaus replied: "All this, my dear,
You have told us justly and well. And truly, though I
Have traveled much about the wide world and known
The minds and hearts of many resourceful men,
I have never seen anyone else so completely dependable
As dauntless Odysseus. Think what he did and endured
In the carved and polished horse when all of us Argive
Leaders sat with him there bearing fateful death
To the Trojans. It was then, my dear, that you arrived—
It must have been by command of some god who wished
To magnify greatly the glory of Trojans—and with you
Godlike Deïphobus. Three times you walked around
That hollow horse and ran your hands over the wood,
And you called out the names of the Danaan chieftains, making
Your voice like the voices of their wives back home in Argos.
I sat with Tydeus' son and great Odysseus
There in the midst of those men and heard you call,
And both of us were eager to get up and leave,
Or right away to call out in answer, but Odysseus
Restrained us, and though we insisted he held us back.
Then all the other sons of Achaeans sat quietly,
With one exception—Anticlus, who alone seemed determined
To call out an answer to you. But quickly Odysseus
Clapped his strong hands tightly over his mouth
And held him so until Pallas Athena led you

Away, and thus he saved all the Achaeans."

  Then finally thoughtful Telemachus spoke to the King:
"Zeus-nurtured Menelaus, son of Atreus and leader
Of your people, so much the heavier his loss to us,
Since none of this could save him from grievous destruction,
Nor could have, though his heart had been of iron. But come,
Show us our beds, that we may rest in sweet sleep
And forget our troubles."

  Now Argive Helen told
Her maids to place two beds in the portico and cover them
With fine purple robes, light spreads, and fleecy warm blankets,
And the girls went out with torches and made the beds.
Then a herald showed the guests where they were to sleep,
Telemachus the Prince and the glorious son of Nestor,
There in the portico of the palace. But the son of Atreus
Slept in the innermost room of the lofty house,
And beside him lay long-robed Helen, loveliest of women.

  As soon as early Dawn of the rosy fingers
Appeared, the warrior Menelaus got up from his bed
And put on his clothes. He slung his keen blade
    from his shoulder
And on his shining feet bound beautiful sandals.
Then, like a god in appearance, he went out of his chamber,
Sat down by Telemachus, and spoke these words to him:

  "My good Telemachus, what need has brought you here
Over the sea's broad back to this our lovely land
Of Lacedaemon? Is your business public or private?
Please tell me your reason in all frankness."

  Then thoughtful Telemachus
Replied: "Zeus-loved Menelaus, son of Atreus
And leader of your people, I have come to learn
What I can concerning my father. My house is being
Devoured, my rich estate destroyed, for always
The place is sadly overrun with hostile men

Who continue their wanton slaughter of my restless sheep
And long-horned shuffling cattle, and these same men
Are the proud and arrogant wooers of my mother. I come
To your knees, hoping that you will be willing to tell me
How my father so miserably died, since perhaps you witnessed
His death yourself or have heard his woeful story
From some other wanderer. For beyond all other men,
He was born to suffer. Do not soften your words
Out of pity or compassion for me, but tell me exactly
How you happened to be there and how my father died.
If ever gallant Odysseus kept a promise to you
Of word or deed in the land of the Trojans, I beseech you
To remember it now and tell me his story unaltered."
    Then greatly indignant, tawny Menelaus replied:
"What folly! for those cowards want to lie in the bed
Of a man truly valiant. It's as if a deer were to leave
Her suckling twin fawns asleep in the thicket-lair
Of a mighty lion and go out to graze on the hills
And in the green valleys, while the lion returns to his bed
And ferociously slaughters them both. Even so will Odysseus
Bring down a doom most wretched on those men!
And now I pray, O Father Zeus, Athena,
And Apollo, that he may come among them with strength
Such as that he possessed when once in populous Lesbos
He wrestled a bout with Philomeleides and threw him
Crashing to the ground, with applause from all the Achaeans—
If only he might come among them with strength such as that,
Then would their wooing be bitter, and swift their destruction!
But concerning this matter of which you so earnestly ask,
I will not swerve from the truth or try to deceive you.
Of all the unerring old man of the sea told me,
Not a word will I conceal or keep from you.
    "Eager though I was to get home, the gods still held me
In Egypt, since I had not made due offering to them

Of unblemished hecatombs, and the gods insist always that men
Be mindful of them. Now out in the rolling sea,
About as far out from Egypt as a well-curved ship
Can sail in a day with a whistling strong wind behind her,
Lies an island called Pharos. In the good harbor there men launch
Their graceful ships, having drawn a fresh water supply
From the dark island pools. But there for twenty full days
The gods held me back, and not once in all that time
Did the winds come up that carry ships out from land
And over the sea's broad back. And now all our supplies
And the strength of my men would surely have been exhausted
If a certain goddess had not had compassion on me
And come to my rescue, the goddess Eidothea, daughter
Of powerful Proteus, the briny old man of the sea.
For my situation had aroused most compassion in her
Of all the immortals, and she met me one day as I wandered
Alone in the island, some distance away from my comrades,
Whose empty bellies drove them all around the coast
Fishing with hooks. She came up close and spoke:
     " 'Is it, my friend, that you don't know any better,
Or do you endure such misery of your own free will
As one who takes pleasure in suffering? For a long time now
You have been held back in this island without a sign
Of deliverance, and the strength of your men is dwindling.'
     "She spoke,
And I answered her thus: 'I am by no means certain
Which goddess you are, but let me assure you it is
By no will of my own that I have been held back here.
It is clear that I must have sinned against the immortals
Who rule the wide vault of heaven, but tell me, since the gods
Know everything, which of you binds me here and keeps me
From my journey, and tell me how I may get home
Over the fish-full sea?'
     "So I answered her,

And the lovely goddess was quick to reply: 'Friend,
I will speak to you in all frankness. Here to this island
An old man is accustomed to come, that unerring old man
Of the brine, immortal Proteus of Egypt, who serves
Poseidon and knows how deep is every sea.
He, they say, is my father. Now if somehow
You can lie in wait and catch him, he will tell you
About your journey, how far it is to your home
And how you may get there over the fish-full sea. All this,
My god-kept friend, he will tell you, and too, if you wish
To hear it, he will tell what has happened back home
       in your palace,
Both the evil and good, since you have been gone on your long
And painful journey.'
    "So she spoke, and I answered her
Thus: 'You yourself must think of some way to ambush
That ancient divinity, so that he won't see me and vanish.
For a mortal man can hardly get the best of a god.'
    "Such were my words, and the lovely goddess was quick
To reply: 'Here then, my friend, is what I suggest.
When the sun is directly overhead and the West Wind darkens
The water with ripples, the profound old man of the brine
Comes up from his salty abode and into the caves
To sleep, and the flippered seals, those brine-bred children
Of the sea's fair daughter, come out of the surf in shoals
And lie down to sleep all around him, giving off an aroma
Of the deep salt sea. At dawn I will take you there
And hide you side by side, for you must pick
Three men to go with you, the best three men you have
By your well-decked ships. But now let me tell you all
The wiles and wizardry of that old man. First
He will count the seals and look them over, but when
He has counted them all by fives and made his inspection,

He will lie down among them like a shepherd in the midst
       of his sheep.
Now as soon as you see him lie down, gather up all
Your strength and courage and hold him there, no matter
How hard he struggles to get away. And it will be
A struggle, for he will transform himself not only
Into all earthly creatures but into water as well
And furious fire. Still you must hold him fast
And bear down ever harder. But when at last
He questions you, resuming the form you saw
When he first lay down, then, staunch man, relax
Your hold and let go, and ask the old man which god
Is so angry at you and how you may yet get home
Over the fish-full sea.'
      "So saying, she disappeared
Beneath the billows, and I with an anxious heart
Returned to where my ships were drawn up on the beach.
When I reached the ships and the sea, we had our supper.
Then immortal night came on and we lay down to sleep
On the surf-beaten shore of the brine. But at the first light
Of rosy-fingered Dawn, I set out along the beach
Of the much-traveled sea, fervently praying to the gods
As I went, and with me I took the three men whom I
Could trust most in any undertaking.
      "Eidothea, meanwhile,
Had gone down beneath the wide water and emerged
      with the skins
Of four newly flayed seals to be used in deceiving her father.
She had scooped out beds in the beach and was sitting there
      waiting
When we came up. Then she had us lie side by side
And covered each man with a skin. But the horrible stench
Of the brine-bred seals was all but lethal, and the morning
Would surely have been most terrible—for none of us

Was accustomed to sleeping with a brute from the sea—
       had the goddess
Not thought of a marvelous remedy and come to our rescue
With sweet ambrosia, which she placed under each man's nose,
Thus killing the beastly stench of the seals. All morning
We patiently waited, and the seals came thronging up
And lay down by one another on the surf-beaten shore.
Then at noon the old man himself came out of the sea,
Found the sleek seals, and inspected and counted them all.
Among them he counted us first, suspecting nothing.
Then he too lay down to sleep, whereupon we sprang up
And seized him, but the artful old man had lost none of his
       cunning.
First he became a bearded lion, then a snake,
A panther, and a gigantic boar—then a running stream
And a great leafy tree, but we gritted our teeth and held on.
When at last the cunning old wizard grew tired, he spoke
And questioned me thus:
    " 'With which of the gods, Menelaus,
Have you been conspiring, that you might waylay me so
And take me against my will? What is it you want?'
    "So Proteus spoke, and I made this reply:
'Why vex me with such a question, old man, when you know
Very well how long I have been held back in this island
Without a sign of deliverance, my heart's hope dwindling
Away—but tell me, since surely the gods know everything,
Who among the immortals binds me here
And keeps me from my journey, and tell me too
How I may get home again over the fish-full sea.'
    "So I spoke, and he answered without hesitation:
'If you wanted to sail the wine-dark sea and get home
With all speed, then you should have made fit offerings to Zeus
And the other gods. Now you will never get back to your friends
And firm-founded palace until once again you have gone

To the Zeus-fed river of Egypt and offered holy hecatombs
There to the immortal gods who inhabit broad heaven.
Then at last they will grant you the journey you so much desire.'
    "By these heavy words the heart in my breast was broken,
For once again I would have to sail over that long
And weary stretch of misty sea that led back
To Egypt. Even so, I managed to make this reply:
'I will do what you say, old man, but tell me this
And speak it truly. What about all those Achaeans
Whom Nestor and I left behind when we set sail from Troy—
Did they all return in their ships and reach their homes
Unharmed, or was any man undone by bitter
Death, either on board his ship or in the arms
Of his friends, though he had already wound up his career
In the war?'
    "Again, without hesitation, he answered:
'Son of Atreus, why do you ask me these things
When you have no real need to know what I know? Nor will
Your eyes be dry when you have heard the whole story.
For, though many survived, many were slain.
But only two leaders of the bronze-clad Achaeans were killed
In returning—you already know who died in the fighting—
And another, I think, still lives but is held a prisoner
Somewhere out there in that vast body of water.
    " 'Ajax went down in the midst of his long-oared ships.
Poseidon dashed him upon the huge rocks of Gyrae,
But saved him from the sea. And surely he would have escaped
That death, despicable though he was to Athena, if only
He had not uttered those blind and arrogant words,
Bragging that he had escaped the sea's great abyss
Despite the will of the gods. When Poseidon heard
This blatant boasting, he took his trident in his powerful
Hands and with a single blow he split the rock
Of Gyrae in two. One part remained where it was,

But the other dropped into the sea, and with it went Ajax
And his blind pride, down into the boiling and boundless
Deep, where he drank the briny water and died.
    " 'Your brother and his ships escaped the fates, with the help
Of queenly Hera, but as he approached the high cape
Of Malea a great wind caught him up and carried him, heavily
Groaning, over the fish-full sea almost to the shore
Of that land which was once the home of Thyestes and then
Of his son Aegisthus. But even from here he was given
A safe return, for the gods made the wind turn back
And at last those men got home. Then indeed Agamemnon
Was glad to step out on the soil of his fathers. Laying hold
Of the earth, he repeatedly kissed it, and many hot tears
He shed, so joyful a sight home was to him.
    " 'But now from his place of vigil the lookout saw him,
The watchful man whom crafty Aegisthus had put there,
Having promised as reward two talents of gold, and already
He had stood that guard for a year, that Agamemnon might not
Get by him unseen and give vent to his furious valor.
He ran to the palace and told Aegisthus, shepherd
Of the people, and he quickly contrived a treacherous plan.
He hid his best twenty men in ambush and ordered
A feast prepared on the other side of the hall.
Then, with a heart full of murder, he went in his chariot
To bring the people's shepherd Agamemnon home.
And home he brought the quite unsuspecting King,
And when he had feasted him killed him, as one might slaughter
An ox at the manger. Of those who took part in that melee,
Whether friends of the son of Atreus or the men of Aegisthus,
Not one survived, but one and all were slain there
In the palace.'
    "When I heard these words, my spirit collapsed.
I sat on the beach weeping and wanting to die,
With no wish at all to see the sunlight again.

But when I had had enough of weeping and writhing,
The briny old prophet spoke again: 'Son of Atreus,
Enough of this senseless sobbing, for thereby we'll accomplish
Nothing. But see how soon you can get back home,
For you may find Aegisthus alive, or, if Orestes
Has gotten there first, you may still arrive in time
For the funeral feast.'

  "He spoke, and once again
A warm and manly courage revived my spirit,
Grieved though I was, and I spoke these winged words
To him: 'Now, of these men I know, but tell me
Who the third one is, he who is living or dead
Somewhere out there in that wide water. Grieved
Though I am, I still want to know.'

  "So I to him,
And he answered without hesitation: 'The son of Laertes,
Whose home is in Ithaca. I saw him weeping out there
In the island home of the nymph Calypso. She keeps him
By force, and he has no ship, no oars, no comrades
To help him get home over the sea's broad back. As for you,
Zeus-loved Menelaus, it is not your fate to die
In horse-pasturing Argos. Instead, the immortals will send you
To the Elysian plain at the outermost bounds of the earth,
Where tawny Rhadamanthus lives and where life is most easy
For men. There it never snows, no storm winds blow,
Nor does it rain, but the cool West Wind blows always
Briskly off the stream of Oceanus to refresh men there.
For you are the husband of Helen, and Helen is the daughter
Of Zeus.'

  "So saying, he vanished beneath the billows,
And I with my godlike companions returned to the ships,
My heart full of darkness. There by the sea we had supper,
And when divine night came on we lay down to sleep
On the surf-beaten shore of the sea, but at the first light

Of rosy-fingered Dawn we dragged our graceful ships
Down to the shimmering sea, set up the masts
And sails, and took our places on board. At the oars
My comrades churned the gray water, and back we sailed
To the Zeus-fed river of Egypt, where we moored the ships.
Then I offered unblemished hecatombs, and when
I had appeased the wrath of the everlasting gods
I heaped up a mound to the unquenchable fame of Agamemnon.
This done, I set sail, and the immortals gave a good wind
And brought me swiftly home to my own dear country.
     "But come, stay with me here in these halls ten days
At least, better still, eleven or twelve. Then
I will send you home in style, with splendid gifts—
Three horses, a gleaming chariot, and a beautiful goblet,
That you may pour libations to the immortal gods
And remember me all your days."
     But thoughtful Telemachus
Replied: "Son of Atreus, don't insist on my staying,
For I would be all too willing to sit here with you
A full year, with no desire at all for home
Or parents, so great is my joy when listening to you.
But already my friends grow weary in sacred Pylos
While you still want me to stay. And as for the gift
You would give me, let it be some kind of keepsake, some treasure.
I'll not take horses to Ithaca, but will leave them here
For you to enjoy. For here you have a wide plain
Covered with clover and grass, with wheat and rye
And broad-eared white barley. But Ithaca is no place to run horses,
And we have no meadows. We have, however, good pasture
For goats, and the country is more picturesque than a land
Where horses graze. In none of the islands that slope
To the sea is there really much room to drive horses, nor have they
Many meadows, and Ithaca least of all."
     So he spoke, and battle-roaring Menelaus smiled,

And giving him a pat with his hand spoke thus:
"Your noble blood, my boy, shows plainly in what
You say. Of course I will change the gifts—no trouble
At all for me. And, of the many treasures
Here in my house, I will give you the one most gorgeous
And costly. I will give you a richly wrought wine-bowl, solid
Silver, with ribs and rim of gold, the work
Of Hephaestus, given to me by royal Phaedimus,
The Sidonians' King, when on my way home I stayed
At his house for a while. Now I want you to have it."

    As they were talking, the feasters arrived at the palace
Of the sacred King. Before them they drove their own sheep
And with them they carried a supply of inspiriting wine,
While their wives, beautifully veiled, sent bread for them.
Even so the Spartans prepared for a feast in those halls.

    But the wooers were enjoying themselves with their usual
        arrogance
In front of the palace of Odysseus, there where the ground
Had been leveled, throwing the discus and javelin, while Antinous
And princely Eurymachus, their leaders and men of most valor,
Were sitting there taking it easy. Then Phronius' son
Noëmon approached them to ask Antinous a question:
    "Antinous, do we or don't we have any idea
When Telemachus is supposed to come back from sandy Pylos?
He went in a ship of mine, and now I need her
For a trip to the wide fields of Elis, where I have
        twelve brood mares
And with them young mules, sturdy but still at the teat.
I want to drive one off and break him in."

    He spoke, and they were amazed, for they had no idea
That Telemachus had gone to Neleian Pylos, but thought
He was somewhere on his estate, out among the flocks,
Perhaps, or with the swineherd. Then Eupeithes' son

Antinous replied:
"Now tell me exactly what happened.
When did he go, and who went with him? Were they picked
Young men of Ithaca, or, as they might well have been,
Hirelings and slaves of his own? And tell me frankly,
Did he take your ship by force, or did he talk you
Into letting him take her?"
Then Phronius' son Noëmon
Replied: "I gave her to him of my own free will.
What else could anyone do when such a man,
His heart full of trouble, asks a favor? Such favors
Are hard to refuse. As for those who went with him, they
Are the finest young men in the land, not counting ourselves.
And the man I saw go aboard as captain was either
Mentor or a god who looked exactly like Mentor.
About this, though, I wonder. For only yesterday, just as
Dawn was breaking, I saw the good Mentor here.
Yet he was certainly aboard my ship when it left
For Pylos."
So saying, he headed for his father's house,
Leaving two proud and now very angry men.
At once they made the wooers stop playing and sit down,
And Antinous, son of Eupeithes, spoke among them,
Deeply disturbed. His black heart ran over with rage
And his eyes were like fire when it blazes:
"Of all the damnable
Deeds, this journey Telemachus has taken is surely
One of the most proud and insolent! and we thought he didn't
Dare. Now this mere boy, in spite of us all
And fussing no further, has chosen the best crew available,
Launched a ship, and set sail. At this rate he'll give us
Real trouble some day, if Zeus doesn't choose to ruin him
Before he reaches his prime. But come, let me have
A swift ship and twenty men, that I may lie

In wait and ambush him in the straits between Ithaca
And craggy Samos. Thus he will learn how sad
And costly it is to go sailing in search of a father!"

So he spoke, and they all had praise for him
And his plan and urged him on. Then quickly the meeting
Broke up and the wooers re-entered the house of Odysseus.

Now Penelope soon found out what the wooers were up to,
For Medon the herald let her know. He had been standing
Just outside the court while the wooers within
Were weaving their plot, and he no sooner heard what they said
Than he took off through the palace to tell Penelope, but she
Started in at him before he got through the door:

"Herald, what business have my lordly lovers sent you on
Now? Is it your job to tell the maids of sacred
Odysseus to stop what they're doing and prepare a feast
For them? If so, may it be their very last—
May they never go wooing or feasting again—yes,
I do mean you, my wooers, who congregate here,
Wildly wasting the goods of prudent Telemachus.
When you were children you apparently paid no attention
At all when your fathers spoke of Odysseus and how
He treated them, how he neither did nor said
Any wrong to anyone of his subjects—which is quite unusual
For sacred kings who may love and hate whom they please.
But he hurt no one at all. As for you, your villainous
Wishes and indecorous behavior are all too obvious,
Nor is there any gratitude now for the good
He used to do."

Then Medon, who understood how she felt,
Replied: "I only wish, my Queen, that this
Were the worst they could do, but even now they are planning
Another evil far more monstrous and much harder
To bear, which I pray that Cronos' son will never
Allow. They're determined to murder Telemachus as he

72

Returns from a trip he's been on, a quest, O Queen,
To sacred Pylos and lovely Lacedaemon, for news
Concerning his father."

    As he spoke these words, her knees
Grew weak, her heart grew faint, and for a long time
She said nothing at all. Her eyes filled with tears
And her sobs were all choked up within her. At last
She found her voice and spoke:

    "But herald, why did
My son go? He had no real need to go boarding swift ships,
Those seagoing horses that sailors use to cross
The wide water. Can it be that he wants to destroy forever
His very name?"

    Then Medon, discreet as ever,
Replied: "Some god, my Queen, or his own heart
Impelled him to Pylos. I don't know which. But he went
To learn of his father's return, or at least to find out
What's become of him."

    So saying, he took his way
Through the house of Odysseus, but she in her deadly grief,
Lacking even the heart to go and sit down in one
Of the many chairs in her beautiful chamber, sank down
On the threshold, moaning with misery, while all the maids
In the palace, both young and old, came whimpering around her.
To them Penelope spoke in the midst of her sobs:

    "Listen, my friends, to one whom the Olympian has given
More grief than to any other woman of my generation.
Years ago I lost my noble husband,
My lion-hearted lord, who among the Danaans was the best
And bravest man, famous throughout all Hellas
To the heart of Argos. And now the blasting winds
Have snatched my darling boy away from these halls
And no tidings return. Nor did I hear one word
Of his leaving. Wretches! not even from you—not one

Of you was considerate enough so much as to call me
From bed, though you knew quite well what was going on
That night when he went aboard his hollow black ship.
For if I had known he was planning this journey, he
Would have stayed here, no matter how much he wanted to go,
Or left me dead in these halls! But one of you
Go quickly and call my old servant Dolius, who was given
To me by my father when I first came here and who now
Is in charge of my orchard. I'll send him straight to Laertes,
That he may sit down by him and tell him everything.
Perhaps Laertes will weave some plot and come forth
In tears to plead with the people, who seem dead set
In their aim to destroy the line that descends from him
And godlike Odysseus."
    To which the good nurse Eurycleia:
"Dear lady, whether you kill me with some ruthless knife
Or let me go on living here, I cannot
Help speaking out. I knew all about his going
And gave him whatever he asked for, bread and sweet wine.
But he made me swear a great oath not to tell you
Until the twelfth day, or until you should miss him yourself
And find out he was gone, for he did not wish that tears
Should stain the flesh of your lovely face. But come,
Bathe yourself and put on some fresh clothes. Then go,
With your women attending, upstairs to your room and pray
To Athena, the daughter of aegis-bearing Zeus, for she
Is still able to save him from even this death, and do not
Trouble an already troubled old man. For I cannot
Believe that the blissful gods so utterly hate
The line of Arceisius' son Laertes. Surely
There will always be someone to own this high-roofed house
And the many rich fields that stretch far away all around it."
    With these words she hushed the sobs of her mistress
        and stopped

Her tears. Then Penelope bathed and put on fresh clothes
And went with her women upstairs to her room, where she poured
In a basket some grains of sacred barley, and prayed
To Athena:
      "O unwearied daughter of aegis-bearing Zeus,
Hear me. If ever resourceful Odysseus, here
In these halls, burnt the fat thighs of heifer or sheep
To you, remember those offerings now and save
My dear son. Protect him from the malice of the arrogant wooers."
      So saying, she raised the sacred wail, and the goddess
Heard her prayer. Meanwhile, the reveling wooers
Were laughing and talking throughout the shadowy halls,
When one of the proud young bullies called out: "Surely
The much-courted Queen is getting ready for a wedding.
She doesn't know about the death we've prepared for her son!"
      Even so they boasted, though they were the ones who had
No idea how things would turn out. Then Antinous got
Their attention: "You fools! are you mad? Now do not utter
Another bragging word of any sort, or someone
May go inside and repeat what you have been saying.
But come, let all of us get up quietly and go
Carry out that plan with which our hearts are so pleased."
      So saying, he picked the twenty best men, and they
Went down to the shore where the swift black ship was lying.
First, they drew her out in deep water, where they set up
The mast and sail, fixed the oars in their locks
Of leather, all shipshape, and unfurled the white sail. Their
          squires,
Proud and excited, brought them their weapons. Then
They moored the ship well out in the water and came
Ashore, where they ate their supper and waited for evening.
      Meanwhile, brooding Penelope lay there in her room
Upstairs, without so much as tasting either food
Or drink, worried as she could be about whether

Her innocent son would escape with his life, or die
A victim of the arrogant wooers. And as a lion
In the midst of crafty men is torn and frantic
With fear as the beaters close in on him, even so
She was fearful and worried, but at last deliciously drowsy,
And sinking back on the bed she fell asleep,
Completely relaxed.
      Now the bright-eyed goddess Athena
Had a plan of her own. She made a phantom in the form
Of a woman, Iphthime, another daughter of great-hearted
Icarius, who lived with her husband Eumelus in Pherae,
And the goddess sent it to the palace of sacred Odysseus
To end the tearful lamenting of grieving Penelope.
It entered her chamber through the hole for the thong in the door,
And hovering above her it spoke:
      "Do you sleep, Penelope,
Your heart full of sorrow? Indeed it is not the will
Of the easy-living gods that you should weep and suffer,
For your son has done nothing at all to offend them, and surely
He will return."
      Then thoughtful Penelope answered,
Sweetly slumbering at the gate of dreams: "My sister,
But why are you here? Your coming is most unexpected,
Since you live so far away. Did you tell me to stop
My grieving and put an end to the anguish that racks
My mind and heart? Well, long ago I lost
My noble husband, my lion-hearted lord, who
Among the Danaans was the best and bravest man,
And the noblest, famous indeed throughout all Hellas
To the heart of Argos. And now my darling boy
Has gone off in a hollow ship, and he a mere baby
Without any knowledge at all of the world's hard ways.
I grieve for him even more than I do for his father.
I'm worried half to death about what could happen to him

In a land of strangers, or at sea. For many evil men
Are plotting against him, all of them eager to kill him
Before he gets home."
      Then the dim phantom replied:
"Be strong, and try not to let fear overcome you, for your son
Has a wonderfully capable guide with him, one
Whose presence men have often prayed for—the mighty
Pallas Athena. And she feels sorry for you
In your suffering, for it is she who has sent me to give you
This message."
      But thoughtful Penelope was still not satisfied,
And she said: "If you are indeed divine and have really
Heard the voice of God, tell me, I beg you,
Of that other unlucky man. Is he still alive
And in sight of sunshine, or is he already dead
And in the house of Hades?"
      And the fading dim phantom replied:
"Of him, alive or dead, I cannot speak
In any detail, and windy inaccurate words
Are worse than useless."
      So saying, the phantom faded
Through the hole in the latch and into the wind outside.
Now the daughter of Icarius awoke quite suddenly, but she felt
Warmly comforted that a vision so vivid had appeared to her
In the early hours of night.
      Meanwhile the wooers
Went aboard and sailed off, with nothing but murder
        in their hearts
For Telemachus. Midway between Ithaca and craggy Samos
Lies the rocky little island of Asteris, small to be sure
But having a harbor with a mouth on either side.
It was there the Achaeans lay waiting to ambush the Prince.

BOOK

V

CALYPSO AND ODYSSEUS

As Dawn arose from beside her lord Tithonus
That she might bring light to gods and mortal men,
The immortals sat down in council and among them Zeus,
Who thunders on high and whose might is supreme. Athena
Was recalling the many woes of Odysseus, and retelling
His story, for she was greatly disturbed at his stay
With the nymph:
    "Father Zeus, and you other happy immortals,
May no sceptered king ever again be generous,
Gentle and kind, nor let his heart be filled
With righteousness. May they all henceforth be cruel and unjust,
Since no one remembers sacred Odysseus, not even
The people whose kind and fatherly King he was.
He stagnates still on an island, suffering much
In the home of the nymph Calypso, who keeps him there
By force, and he has no ship, no oars, no comrades
To help him get home over the sea's broad back. And now
They're determined to murder his own dear son as he
Returns from a trip he's been on, an urgent journey

To sacred Pylos and lovely Lacedaemon for news
Concerning his father."
  Then cloud-gathering Zeus replied:
"My child, what words are these that you let by
The barrier of your teeth! Was it not all
Your own idea? Don't you plan for Odysseus to come
And make them all pay for their wrongs? As for Telemachus,
You are quite able to take care of him yourself.
See him safely home, and let the wooers sail back
Completely baffled."
  So saying, he turned to Hermes,
His own dear son, and spoke: "Hermes, since you
Have been our messenger before, go tell the nymph,
Whose hair is so beautifully braided, what we have decided,
That patient Odysseus must be allowed to return,
But without the guidance of gods or mortal men.
He must suffer alone in a boat built by himself
Till on the twentieth day he reaches Scheria,
The loamy rich land where live the close kin of the gods,
The Phaeacians, who will heartily honor him, as though he
Were a god. Then in a ship they will send him to his own
Dear country, with a store of gifts from them of bronze,
Garments, and gold, more than Odysseus could ever
Have won from Troy, though he had returned without hurt
And with his due share of the spoil. For even so
He is destined to reach his own country and high-roofed home,
Where again he will see his friends."
  He spoke, and swift Hermes,
Slayer of Argus, obeyed him, putting on his bright sandals
Of magic immortal gold, which bear him always
Swift as the wind over boundless earth and sea.
And he took the wand with which he can lull to sleep
Or wake from the deepest slumber whomever he wishes.
With this in his hand the mighty slayer of Argus

79

Flew down from the upper air to the peaks of Pieria,
And from there he swooped to the sea, skimming over the waves
Like a gull that searches for fish amid the dread gulfs
Of the unresting sea and drenches its wings in the spray.
Thus over the endless waves swift Hermes flew
Till he reached the far island. Coming in from the violet sea,
He landed, and quickly made his way inland on foot
To the spacious cave, where the nymph with the beautiful braids
Made her home. On the hearth a great fire was blazing,
                    and all over
The island was a fragrance of split cedar and juniper burning.
Inside the cave the nymph was sweetly singing
As with a golden shuttle she wove at her loom.
Outside was a flourishing forest of alder and poplar
And sweet-smelling cypress, where the long-winged birds
                    were nesting,
Horned owls and hawks and clamoring long-tongued sea-crows,
Who all depend on the sea for a living. And there
About the cave a vigorous grapevine was growing,
Heavy with opulent clusters. And in a row
Four fountains close together sent their bright water
Tumbling in different directions, while all around
Lush fields of violets and parsley were blooming. There
Even a god might gaze in wonder and delight,
And there indeed swift Hermes, slayer of Argus,
Stood and marveled at the scene before him. Then quickly
He entered the wide cave, and the beautiful goddess Calypso
Knew him at once, for the immortals are not unknown
To each other, though one may dwell in a far distant home.
Great-hearted Odysseus, however, he did not find
In the cave. He, as often, was down on the beach
Tormenting himself with sorrows, groaning and tearful,
As he sat looking out on the barren and unresting sea.
Calypso seated her guest in a splendid bright chair

80

And questioned him thus:
   "Hermes of the golden wand,
To what do I owe this visit? You are indeed
An honored and welcome guest, but your visits to me
Have not been frequent. So say what you have in mind,
And if it can be done and done by me
Then my heart says do it. But follow me further, that I
May set some refreshment before you."
   So saying, the goddess
Drew up before him a table filled with ambrosia
And she mixed the ruby nectar for him to drink.
Now when the swift slayer of Argus had eaten and drunk
As much as he wanted, he answered her in these words:
   "You are a goddess and I a god, but since
You ask why I've come, I'll tell you. Quite against my will
Zeus ordered me here, for who would willingly travel
Over that unspeakable stretch of salt sea-water?
Out there is no city where mortal men make sacrifice
To the gods and offer choice hecatombs. But the will of Zeus,
Who bears the aegis, no other god can escape
Or change. He says that you have with you here a man,
The most woebegone man of all the men who fought
For nine years round the city of Priam, sacked it in the tenth,
And set out for home. But on the way they sinned
Against Athena, who proceeded to send on them
A most wicked wind with waves both heavy and high.
There all his comrades were lost, but he was brought here
By wind and wave. Now Zeus bids you send him away
As soon as you can, for here, so far from his friends,
It is not his doom to die. He is still destined
To reach his own country and high-roofed home, where again
He will see his friends."
   At this the lovely Calypso
Shuddered, then answered him with these winged words:

81

"O cruel! but then you begrudging gods are ever so
When goddesses would lie with mortal men and do it
With no deception. Right well I recollect what happened
When Dawn, that rosy sweet lass, thought to have
Orion for herself. You slothful gods
Begrudged her him, of course, till in Ortygia
Cold Artemis killed him with her painless arrows. So too
When fair-haired Demeter gave in to her yearning and lay
In love with Iasion in that thrice-plowed fallow field.
Zeus soon heard of it, and with his thundering bright bolt
Demolished her lover. And now I am the one you begrudge—
Cruel gods, that can't abide to see a mere mortal
Living with me, a man I once saved when he
All alone was adrift astride the keel of his ship,
For Zeus with his thundering bright bolt had struck, had shattered
That man's swift ship in the wine-dark sea. There all
His comrades were lost, but he was brought here by wind
And by wave. I welcomed him warmly, fed him, even promised
To make him immortal and ageless forever. But since
No other god can escape or change the will
Of aegis-bearing Zeus, let him go, if that
Is what Zeus wants, over the barren and unresting sea.
But I myself can give him no convoy, since I have
No ships, to say nothing of men to man oars, but I'll give him
Some advice, both gracious and candid, that he may reach
His own country completely unharmed."

      Then the swift slayer
Of Argus: "Well good, show respect for the will of Zeus,
For if you cross him in this, he'll surely make life
More than difficult for you."

      So saying, mighty Hermes departed,
And the graceful nymph, with the message of Zeus uppermost
In her mind, went looking for great-hearted Odysseus. She
            found him

On the beach, sitting there with eyes full of tears, his sweet life
Trickling away in his mournful yearning for home.
The nymph he no longer found pleasing, though at night
        he still slept
With her in the looming caves, an unwilling man
By a nymph not at all that way. But during the day
He would sit on the rocky beach tormenting himself
With sorrows, groaning and tearful, wistfully looking
On the barren and unresting sea. Now the beautiful goddess
Drew near him and spoke:
      "Unlucky man, waste
No more of your life in sorrow here with me,
Since now I am ready and willing for you to go.
But come, with tools of bronze you must hew tall timbers
And build yourself a boat, sufficiently broad-beamed
And high-decked to carry you over the misty deep sea.
I will stock it with bread and water and warming red wine,
So you won't be hungry, and give you some clothes,
        and a tail wind
Too, that completely unharmed you may reach your own country,
If that is the will of the gods who rule the wide sky
And have more power than I both to plan and fulfill."
      At this the noble, long-suffering Odysseus shuddered,
Then answered with these winged words: "Surely, goddess,
Something other than my safe passage is in your mind
When you bid me cross the great and engulfing sea
In such a craft. So hard and dreadful it is
To cross that wide water that even the graceful swift ships
That exult in the Zeus-sent wind, even they can't do it.
At any rate, till I am sure your good wishes are with me,
I'll not set foot in a boat—no, goddess, not until
You can bring yourself to swear a great oath that you will not
Plot some new evil against me."
      Lovely Calypso

Smiled and gently caressed him, then answered him thus:
"You may be a rascal, but such a speech surely proves
That there's nothing stupid about you. Now then, let earth
Be my witness and broad heaven above and the tumbledown
       waters
Of subterranean Styx—which to the gods
Is the oath most great and terrible—that I will not plot
Any new evil against you. Far from it, my plans
For you are quite the same as I'd make for myself
Were I in your place. After all, I have a sense
Of fair play, and my heart is not made of iron. My heart
Is full of compassion."
      Then the beautiful goddess walked quickly
Away and he followed. Goddess and man, they reached
The great cavern together, and he sat down in the chair
From which Hermes had lately arisen. Before him the nymph
Placed all sorts of food and drink such as mortals delight in,
Then seated herself across from sacred Odysseus.
Her maids set ambrosia and nectar in front of her
And they both helped themselves to the good things spread out
      before them.
When they had eaten and drunk as much as they wanted,
The lovely goddess Calypso broke the silence:
      "Zeus-sprung son of Laertes, resourceful Odysseus,
Do you really desire to leave right away for home
And your own dear country? Even so, I wish you joy.
But if in your heart you knew what a measure of woe
You will have to fulfill before you reach your own country,
You would stay right here, ageless forever, and keep
This house with me through countless immortal years
To come. You would, despite that constant yearning
To see your wife. Surely, I cannot be
Less lovely than she, in face or in figure, nor is it
Very becoming for a mortal woman to compete

With a goddess in this respect."
     Then resourceful Odysseus
Replied: "Great goddess, don't be angry with me
About this. I am well aware that thoughtful Penelope
Is much less attractive than you, in face and in figure,
For she's a mere mortal, while you are immortal and ageless.
Even so, all the time I yearn for my home and the day
I'll return there. And if once again some god undoes me
In the wine-dark sea, I'll bear it, for the heart in my breast
Is a patient heart. Already, through waves and war,
I have toiled and suffered much. Let this be added
To that."
     When darkness came they retired far back
In the depths of the cave, where they made delightful love
And slept side by side all night.
     At the first pink light
Of Dawn, Odysseus quickly put on a tunic
And cloak, while the nymph slipped into a shimmering
             white gown—
Long, lovely, and very sheer. Then,
Having cast about her waist an exquisite golden sash
And arranged a veil high up on her head, she began
To concentrate on the sending of great-hearted Odysseus.
     She gave him
A huge bronze ax, its double-bladed head tightly set
On a beautiful olive-wood handle that fitted his hands
To perfection. This and a gleaming adze she gave him,
Then led the way to the outskirts of the island where tall trees
Had grown, alder and poplar and sky-lofty pine,
Long sapless and dry, well-seasoned timber that would surely
Float lightly for him. Now when the beautiful goddess
Had shown him where the tall trees were, she went back
To the cave, but he started in to cut timber and made
The chips fly. He felled twenty trees in all and lopped

Their branches, then skillfully hewed them and smoothed them
    straight
To the line. Meanwhile, the lovely Calypso brought augers
And he bored and fitted all the pieces just right and joined them
With pegs driven through the lined-up holes. The beam
He made just as wide as one that a skillful shipwright
Marks out for the hull of a broad trading vessel. The decking
He fitted to the close-set ribs and finished it off
With long gunwales. He set up a mast with fitted yard-arm
And made a large oar to steer with. Then, from stem
To stern he reinforced her sides with willow withes to ward off
The waves and covered the bottom with brushwood. Meanwhile,
The lovely Calypso had brought him cloth for a sail,
And he made that too, very expertly. He lashed
In their places on board the braces, halyards, and sheets,
And then on rollers he eased her down the beach
Into the bright water.
      All this he did in four days,
And on the fifth the beautiful Calypso, having bathed him
And fragrantly dressed him, sent him off on his way
        from the island.
In his boat the goddess put a skin of dark wine and another,
Much larger, of water, and a leather bag quite full
Of good things to eat, and she caused a gentle warm wind
To spring up. Then joyfully good Odysseus spread
His sail to the wind and skillfully steered with the oar.
He sat there, sleeplessly steering, as he watched the Pleiads
And late-setting Boötes, but most of all his eyes
Were on the Great Bear, by some called the Wain, which circles
In its place, its eyes on Orion the Hunter, and never
Sinks in the baths of Oceanus. For this constellation
The beautiful goddess Calypso had told him to keep
On his left as he sailed. So he did for seventeen days,
And then on the eighteenth he sighted the shadowy mountains

Of the Phaeacians, which show like a shield in the misty sea.
    But then from the far-off mountains of the Solymi, Poseidon,
The imperial Earthshaker, booming home from Ethiopia,
Caught sight of Odysseus sailing the sea, and his spirit
Boiled up in rage as he shook his head and spoke thus
To his heart:
    "Confound it all! While I was away
The gods have apparently changed their minds about Odysseus,
And now he's nearing Phaeacia, where he's destined to lose
Those mighty toils of woe which have fallen upon him.
But still I think I can give him his bellyful of misfortune!"
    So saying, he gathered the clouds and seizing his trident
Stirred up the deep sea. He aroused the battering blasts
Of all the winds and hid both land and sea
With a cover of clouds, and suddenly darkness descended.
Then the jostling, sky-born winds from the East and South
And West and North crashed in confusion together,
And out of that foamy tumult a great wave came rolling.
The knees and heart of Odysseus were themselves like water
As out of his anguish he spoke to his own great spirit:
    "Miserable wretch that I am, what end will be mine?
I'm afraid the goddess spoke all too truly in foretelling
The measure of woe I would have to fulfill before reaching
My own native land. Everything so far is happening
Just as she said, for Zeus has crammed the wide sky
With clouds and stirred up the sea, and here I am
In a maelstrom of blasting winds, my destruction sure.
Thrice and four times blessed were the Danaans who died
On the wide plains of Troy serving the sons of Atreus.
I wish I'd been equally lucky that day when throngs
Of Trojans hurled bronze-headed spears at me as we fought
Round the corpse of Achilles. Then at least I'd have had a funeral
And far and wide the Achaeans would have carried my fame.

But now it seems I was fated to die most dismally."
     Even as he spoke, the towering great wave came crashing
Down on him with terrible force and sent his boat spinning
Around. The steering-oar wrenched from his hands and he
Was thrown far from the boat. Then a mighty blast of wind,
Rushing out of that roaring tumult, snapped the mast,
And both sail and yard-arm fell far out in the sea.
Odysseus was kept a long time under water, for he found it
No easy matter to fight his way up through the downrush
Of that huge wave, weighed down as he was by the clothes
Which beautiful Calypso had given him. But at last he came up
And spit out the brine as rivulets streamed from his head,
Nor did he forget his boat, half-drowned though he was.
He sprang through the waves and caught her, then crouched
         amidships,
Avoiding sure death, while a great wave bobbled the boat
This way and that with the current. As when in autumn
The North Wind blows close-clinging balls of thistles
About the fields, even so the winds were driving
That boat of his this way and that on the sea.
Now the South Wind would toss it for the North to carry awhile,
Now the East would yield that the West might chase it in turn.
     But the daughter of Cadmus, trim-ankled Ino, she
Who was once a mortal woman with speech like ours
But now as Leucothea in the sea's deep brine is honored
By the gods, she both saw and pitied the plight
Of Odysseus as he wandered in such great suffering, and now,
Rising up from the deep like a gull on the wing, she perched
On the well-bound boat and spoke:
        "Poor man, how is it
That you are so terribly odious to earth-shaking Poseidon
That he sows these many disasters in your way?
He shall not destroy you completely, no matter how much
He rages. But come now, use your good sense and do

As I say. Take off those clothes, leave your boat
To the winds, and swim for all you're worth to the coast
Of Phaeacia, where it is your fate to be free. Here then,
Take this veil and tie it around your waist.
With its immortal protection you will suffer no injury
Or death. But when you lay hold of dry land, take it off
And throw it well out from shore in the wine-dark sea,
Turning away as you do."
    Then she gave him the veil
And back like a gull she plunged in the swollen sea
To vanish amid the dark waves. But good Odysseus,
Long-suffering as ever, was left deeply moved and perplexed.
Thus he spoke to his own great heart:
    "O misery! this order
To abandon my boat—let it not be once again
Some god-woven snare for me. But I'll not do it!
For with my own eyes I have seen how far the land is
Where she said my deliverance would come. So I'll do what I
Think best. As long as these planks hold together, I'll stay here
And suffer this woe, but when the waves have beaten
This boat to pieces I'll swim as a last desperate chance."
    Even as he was pondering this plan in his mind and heart,
Earth-shaking Poseidon raised another great wave. Grim
And terrible it curled high above him, then crashed down
And scattered his boat's long timbers like a dry heap of straw
Struck by a hurricane wind. But Odysseus got astride
One plank, as though he were riding a horse, and stripped off
The clothes that lovely Calypso had given him. Then quickly
He tied the veil around his waist and with arms
Outstretched plunged headlong into the sea and struck out,
Greatly determined. And the mighty creator of earthquakes
Saw him, shook his head, and muttered to himself:
    "So be it! Now make your miserable way through the waves
Till you reach the home of a god-sprung people. Even so,

I don't think you'll make many jokes about what you've
      been through!"
    So saying, he lashed his beautiful mane-tossing horses
And came to Aegae, where he has his glorious palace.
    But Zeus's daughter Athena had plans of her own.
All winds but the North she checked in their courses
      and bade them
Leave off and go sleep, but the tearing North Wind she sent
To beat down the waves in the path of Zeus-sprung Odysseus,
That he might reach the oar-loving Phaeacians, escaping
Death and the fates.
    For two days and two nights he was driven
By the battering waves, and many times he thought he was
      done for.
But when with fair-haired Dawn the third day came,
The wind died down to a calm, and he, from the top
Of a wave, looked hard ahead and caught sight of the shore
Near by. And then as a dying man's children are glad
When the demon disease is broken and their father, who pined
In pain for so long, is released from suffering and death
By grace of the gods, even so Odysseus rejoiced
At the sight of land and trees, and swam on, more than eager
To set foot on that shore. But when he came within call
Of land, he heard only the boom of the sea on the reefs,
The great waves thundering and belching on the rock-bound coast,
Where all was veiled in the spume and spray of the brine.
For there were no harbors for ships, nor so much as a cove,
But everywhere cliffs jutted out, craggy headlands and reefs
Of sheer rock. And the knees and heart of Odysseus grew weak
And dissolved, as out of his deep disappointment he spoke
To his own great spirit:
    "O misery! when my hopes were gone,
Zeus finally granted me a glimpse of land,
And I've managed to swim the distance only to find

No escape from this gray sea. The reefs offshore
Are jagged and sharp and the waves crash around them
       with bellow
And moan, while behind them a cliff of sheer rock rises up
From the sea, which even in there is surely too deep
For me to get my feet on the bottom and escape
This destruction. If I try to get in, a great wave may rush me
Against a sharp rock, making all my striving quite vain.
But if I keep on swimming in hope of a harbor
And sloping beach, a gale may seize me again
And bear me, groaning, far out in the fish-full sea,
Or from the deep some demon may send a great monster
Against me from the numerous brood of renowned Amphitrite.
For all too well I know that the glorious Earthshaker
Hates me most heartily."
     Even while he was pondering these things
A huge wave rushed him in toward the craggy shore,
Where the reefs would have stripped him of skin and broken
       his bones
Had he not been inspired by the bright-eyed goddess Athena
To lay hold of a rock with both hands and hang on to it, groaning,
While the great wave roared by. But he had no sooner escaped it
Than it poured back upon him in its rushing withdrawal
      and bore him
Well out to sea. And pieces of skin were torn
From his strong hands and left clinging there on the crag
Like pebbles that cling to the suckers of a writhing squid
Torn from his hole. Odysseus was lost in the surge
Of that great wave, and then, before his time,
That unlucky man would surely have been destroyed
Had not the bright-eyed goddess Athena helped him
To think. Now out beyond where the shore-bound billows
Were breaking, he swam along looking landward for a harbor
And sloping beach. Afterwhile he came to the mouth

Of a fair-flowing river, which seemed most likely to him,
Since free of stones and sheltered from the wind. He felt
The current of the stream and prayed to it thus in his heart:
  "Hear me, Royal River, whoever you are,
For I come as to one much prayed to, seeking deliverance
From the sea and the wrath of Poseidon. Even to the gods
That man is sacred who comes a wayfaring stranger,
As I, having toiled and suffered much, come now
To you and your stream for help. Pity me, my lord,
For I am your suppliant."
    Then the river checked its flow
And held back the waves and through the calm water
    brought him safely
To shore at its mouth. He sagged at the knees and his strong arms
Hung limp, for his heart was brine-broken and his whole
    body swollen.
The sea-water gushed from his mouth and nose and he lay there
Winded and speechless, too terribly weary to move.
But when his spirit returned, he untied the veil
Of the goddess and let it drop into the sea-mingling river,
And a great wave bore it downstream and into the hands
Of Ino. Then turning away from the water, Odysseus
Sank down in the reeds and kissed the grain-giving earth,
And still deeply troubled he spoke to his own great heart:
  "If I stay here all night in the bed of this river,
Awake and weary, the deadly frost and dew
That's bound to be heavy may overcome me. Just
Before dawn the breeze off a river blows cold, and I,
In my weakened condition, might very well give up the ghost
For good. But if I climb up the slope to the shade
Of those trees and lie down for a while in the thick underbrush,
Trying to get warm again and rested, I'm afraid

Sweet sleep would come on me and I would be nothing but prey
For wild beasts to devour."

　　　But he soon decided in favor
Of the woods and made his way to some trees that stood
In a clump not far from the water. Here he crawled under
Two olive bushes, one of them wild, that grew
From out the same spot and entwined so thickly together
That no raw wind or rain or blazing hot sun
Could pierce them, and with his hands he raked up a broad bed
Of the leaves that had fallen and littered the ground in sufficient
Abundance to shelter two or three cold men from the rage
Of winter's worst weather. Odysseus, having suffered so much,
Could hardly help gloating as he looked at that bed, and then
He lay down in the middle and covered himself with dry leaves.
As when a man on an outlying farm, a man
With no neighbors, heaps ashes upon a live coal, that he
May keep it alive and not have to go elsewhere for fire,
Even so Odysseus covered himself with dry leaves.
And Athena shed sleep upon him, that he might close
Weary eyes and be free at last from all that toil.

BOOK

VI

NAUSICAA

As the noble, long-suffering Odysseus, completely exhausted,
Lay there asleep, Athena arrived in Phaeacia
And entered the city. At one time the Phaeacians had lived
In broad Hypereia not far from the arrogant Cyclopes,
Who had used their greater strength to plunder them constantly.
Finally, sacred Nausithous had led them far away
From all civilized men and into Scheria, where they settled.
Here, under his direction, they laid out a wall
Around their new city, built themselves houses and temples
To the gods, and divided the arable land. But Nausithous
Long since had yielded to fate and made the journey
To Hades, and now god-guided Alcinous was King.
Straight to his palace went the bright-eyed goddess Athena,
Still busy about the return of great-hearted Odysseus.
There she came to the richly wrought chamber in which
A certain young lady was sleeping, a girl with the face
And figure of an immortal goddess, Nausicaa, the daughter
Of great-hearted Alcinous, and with her, one by each
Of the door-posts, slept two of her ladies, whom the Graces
        themselves
Had made lovely. The bright doors were closed, but the goddess
        passed through

Like a breeze to where the girl slept and hovered above her.
Then, in form like the seaman Dymas's daughter,
A lovely girl of Nausicaa's age and one
She adored, the bright-eyed goddess Athena spoke:
          "Nausicaa, with a mother like yours, how can you be
So lazy? You let your lovely clothes lie around
Uncared for, and yet your wedding can't be far off,
And then you'll need these nice things, for yourself and those
Who attend you. Attention to such details, you know,
Makes a girl well thought of and her parents proud. At
          dawn, then,
Let's go wash them all. I want to go too
And help you get ready more quickly for that wedding
          that's bound to be
Soon. For already the finest young men in the land
Are your suitors, Phaeacians as nobly descended as you are.
So come now, go to your famous father at dawn
And ask to have mules and a wagon made ready for you
To carry all the sashes and robes and bright blankets. A wagon
You'll surely appreciate, for the pools are far from the city,
Much too far to walk."
          So saying, the bright-eyed goddess
Athena left for Olympus, which they say is the home,
Eternal and strong, of the gods. For never is it shaken
By winds, never drenched with rain, never covered with snow,
But the sky stretches cloudless above them and everything glows
With a radiant white light. There the blessed gods
Are happy forever, and that is where bright-eyed Athena
Went, having seen the girl and had her say.
          Quickly Dawn rose from her glorious throne and awakened
The beautifully-gowned Nausicaa. Briefly she marveled
At her dream, then hurried through the palace to tell her
          dear parents.
Her mother sat at the hearth with her ladies, spinning

The sea-blue yarn. But her father she met at the door
On his way to join the elders in a council to which
Those august Phaeacians had called him. Coming up to him close,
She said:
     "Papa, won't you please have a wagon, a high one
With strong wheels, made ready for me so I can take
Those fine mussed clothes of mine to the river for washing?
And besides, you ought to have on completely clean clothes
When you sit in council with princes. And here in these halls
You have five sons—two married, but three blooming bachelors—
Who all insist on fresh clothes when they go to a dance.
And it's up to me to see that all this gets done."
     So she spoke, for she was too modest to mention
Her own ripe plans for a wedding, but Papa understood
Perfectly, and thus he replied: "I don't begrudge you
The mules, my child, or anything else. Go ahead.
I'll have the servants get a wagon ready for you,
A high one with strong wheels and fitted with an awning besides."
     Then he called to the servants and they got a
          well-running mule wagon
Ready outside the palace, brought up the mules
And put them in harness. Nausicaa brought the bright clothes
From her room and put them in the gleaming wagon,
          while her mother
Filled a box with all sorts of good things to eat and poured wine
In a goatskin bottle. The girl climbed aboard and her mother
Gave her a golden flask of soft olive oil,
That she and her ladies might use it after their bath.
Then Nausicaa picked up the glossy reins and the whip
And gave the mules a flick to get them started.
Off they clattered, pulling the girl and her garments
At a goodly clip, and her ladies followed, that the Princess
Might not go alone.
     When they reached the beautiful river

Where the pools are always full of clear water, burbling up
And away in sufficient abundance to cleanse any clothes
No matter how dirty, there they unyoked the mules
From the wagon and drove them along the swirling stream
To graze on the wild and honey-sweet grass. Then
From the wagon they took the clothes in their arms
      and carried them
Into the dark water, where they vied with each other
      in trampling them
Clean in the troughs. When every spot was gone,
They spread them out on the beach where the sea had come up
And washed the pebbles clean, and they, having bathed
And rubbed themselves richly with oil, ate their lunch
      on the banks
Of the river and waited for the clothes to dry in the bright
Light of the sun. When the pleasant meal was over,
The maids and their mistress threw off their brief veils and began
To play with a ball, while white-armed Nausicaa led
In the song. Now whenever Artemis the archer descends
The high ridges of Mount Taÿgetus or Mount Erymanthus
To joy in the chase of wild boars and the nimble deer,
The heart of her mother Leto is filled with delight,
For the rural nymphs, daughters of aegis-bearing Zeus,
Join in the sport, and, though all are lovely,
Artemis stands a head taller than any of the others
And is easily known. Even so, that virgin Princess
Shone among her ladies.
      When the time had come
To go home, Nausicaa was about to yoke the mules
And fold the fine clothes, but bright-eyed Athena had plans
Of her own. She wanted Odysseus to wake up and see
The lovely girl, who soon would be his guide
Into the Phaeacian city. So when next the Princess
Tossed the ball to one of her ladies, she threw it

97

Wide of her mark and into a deep swirl of the river.
At this they all gave a loud shriek, and the noble Odysseus
Awoke, sat up, and began to think things out:
    "O misery! among what manner of mortals can I
Be now? Are they cruel, unjust, and completely uncivilized,
Or god-fearing, hospitable men? Just now I thought
I heard the sound of maiden voices, the cry
Of nymphs, perhaps, ladies who haunt the high hills,
The springs where rivers rise, and the grassy fields.
Or can it be that I'm really close to men
With speech like mine? I'll go and see for myself."
    So saying, the good Odysseus crept out from beneath
The bushes and with his great hand reached into the thicket
And broke off a leafy branch to hide his nakedness.
Then on he went like a bold lion of the mountains
Who goes through wind and rain with his eyes of fire
In search of cattle, sheep, or wild deer, and when
His belly bids him right into the close-barred fold
To attack the flocks therein. Even such was the need
Of Odysseus as he went in his nakedness to approach that party
Of girls with hair so beautifully braided. And to them
He appeared very terrible indeed, all encrusted with brine
As he was, and they scurried in all directions mid the jutting
Banks of sand. Only Alcinous' daughter
Remained. Made brave by Athena, who took the fear
From her limbs, she stood and faced him, while Odysseus tried
To decide whether he should embrace the lovely girl's knees
And so make his plea, or stay where he was and softly
Beseech her to give him some clothes and show him the city.
Thus pondering, he decided to stay where he was and speak softly
To her, since she might take offence at his embracing
Her knees. So without more delay he spoke these shrewd
And gentle words:
    "I implore you, O Queen—but are you

Goddess or woman? If you are a goddess, one
Of those who rule the wide sky, then surely in grace
Of face and figure you're most like Artemis, the daughter
Of almighty Zeus. But if you're a mortal, one
Of those who live here on earth, thrice-blessed are your father
And fortunate mother, and thrice-blessed your brothers are too.
I can well imagine the wonderful warmth and joy
You give them as they watch so lovely a flower taking part
In the dance. But happiest of all will be that man
Who wins you with the gifts of a wooer and takes you home
As his wife. For never before have I seen such a mortal
As you, whether man or woman. I gaze, completely
Astounded. Once indeed in Delos I saw something like you,
A lovely young palm shooting up by Apollo's altar—
In Delos, where I had gone with an army on a journey
Very rich in misfortunes for me—even so, when I saw
That tree, I marveled long in my heart, for never
Has there been such another curving up from the earth. As I look
At you now I feel that same amazement, an awe
That keeps me from clasping your knees, though terrible
             are the things
That have happened to me. Just yesterday I came out
Of the wine-dark sea after nineteen days of high wind
And waves that bore me from the island Ogygia. Now
Divine power has marooned me here to suffer I know not
What, for surely the gods have plenty of evils
In store for me yet. Have pity, O Queen, for you
Are the first to whom I have come after all my suffering
And toil, nor do I know any of the others who own
This land and this city. Give me some rag to put on—
An old wrapper from the laundry will do—and show me the city.
And as for yourself, may the gods grant all the desires
Of your heart—a husband and home and a wonderful oneness
Between you, for nothing is better or greater than a home

99

Where man and wife are living harmoniously together,
The envy of evil minds, but a very great joy
To men of good will, and greatest of all to themselves ."
      Then the white-armed maiden replied: "Stranger,
              since it seems
That you're neither evil nor stupid, this misery of yours
Must be the will of Olympian Zeus himself,
Who gives happy fortune to men, whether good or bad,
To each as he sees fit. So you must, of course,
Endure it. But now that you've come to this land and city
Of ours, you shall not want for clothes or anything
Else that a wayworn castaway needs for his comfort.
I'll show you the city and tell you who we are.
This is the country and city of the Phaeacians,
And I am the daughter of great-hearted Alcinous, upon whom
The people depend for all the strength they have."
      She spoke, and called to her ladies with the beautiful braids:
"Hold on! my friends. Since when do you run at the sight
Of a man? Surely you didn't think he would harm us.
That man doesn't live, nor shall he ever, who could come
Bearing malice to this land of Phaeacia, since the immortal gods
Love us too much for that. And besides, we live
Far out in the billowing sea, the remotest of men,
And no other mortals have any designs on us.
But this is some unlucky wanderer, and we must take care
Of him, for all strangers and beggars are surely from Zeus,
And a kindness that we think small is not so to them.
So come, my ladies, find food and drink for our guest
And bathe him in the river in a spot that's sheltered
              from the wind."
      At this they stood for a while and urged one another,
Then seated Odysseus in a sheltered spot, just as
The royal daughter of great-hearted Alcinous had said,
And beside him for clothes they laid out a tunic and cloak.

100

Then they gave him the golden flask of soft olive oil
And urged him to bathe in the stream that ran by them. But he
Had this to say:
    "Ladies, stand back over there
While I wash the brine from my shoulders and rub my body
With oil, as I haven't done for so long. I'll not
Take my bath in front of you, for I'm ashamed
To be naked in the midst of such young and lovely-haired ladies."
    Thus he spoke, and they all went over and told
The Princess. Now gallant Odysseus scrubbed off the brine
Which was caked on his back and broad shoulders, and from
        his head
He scrubbed the scurf of the barren and unresting sea.
When he had finished his bath and rubbed himself
With the oil, he put on the clothes which the bride-to-be
Had provided for him, and Athena, the daughter of Zeus,
Made him seem taller and better built and caused
His hair to curl like the hyacinth in bloom. As a craftsman
Who learned his art from Hephaestus and Pallas Athena
Overlays silver with gold and produces a work
Full of charm, so the goddess shed grace on the head and shoulders
Of Odysseus. Then he went over and sat on the beach
By himself, resplendent with masculine charm, and the Princess,
Admiring him greatly, spoke thus to her fair-haired companions:
    "Listen, my ladies. I have something to tell you.
This man's arrival among the godlike Phaeacians
Was not without the will of all the gods
Who live on Olympus. At first he seemed to me
Rather crude and unattractive, but now he looks like one
Of the sky-ruling gods himself. I would like to have
Such a man for my husband here in Phaeacia, and I hope
He decides to stay. But come, my ladies, get food
And drink for our guest."
    Quickly her ladies set food

And drink in front of the noble, long-suffering Odysseus,
And he fell to ravenously, for he had not tasted food
In a very long time.
     Meanwhile, Nausicaa had made up
Her mind. Having folded the clothes, she put them away
In the excellent wagon, hitched up the hard-hoofed mules,
And climbed into the wagon herself. Then she spoke thus
To Odysseus:
     "Stranger, it's time we set out for the city,
That I may show you the way to my good father's house,
Where you'll be sure to meet all of the best Phaeacians.
But do this, if you will, for you seem to be a man
Of discretion. So long as we pass through the fields and the farms,
I want you and my ladies to keep up with the mules
     and the wagon,
While I take the lead, but when we get close to the city—
Well, the way leading in is narrow, and since
A fine harbor lies on either side, curved ships
Are pulled up in private docks along the road.
And there around Poseidon's beautiful temple,
Where the huge quarried stones are set deep in the ground,
     the sailors
Congregate. Here they busy themselves with the tackle
Of those black ships, the ropes and the sails, and here too
They shape their thin oar-blades. For Phaeacians take no interest
In bow or quiver, but delight in masts and oars
And shapely ships, wherein they go gaily and cleave
The gray sea. Now it's their uncouth remarks I would like
To avoid, for surely we have our share of crude fellows,
Any one of whom might see us and thus presume:
     " 'Aha! who is this tall and handsome stranger
That follows Nausicaa? And where did she find him? No doubt
She'll marry him—some wandering foreigner she's brought

From his ship, for there's nowhere close he could possibly
                come from—
Or some god perhaps has heard her prayers and come down
From heaven to be her husband so long as she lives.
And surely it's better that now she's gone out and found
Herself a husband from somewhere else, for she spurns
Her suitors here among her own people, though they
Have been many and noble.'
     "Such talk would do me no good,
And I myself would blame any girl who defied
Her dear father and mother by running around with men
Before she was properly married—but now listen to what
I tell you, stranger, that you may win from my father
A quick and convoyed return to your home. You'll come
To a beautiful grove of Athena right next to the road,
Fine poplar trees with a spring welling up in their midst
And a meadow stretching out on all sides. There, within call
Of the city, is my father's park and fruitful vineyard.
Sit down right there and wait till you think we've gotten
In town and reached my father's palace. Then you
Come into the city yourself and ask for the house
Of my father, great-hearted Alcinous. It's easily known
And the merest baby could show you which one it is,
For no other Phaeacian house is built at all like
The palace of King Alcinous. Now when you have passed
Through the court and entered the house, go quickly through
The great hall to where my mother sits at the hearth—
A wonderful sight as she leans against a pillar
There in the firelight and spins the sea-blue yarn
With her maids sitting behind her. Against the same pillar
Is the throne of my father, and there he sits drinking his wine
Like a god. Walk past him and clasp the knees of my mother,
That you may see your joyful day of return
With little delay, no matter how far from home

You may be. For if you win her favor, then indeed
You may hope to reach your own country and firm-founded house
And be with your friends and loved ones again."

    So saying,
Nausicaa lashed the mules to a trot, and quickly
They left the river behind them. But she as driver
Laid on the lash with care, so that her ladies
And Odysseus might have no trouble keeping up on foot.
At sundown they came to the sacred and glorious grove
Of Athena, and there Odysseus sat down. Then without
More delay he prayed to the daughter of almighty Zeus:

    "O invincible child of Zeus who bears the aegis,
Hear me now, since you paid no heed before
When the famous Earthshaker shattered my ship and me.
Grant that I may be pitied and receive a warm welcome
From the Phaeacians."

    He prayed, and Pallas Athena
Heard him, but still she did not appear before him,
For she had great respect for her uncle Poseidon,
Who continued his frenzied wrath against Odysseus
Till finally that godlike man reached his own country.

BOOK

VII

THE PALACE OF
ALCINOUS
AND ARETE

While the godly, long-suffering Odysseus was praying there,
The two strong mules brought the Princess into the city.
When she came to her father's palace, she drew up at the gate,
And her godlike brothers crowded around her, unharnessed
The mules from the wagon, and carried the clothes inside.
Then she too went to her room, where a fire was kindled
For her by the chambermaid Eurymedusa, an old woman
From Apeira, whom Phaeacian sailors long ago had brought
In their curved ships as a gift for their King Alcinous,
Since he ruled all the Phaeacians and was respected
By them like a god. It was she who had seen to the rearing
Of white-armed Nausicaa there in the palace, and she
It was now who got supper ready for her in her room.
  Meanwhile, Odysseus arose to go into town,
And Athena, who loved him, shed a thick mist about him,
That no high-hearted Phaeacian might meet and insult him
And ask who he was. And now, just as he

Was about to enter the truly exquisite city,
The flashing-eyed goddess herself stood in his way,
Disguised as a girl carrying a pitcher, and thus
The gallant Odysseus questioned her:
    "My child,
Would you be so good as to guide me to the house of Alcinous,
The man who is your King? For I am a stranger
Here, wayworn and weary, from a far distant country,
And I don't know a single soul in this city or land."
    Then the bright-eyed goddess Athena replied: "Sir,
I'll gladly show you the house you ask about,
Since it lies very close to the house of my own good father.
But you must follow me quietly, staring at no one
And asking no questions, for our men are not very fond
Of strangers, and the welcome they give to foreigners is something
Less than warm. Their trust is in the speed
Of their swift ships, in which they cross the sea's
Great gulf, for the mighty Earthshaker has granted them this,
And indeed their ships are swift, swift as a bird
In flight, or thought itself."
    So Pallas Athena
Quickly took the lead and he followed in her
Divine footsteps. And as he went through the city in the midst
Of ship-famous Phaeacians, they noticed him not, for Athena,
That awesome goddess with the beautiful hair, out of her
Most tender regard for him, shed a wonderful mist
About him, so that none could see. But he saw and marveled
At the harbors and graceful ships, at the meeting-places of those
Great seamen, and at their long and lofty walls
Topped with sharp stakes, wondrous indeed to behold.
When they reached the splendid home of the King, Athena,
Her blue eyes shining, turned to him and said:
    "Here, good sir, is the house you asked me to show you.
Inside you will find the god-sprung princes feasting,

106

But go right in and be afraid of nothing,
For a bold man is always best, whether he is a stranger
Or not. Head straight for Queen Arete, who comes
From the same royal line as King Alcinous himself.
First came Nausithous, the son of earth-shaking Poseidon
And the loveliest of women, Periboea, the youngest daughter
Of great-hearted Eurymedon, him who once was King
Of the haughty Giants, till he brought ruin on them,
A blindly arrogant people, and himself as well.
But Poseidon lay with fair Periboea and made her
The mother of Nausithous, a son of great spirit, who ruled
The Phaeacians. And he had two sons, Rhexenor and Alcinous.
Rhexenor died in his great hall when Apollo
Of the silver bow struck him down. Hardly
More than a bridegroom, he died sonless, but left
An only daughter, Arete. Alcinous made her
His wife and honored her as no other woman
On earth is honored, of all the women who keep house
For their husbands in the world today. Such deep devotion
She receives, and always has, from her children
And husband and from the people too, who regard
And greet her as a goddess when she goes through the city. For she
Has an excellent mind and can, when so disposed,
Resolve even the quarrels of men. So you have
But to win her favor, and then indeed you may hope
To reach your own country and high-roofed home and be
With your friends again."

           So saying, bright-eyed Athena
Left lovely Scheria and crossed the unresting sea
To Marathon and the broad streets of Athens, where she entered
The well-built home of Erechtheus. But Odysseus approached
The splendid palace of Alcinous, and many were his
Misgivings, as he paused on his way to the threshold of bronze.
For from the lofty palace of the great-hearted King

Came a radiant glow like that of the sun or moon.
Walls of bronze with a molding of blue enamel
Extended from the threshold to the innermost part of the palace.
Golden doors hung on the silver posts
That were set in the threshold of bronze. The lintel was silver,
The door-handle gold, and on either side stood gold
And silver dogs, made with great skill by Hephaestus,
Immortal and ageless guardians, their charge the palace
Of great-hearted Alcinous. Inside, tall chairs were fixed
Along the walls from the entrance to the innermost chamber,
And on them soft robes were thrown, wonderfully woven
By women. Here the Phaeacian leaders would sit
To enjoy their unfailing stores of food and wine,
While golden boys, standing on sturdy pedestals,
Held blazing torches, enlightening the night for feasters
In the hall.
      Fifty women servants keep busy
Within the palace. Some turn the mill by hand
That grinds the golden grain. Others weave
At the looms, or sit and twirl the yarn, their hands
Fluttering like leaves on a tall poplar tree, while a wash
Of soft olive oil drips down from the close-woven cloth
They are giving a gloss to. For just as Phaeacian men
Excel in handling swift ships at sea, even so
Their women have wonderful skill at the loom, for Athena
Has given to them surpassing cleverness and excellence
Of mind.
      Outside the palace yard, stretching out
From the gates, lies a fine four-acre orchard, with a hedge
On either side. Here tall trees are thriving,
Heavy with pears and pomegranates, with glossy apples,
Sweet figs and luscious plump olives. Year round, winter
Or summer, their fruit never fails, but here is always
Fruit for the West Wind's breath to quicken and ripen,

Pear upon pear, apple on apple, cluster
On cluster of grapes, and fig upon fig. Here too
His fruitful vineyard is planted, in one part of which
Is a level spot in the sun where grapes are drying,
While pickers are gathering other grapes and treading
Still others, and in the front rows are unripe clusters
Just shedding their blossoms or beginning to turn. Beyond
The last row of vines, trim vegetable beds are laid out,
Green and growing all year long. Two springs
Well up in the midst, one of which runs in rills
Throughout the garden, while the other flows under the courtyard
Gate and on to the lofty palace itself,
And from this spring the townsfolk draw their water.
Such were the gods' good gifts at the home of Alcinous.
        The noble, long-suffering Odysseus stood there in front
Of the palace, marveling in his heart at the splendors
Around him. Then quickly he crossed the threshold and entered
The house. There he found the Phaeacian leaders
And counselors with goblets in hand, pouring libations
To the keen-eyed slayer of Argus, to whom it was
Their custom to pour last of all before they retired.
But the noble, enduring Odysseus walked through the hall,
Enclosed in the cloud which Athena had shed about him,
Until he came to Arete and Alcinous the King
And threw his arms around the knees of Arete.
At once the marvelous mist disappeared, and a hush
Fell on the feasters throughout the hall at the sight
Of him there. They stared in amazement as Odysseus made
His plea:
        "Arete, daughter of sacred Rhexenor,
After many miserable labors, I come to your husband
For help, and here at your knees I make my appeal
To you and those who are feasting here. May the gods
Grant them good life, and may each of them hand down

To his children the wealth of his house and the gifts of honor
Which the people have given to him. But as for me,
Please help me get home as soon as possible, for I
Have suffered long and much far away from my friends."

    Then he sat down in the ashes there by the fire
On the hearth, and still all the feasters were silent. But finally
The aged lord Echeneus spoke out, an elder
Among the Phaeacians, a most eloquent man, wise
In the wisdom of old. He, with great good will,
Addressed the King:

    "Alcinous, that a stranger should sit
On the ground in ashes by the hearth is not at all seemly
Or well, but the feasters hold back, awaiting some word
From you. Come then, raise up the stranger and seat him
On a chair all studded with silver, and bid the heralds
Mix wine, that now we may pour libations to Zeus,
The hurler of lightning, for he is ever the friend
Of sacred strangers. And let the housekeeper bring out
Some supper for this our guest."

    When the sacred King
Alcinous heard these words, he took the hand
Of the wise and wary Odysseus and raised him from the hearth
And seated him in the gleaming chair next to
His own, from which his favorite son Laodamas
Arose at his father's request. Then a maid brought lustral
Water in a golden pitcher and poured it out
Above a silver basin, that he might wash his hands,
And the girl drew up before him a polished table.
On this the respected housekeeper put generous helpings
Of bread and other good things to eat. And now,
While the noble, long-suffering Odysseus ate and drank,
The mighty Alcinous spoke thus to the herald:

    "Pontonous,
Mix a bowl and serve out wine to all

In the hall, that now we may pour libations to Zeus,
The hurler of lightning, for he is ever the friend
Of sacred strangers."
      At this, Pontonous mixed
The honey-hearted wine, and served it out to all,
First pouring libation drops into their goblets.
But when they had made their drink-offering and drunk as much
As they wished, Alcinous addressed them:
      "Leaders and counselors
Of the Phaeacians, your attention please, while I speak
What the heart in my breast commands. Now that our feast
Is over, let each of you go home and to bed.
But in the morning we'll call a larger gathering
Of elders, that we may entertain our guest in these halls
And to the gods offer fit sacrifice. Then
We will turn our attention to providing an escort for him,
That this our guest may get home without any more toil
Or trouble at all, and that very quickly, no matter
How far it may be. Nor shall he suffer any evil
Or harm until he is safe within his own country,
But from that moment on he shall suffer whatever fate
The ruthless Spinners spun with the thread of his life
On the day his mother bore him. But if he is
An immortal come down from the sky, then this is something
Truly new that the gods are contriving. For always,
Up until now, when we have offered to them
Fine hecatombs, they have appeared to us in their own
True forms. Even so, they sit and feast with us,
And whenever one of our people alone on the road
Encounters them, they use no disguise at all,
For we are close kin to them, as are the Cyclopes
And the savage race of Giants."
      Then resourceful Odysseus
Replied: "Alcinous, you've nothing to worry about there,

111

For I'm a mere mortal, and neither in stature or form
Am I like the immortals who rule the wide sky. I am far
More like the men you know whose burden of pain
Is the greatest. To them indeed I might compare
Myself and my sorrows, and I think I could tell a tale
Somewhat longer than theirs of all the hardships I've borne
By will of the gods. But first let me finish my supper,
In spite of my troubles. For nothing is more dog-shameless
Than the hateful belly, which makes a man mindful of it
No matter how worn-out and weary, no matter how grieved
He may be. Even so is my heart heavy with grief,
But my belly continues its usual demands for food
And for drink, makes me forget what I've been through,
        and bids me
Eat till I'm full—but when morning comes, please hurry,
That you may set this unlucky guest of yours
On the soil of his own dear country. My trials have been many,
And I ask no more before death than to see once again
My treasures, my slaves, and my lofty great house."
      He spoke,
And so well that they all had praise for his words and favored
His sending. Then, having poured libations, and drunk
What they wished, they all went home and to bed, leaving
Noble Odysseus there in the hall, and with him
Sat Arete and sacred Alcinous, while the maids
Cleared all the dinner things away. The first
To speak was white-armed Arete, for she, in observing
His beautiful clothes, had recognized the mantle and tunic
Which she herself had made with the help of her ladies.
So now she spoke these winged words to him:
      "Sir, first a few questions from me. Who are you?
Where are you from? And who gave you those clothes you
      are wearing?
Didn't you say that you came wandering here

From over the sea?"

    Then Odysseus, still cautious, replied:
"Very hard, O Queen, it would be to tell the whole tale
Of my sorrows, since to me the heavenly gods have given
A profusion of woes, but I think I can answer your questions.
Far out at sea lies an island, Ogygia by name,
And therein is the home of the fair-haired daughter of Atlas,
The cunning Calypso, a much-feared goddess, whom
Both gods and men leave strictly alone. But fate
Brought miserable me to her hearth, and all by myself,
For Zeus with his blinding bright bolt had struck my swift ship
And shivered its timbers in the wine-dark sea. There all
My good friends were lost, but I threw my arms around the curved
Ship's keel and drifted on for nine days. Then,
On the tenth black night, the gods washed me ashore
On Ogygia, the island home of that dread goddess,
Calypso of the beautiful braids. She took me in,
Welcomed me warmly, fed me, and declared she would make me
Not only immortal but ageless forever. But she
Never won the consent of the heart in my breast, though there
I remained without change for seven long years, daily
Bedewing with tears the immortal garments she gave me.
The eighth year had arrived, when either because of some message
From Zeus, or a change in her own way of thinking, she urged me
To go and sent me on my way, clad
In wonderful clothes, and bearing, as further gifts
From her, an abundant supply of bread and sweet wine.
She caused a fine breeze to spring up, both gentle and warm,
And for seventeen days I sailed on and on through the sea,
Till on the eighteenth day I joyfully sighted
Your shadowy mountains. But still I was under a curse,
And great misery was still to be mine, sent on by Poseidon,
Creator of earthquakes. He worked up the winds against me
And caused the sea to run unspeakably high,

113

So completely halting my progress that I, now frantically
Groaning, no longer even drifted with the waves. In fact,
My boat came apart in the storm, but I swam my way through
That engulfing abyss out there, till wind and wave
Brought me in to the coast of your country. But there I could not
Come ashore, since the waves would have hurled me
        against the great rocks
At a place unpleasantly craggy. So I swam out some distance
And then along shore till I came to a river and spotted
What seemed the best place to land, since free of stones
And sheltered from the wind. I staggered out,
Collapsed, and lay there gasping for breath. Then,
As immortal night came on, I left the shore
Of the god-sprung river and lay down in a nearby thicket,
Covering myself with leaves. Then boundless sleep
God shed upon me, and there in the leaves I slept,
Completely worn-out as I was, right through the night
Until dawn, and then until noon. It was not, indeed,
Till the sun had begun to go down that I was released
From that delicious sleep and became aware
Of your daughter's companions at play on the beach, and she
Herself was there like a goddess among them. To her
I made my plea, and she showed, I assure you, a wisdom
You would scarcely expect in one so young, for the young
Are usually thoughtless. She furnished me bread and bright wine,
Bathed me there in the river, and gave me these clothes.
I haven't felt much like talking, but all this I've told you
Is true."

    And Alcinous replied: "Sir, my daughter
Did wrong in not bringing you straight home with her ladies.
She, I believe, was the first to whom you made
Your plea."

    Then resourceful Odysseus answered him thus:
"My lord, for that I hope you'll not rebuke

114

Your blameless daughter. She, I assure you, told me
To follow along with her ladies, but I, ashamed
And fearful, would not do it—afraid of offending
You. For we men, all over the earth, are a jealous
Lot and quick to anger."

    And Alcinous replied:
"My heart, sir, is not the sort to be wantonly
Wrathful. Moderation is always best. In fact,
Since you're a man of parts and think very much
As I do, I heartily wish by Father Zeus,
Athena, and Apollo too that you would remain here
And be my son-in-law, with a house full of treasures
As a present from me. But the choice is yours. God
Forbid that any Phaeacian should against your will
Detain you. For your reassurance, I shall set a time
For your sending. Let tomorrow be the day. Then,
While you lie fast asleep, my men shall row you
Across a calm sea to your country and home, or wherever
You wish, though it be even much further than the land
Of Euboea, and those of our people who saw it when they carried
Blond Rhadamanthus to visit the son of Gaea,
Tityos by name, say that Euboea is the furthest
Land of all. But they made the trip there and back,
And made it without fatigue, in a single day!
You shall find out for yourself how far my ships
Are the best and how much my young men excel at beating
The brine with an oar-blade."

    At these words the patient Odysseus
Rejoiced, and thus in prayer he lifted his voice:
"O Father Zeus, grant that Alcinous may do
All that he says. Then indeed will he have renown
Unquenchable throughout the grain-giving earth, and I
Will get home again."

    While they were talking, white-armed

115

Arete told her maids to place a bed
In the portico and cover it with fine purple robes,
Light spreads, and fleecy warm blankets, and girls with torches
Went out and quickly made the strong bed. Then they came
To Odysseus and said: "Come, sir, your bed is ready."
And he was more than glad that it was. And there,
On a corded bed beneath the echoing portico,
The noble, long-suffering Odysseus slept all night.
But Alcinous lay down to sleep in the innermost chamber
Of the lofty palace, and beside him lay his wife
The Queen, who prepared and shared the royal bed.

BOOK

VIII

PHAEACIAN SONG
AND GAMES

At the first pink signs of Dawn, royal Alcinous,
The strong and sacred, arose from his bed, as did
Odysseus, the god-sprung taker of towns. And the King
Conducted his guest to the Phaeacians' place of assembly
Which had been constructed for them close by the ships.
Here they sat down together on the glistening marble.
But Pallas Athena, disguised as one of the heralds
Of wise Alcinous, went up and down the city
Preparing for the return of great-hearted Odysseus,
Speaking thus to the men she approached:
                                   "Come, O leaders
And counselors of the Phaeacians, come to the place
Of assembly, that you may learn of the stranger, in form
Like one of the gods, now newly arrived at the palace
Of wise Alcinous, after wandering all over the sea."
    So saying, she left them curious and eager, and quickly
The assembly seats were filled with the gathering men,
Throngs of them who sat gazing in wonder at the subtle
Son of Laertes. For the grace Athena shed over

His head and shoulders was marvelous indeed to behold,
And she made him look taller and more powerfully built, so that
The Phaeacians would welcome him with honor and awe
And he might acquit himself well in the many contests
Wherein the Phaeacians might make trial of him.
Now that they were assembled, Alcinous addressed them:
    "O leaders and counselors of the Phaeacians, your attention
Please, while I speak what the heart in my breast commands.
This guest of ours—and I don't know who he is—
Has come in his wanderings here to my house, whether
From men of the East or men of the West, again
I do not know. But he is anxious to go,
And prays for our help. So let us do now, as we
Have done before, and speed him on his way,
For surely no guest of mine chafes long in this land
For lack of transportation. Come then, let's launch a new
Black ship upon the bright sea, and let us pick
As crew fifty-two of our best, already proven
Young men. And when they have lashed their oars to the benches
Securely, let them go ashore and prepare
With all haste a feast at my house, where I'll provide plenty
For all—this for the young men only. But as
For the sceptered kings among you, let them come
To my fair palace and help me entertain our guest
Within its halls. In this, may no man refuse me.
And summon the sacred bard Demodocus, for God
Has granted him skill above all others to delight
His hearers with whatever song his spirit prompts him
To sing."
    So saying, he left with the sceptered kings
Behind him, while a herald set out to fetch the glorious
Poet. The fifty-two select young men
Proceeded, as ordered, to the shore of the unresting sea.
Having reached the beach, they drew the black ship down

Into the deep water, put mast and sails aboard,
Made fast the oars in loops of leather, and hauled up
The white sail. Then anchoring the ship well out in the harbor
They headed for the spacious home of wise Alcinous.
There the porticoes, courts, and chambers were filled
With the gathering throng of men both young and old,
For whom Alcinous sacrificed twelve sheep, eight boars
With white tusks, and two shambling steers. These they flayed
And prepared for the table, and so made a fine feast ready.
    Then the herald returned, leading the faithful bard,
Whom the Muse loved most of all, though she had given
To him both good and evil, for she had taken
His sight but bestowed on him the gift of sweet song.
For him Pontonous the herald set a silvery chair
Mid the feasters against a tall pillar, and from a peg
Above his head he hung the clear-toned lyre
And showed him how to reach it with his hands.
A lovely table he placed in front of him
And on it a basket and goblet filled with wine,
That he might drink at will. Then they all helped themselves
To the good things lying before them. But when they had eaten
And drunk as much as they wished, the Muse inspired
The bard to sing the famous deeds of men,
That song whose renown had already reached the wide sky,
The quarrel of Odysseus and Peleus' son Achilles,
How once with violent words they contended at a rich
Ceremonial feast for the gods, and the king of men
Agamemnon was secretly glad that the best Achaeans
Were quarreling, for thus had Phoebus Apollo foretold
To him in holy Pytho when he had crossed
The marble threshold there to consult the oracle
Concerning the wave of woe that by the will
Of almighty Zeus was just beginning to roll
On Trojans and Danaans alike. This was the song

119

The famous bard sang, whereupon the strong hands of Odysseus
Drew his great purple cloak down over his head,
Thus hiding his handsome face so that the Phaeacians
Could not see him weeping. And whenever the sacred bard
Stopped singing, Odysseus would wipe his tears, draw the cloak
From his head, and taking the two-handled cup he would pour
Divine libations. But each time the bard began singing
Again, urged on by the princely Phaeacians, whom his words
So delighted, Odysseus would cover his head once more
And moan. Now from all of the others he hid the tears
He was shedding, but Alcinous could not help noticing, for he sat
Beside him and heard his deep groaning. So without hesitation
He spoke to his sea-loving people:
      "O leaders and counselors
Of the Phaeacians, your attention please. Now
That we have regaled ourselves with fine food and its
Companion the lyre, let us go out and try
Our skill in the various athletic events, that our guest,
When he returns home, may tell his friends how superior
We are at boxing, wrestling, jumping, and running."
      He led and they followed, while the herald
             hung the clear-toned lyre
On its peg, took the hand of Demodocus, and led him
             from the hall
In the same direction the Phaeacian nobles had taken
On their way to the games. They all set out for the place
Of assembly, accompanied by a countless throng. There
To take part in the games were many splendid young men—
Acroneus, Ocyalus, Elatreus, Nauteus, and Prymneus,
Anchialus, Eretmeus, Ponteus, Proreus, Thoön,
And Anabesineus, and Amphialus, son of Polyneus
And grandson of Tecton. And Naubolus' son Euryalus
Arose, the equal of man-slaughtering Ares. He,
In looks and physique, surpassed all the Phaeacians but one,

Matchless Laodamas, who was also there to compete,
Along with his brothers, Halius and godlike Clytoneus,
All three the sons of royal Alcinous. The first
Event was a race. A course was laid out for them
And they all ran swiftly, beating up dust from the plain,
But the able Clytoneus was so far the swiftest that he
Outran them all by the length of a furrow such as mules
Plow in the fallow, and so was first to arrive
At the crowd about the finish. Next they strove
At hard wrestling, and in this Euryalus defeated all comers.
Amphialus beat everyone else at jumping, and Elatreus
Was much the best with the discus, as the skillful son
Of Alcinous, Laodamas, was in the boxing. When all
Had had their fill of delightful competition, Laodamas,
Son of Alcinous, spoke thus among them:
      "Come on,
My friends, let us ask our guest over there what games
He's good in. He's built like a man indeed, what with
Those legs and arms and that powerful neck of his.
He's bound to be strong, and surely he's still young enough,
Though broken by many misfortunes. In my opinion
There's nothing worse than the sea to confound a man,
No matter how strong he may be."
      And Euryalus said:
"Laodamas, I quite agree with what you say.
Go over and speak with the stranger and deliver our challenge."
      At this the fine son of Alcinous took his stand in the midst
Of the crowd and spoke to Odysseus: "Come, good sir,
Take part in the games, if you have any athletic skill,
And have it you must, for there's no greater glory in life
Than that which a man may win with his feet and hands.
So come, throw your worries away and do what you can.
You'll soon be on your way home. Already your ship

Has been launched and the crew is waiting."
　　　Then resourceful Odysseus
Replied: "Laodamas, why do you mock me this way?
My mind is far more full of grief than games.
I have suffered and toiled a great deal, and now I am interested
Only in my return home, as I sit in this gathering
Of yours and make my plea to the King and all
Of his people."
　　　Euryalus answered with an obvious insult:
"Truly, stranger, I wouldn't take you for an athlete
Anyway, though many men have such skill. To me
You look far more like a captain of seagoing merchants,
One who goes back and forth in his many-oared ship
With a mind full of freight and the greedy profit he'll make
By his trip. No, you surely don't look like an athlete!"
　　　At this the quick-witted Odysseus scowled, and replied:
"That, sir, was not well spoken, the speech of a fool,
But then the gods aren't accustomed to give their good gifts
Of physique and mind and eloquence to all alike.
Sometimes a man is not handsome at all, but God
Bestows on his words such form and grace that men
Look on in delight as he speaks in a way that combines
Unfaltering technique with an obvious lack of conceit.
He alone stands out among them, and whenever he goes
Through the city, he is gazed upon like a god. But another
Is like the immortals themselves in appearance, but no crown
Of grace is bestowed on his words. Even such are you,
For in looks you stand out from the rest—no god could
　　　improve them—
But you're sadly lacking in brains. And now your bad manners
Upset me. I'm not, despite what you say, at all poor
In sports, but was, I believe, among the first
So long as I could rely on my youth and my hands.
But now I'm oppressed by all that I've suffered in war

122

And the weltering waves. But in spite of all that sorrow,
I will compete in your games, for your words bite deep
In my heart and provoke me."
      With this he sprang up, and not even
Removing his mantle he seized a large discus, thick
And a good deal more weighty than those the Phaeacians used
In their competition. He spun and let it fly
From his powerful hand, and the stone went whizzing away
As the long-oared, ship-famous Phaeacians ducked down
          beneath it.
Swiftly it left his hand and whirred through the air
Beyond all the other marks, and Athena, in the form
Of a man, set a mark for it and called back to him:
      "Even a blind man, sir, would know your mark
Just groping around with his hands, for it's not even close
To the others, but first by far. You may rest easy
About this event at least. No Phaeacian will equal
This throw, much less surpass it!"
      So spoke the goddess,
Delighting the patient Odysseus, who was glad to see
A true friend in the crowd, and now he addressed the Phaeacians
In a much lighter mood: "Now let's see you youngsters
      match that!
Pretty soon, I think, I'll toss out another as far
Or farther. As for you others, if any man feels
His heart and soul so moved, let him come forth
And compete with me—for you have offended me deeply—
At boxing, wrestling, or for that matter running. I don't
Really care. I'll take on all comers except Laodamas,
For who would quarrel with his host? Both stupid and worthless
Is he who would challenge the man who befriends him abroad.
He would but spoil his own chances. But as for the rest,
I'll neither back down nor belittle. I'm eager indeed
To take on all comers and try my strength against theirs.

For I am not half bad in any event
Performed among men. I do very well, for instance,
With the polished bow, and I would always be first
To pick off my man in the thronging enemy ranks,
No matter how many stood with me and shot at the foe.
At Troy, Philoctetes alone did better than I
When we Achaeans shot. But I claim to be best
By far of all other bread-eating mortals now living
On earth. With men of old, however—with Heracles
Or Oechalian Eurytus—I would not wish to compete.
With the bow those two strove even with gods, and so
The great Eurytus met sudden death, nor did he live
To be old in his palace. For when he challenged Apollo
To shoot with the bow, the god grew angry and killed him.
But I can throw the spear farther than any
Other mortal can shoot an arrow. At running, however,
I have my doubts about winning, for there was in my ship
No exhaustless supply of provisions, and I was badly battered
Mid many waves. So my legs are in very poor shape."
    Then they all remained silent till Alcinous answered
        him thus:
"Stranger, since not without grace and charm you have spoken
These things, wishing to show the fine abilities
You obviously have and angry at him who came up
To you in the crowd and made light of your prowess, as no
Well-mannered mortal would do—but come now, hear
What I have to say, that when you are home in your halls
And feasting once more with your wife and your children, you
May remember us and tell your peers of those feats
In which Zeus has given us skill from our forefathers' time
Until now. In boxing and wrestling, it's true we're not perfect,
But we're fast on our feet and the best of all sea-going men,
And always we love the feast, the lyre, and the dance,
Fresh clothes, hot baths, and the bed. But come, let all

The best dancers among the Phaeacians show us their art,
That when our guest gets home he may tell his friends
How far we surpass all others in seamanship and running
And dancing and singing. Someone go quickly and bring
The sweet lyre to Demodocus. It's back there somewhere
            in the palace."
        So spoke sacred Alcinous, and the herald took off
For the home of the King to bring back the deep-curving lyre.
Then the officials, nine chosen men, who were
At these meetings in charge of such things, marked out a large ring
And cleared it for dancing. The herald returned with the lyre,
So vibrant-sweet, for Demodocus, who now moved to the center
Of the vigorous and skillful young dancers. And as they began
To dance on the sacred floor, Odysseus gazed
With delight at their flashing feet and marveled within.

        The bard played chords in prelude to his sweet song,
Then sang the love of Ares and fair-crowned Aphrodite,
How first they made secret love in the house of Hephaestus.
To her Ares gave much and dishonored the bed
Of lord Hephaestus. But they were seen by Helios,
As they lay making love, and he came with news for Hephaestus,
Who no sooner heard the distressing account than he went
To his forge, brooding evil deep in his heart. He placed
The great anvil on the great anvil block and forged a net,
A snare for the lovers, that could not be broken or loosed.
Having hammered out this device in his wrath for Ares,
He went to his room and suspended the net from the beams
And spread it about the bed-posts. Fine as cobwebs,
It was made with such craft that the blessed gods themselves
Could not see it. When his trap round the bed was ready,
            he pretended
To be leaving for Lemnos, a fine town in a land he prefers
To all others. Now Ares of the golden bridle kept no
Blind watch. When he saw renowned Hephaestus leave,

125

He headed for the great craftsman's home, impatient indeed
For the love of fair-crowned Aphrodite. She had just returned
From a visit to her father, the almighty son of Cronos,
And had just sat down, when eagerly in came Ares,
Took her by the hand, and said:
    "Come, my sweet,
Let's go to bed and enjoy each other there,
For Hephaestus is no longer home, having gone, I believe,
To Lemnos to visit the Sintians, so rude in their speech."
    Now she was only too glad to sleep with him,
So the two of them went over to the bed and lay down,
Whereupon the subtle toils of cunning Hephaestus
Clung close about them, so close they could not move a limb,
Much less get up. They soon saw there would be no escape
This time, and the great lame god himself was coming
Steadily nearer. For he, on word from Helios,
Keeping watch for him, had turned back before reaching Lemnos,
And now with deep gloom in his heart he stood at the gate
Of his house, and thus in the grip of fell fury called out
In a terrible voice to all of the gods:
    "Father Zeus
And you other everliving happy gods, come here and see
This cruel, ridiculous deed, how Zeus's daughter
Aphrodite despises me for my lameness, but adores
Destructive Ares, since he has good looks and sound limbs,
While I was born crippled. Nor is there anyone else
To blame but my parents. I heartily wish they had never
Begotten me! But you shall see for yourselves—
These two in my bed, lying in love together.
For me it's a truly painful sight, though I
Have a notion they won't want to lie there long, not even
For a moment, in fact, no matter how loving they are.
Very soon, I think, they won't be sleepy at all,
But that cunning web of mine will hold them there

Till her father hands over to me every last one
Of the gifts I gave him to win this bitch of a girl,
His daughter, who is lovely indeed but has no inhibitions!"
      He spoke, and the gods came in answer to the house of
           bronze floors.
Earth-holding Poseidon and helpful Hermes were there
And lordly far-working Apollo. The goddesses, embarrassed,
Stayed in their houses. But the gods, from whom our blessings
Come, gathered outside the doors, and laughter
Unquenchable roared throughout that happy crowd
When they saw the clever contrivance of cunning Hephaestus.
Thus one, with a glance at his neighbor, would say:
      "Evil deeds
Don't pay. The slow catches the swift, even
As now Hephaestus, who is surely slow, has outstripped
Ares, the fastest god on Olympus. Lame
But crafty—that's Hephaestus! And now Ares
Must pay an adulterer's fine."
      So they remarked,
But to Hermes, lordly Zeus-sprung Apollo spoke thus:
"Hermes, son of Zeus, good guide and messenger
And bestower of blessings, would you really like to be
In that bed with golden Aphrodite, in spite of those
Unbreakable bonds?"
      And the speedy slayer of Argus
Replied: "If only I might, my far-darting lord
Apollo, I wouldn't object to three times as many
Unshakable shackles. Nor would I mind having you gods
For an audience—and all the goddesses too—if only
I might be in bed with golden Aphrodite!"
      This got a good laugh from the immortal gods—from all
But Poseidon, who was much too busy beseeching that renowned
Artificer, Hephaestus, to let Ares go, pleading thus

127

In these winged words:
      "Release him and I guarantee
He'll make whatever atonement you may demand
Here in the midst of immortal gods."
      But the great
Ambidextrous god replied: "Earth-girdling Poseidon,
Don't ask me to do it. Pledges for the worthless are worthless.
How could I hold you in chains mid immortal gods
If Ares should go and leave both debt and net
Behind him?"
      Then again earth-shaking Poseidon replied:
"Hephaestus, if Ares flees without paying, I myself
Will pay what you ask."
      And now the famous lame god:
"To this from you it would hardly be right to say no."
      So saying, mighty Hephaestus undid the shackles,
And the lovers were no sooner free from those strong toils
Than they both sprang up and fled, Ares to Thrace,
And laughter-loving Aphrodite to Cyprian Paphos,
Where she has a grove and temple and altar fragrant
With incense. There the Graces bathed her and rubbed her
            with oil,
The immortal oil that gleams on the deathless gods,
And they dressed her in lovely clothes, bewitching to see.
      This was the song the famous bard sang, and Odysseus
Listened with delight in his heart, as did the long-oared,
Ship-famous Phaeacians.
      Then Alcinous asked Halius and Laodamas
To dance by themselves, since they had no real competition.
So taking the fine purple ball that skillful Polybus
Had made for them, one would bend back and toss it
Toward the shadowy clouds, and the other would leap in the air
And gracefully catch it before coming down again.
Having shown their skill at high tossing and catching, the two

Struck up a dance on the bountiful earth, quickly
Throwing the ball back and forth, while the other young men
Stood by and beat time, loudly stamping their feet.

Now noble Odysseus spoke to Alcinous: "Great King,
Most distinguished of men, you said that your dancers were best,
And your boast is made good. I can only watch them and wonder."

At this the strong and sacred Alcinous rejoiced,
And without hesitation spoke thus to his sea-loving people:
"Hear me, O captains and counselors of the Phaeacians.
This guest of ours is obviously a man of fine judgment.
So come, let us make him some truly suitable gesture
Of friendship. Twelve pre-eminent kings rule here
In our land, thirteen including myself. Now I
Want each of you twelve to bring to this place, right away,
A fresh cloak and tunic and a talent of precious gold
As gifts for our guest, that he may go to his supper
With a heart full of joy. Let Euryalus make his apology
To him with words and a gift as well, for surely
He spoke with no regard at all for good manners."

They all agreed with the King and spoke well of his words.
Then each dispatched a herald for the presents, and Euryalus
Spoke thus in reply: "Mighty Alcinous, most eminent
Of men, I'll gladly do as you say in making
Amends to our guest. I'll give him this solid bronze blade
With silver hilt and a close-fitting scabbard of newly sawn
Ivory—a gift I am sure he'll appreciate."

So saying,
He placed the sword, bright-studded with silver, in the hands
Of Odysseus, and addressed him with these winged words:

"All joy
To you, O father and guest, and if any harsh word
Has been spoken, may the storm-winds whirl it away, and may
The gods grant your return to wife and home, since

For so long you have suffered so far from your friends."
    And resourceful
Odysseus replied: "To you too, friend, all joy.
May the gods richly bless you, and I hope you will never have
        need
Of this sword you have given me here with such kind words."
    He spoke, and hung the silvery sword from his shoulder,
And now the sun set and the glorious gifts were brought him.
These the high-born heralds took on to the palace,
Where the sons of peerless Alcinous received them and set them
In all their beauty before their honored mother.
Alcinous, sacred and strong, walked home with his friends,
And they all came in and sat down in the high-backed chairs.
Then mighty Alcinous spoke to Arete:
    "My dear,
Bring here to us the very best chest we have,
And you yourself put in it a fresh cloak and tunic,
And warm a cauldron of water, that our guest may bathe
And see all of his gifts from the noble Phaeacians packed safely
Away. Then he can fully enjoy the feasting
And hearing the hymns of the bard. And I will give him
This lovely golden chalice, so that all of his days,
Whenever at home he pours libations to Zeus
And the other gods, he may remember me."
    So he spoke, and Arete told her maids
To put a great three-legged cauldron on the fire right away.
They set the cauldron over the coals and poured in
Water for the bath and beneath it heaped wood. Then,
As the flames leaped round the cauldron's belly, warming
The water, Arete brought from an inner chamber
An exquisite chest for the stranger, and in it she put
The fine Phaeacian gifts of clothing and gold,
To which she added a cloak and a beautiful tunic.
And thus with winged words she spoke to Odysseus:

"Now you must look to the lid and make haste to tie it
Securely, so that on the way when you lie in sweet sleep
In the sailing black ship, no one will be able to rob you."
    When Odysseus, the nobly enduring, heard her
        suggestion,
He lost no time in fitting the lid on and making
It fast with a cunning elaborate knot great Circe
Had taught him. And now the housekeeper suggested that he
Go bathe, and truly his heart rejoiced when he saw
The hot bath, for such comfort had been something less
        than frequent
Since he left the home of fair-haired Calypso. While there,
However, he was constantly cared for like a god.
    When the maids had bathed him, rubbed him with oil,
        and dressed him
In a splendid tunic and mantle, he left the bath
And walked over to join the men at their wine. But Nausicaa,
Divinely beautiful, stood by one of the pillars
On which the thick roof rested, and as she gazed
In wonder at Odysseus she spoke these winged words:
    "Good luck, stranger, and someday in your own country
Perhaps you'll remember me, for to me most of all
You owe your life."
    And resourceful Odysseus replied:
"Nausicaa, daughter of great-hearted Alcinous, if the husband
Of Hera, loud-thundering Zeus, allows my return
Home again, there for the rest of my life I will worship
You like a goddess, for you, young lady, have given
Me life."
    He spoke, and took his seat in a chair
By King Alcinous, for already they were carving the meat
And mixing the wine. The herald came in, leading
The faithful bard Demodocus, dear to the people,
And seated him mid the feasters, having leaned his chair

131

Against a tall pillar. Then thoughtful Odysseus, carving
A portion from the succulent chine of a white-tusked boar,
Spoke thus to the herald:
    "Here, sir, take this meat
To Demodocus, that he may eat. Him I hail
With all warmth, whatever my grief, for throughout the earth
The portion of poets is honor and reverence, since the Muse
Loves all of them dearly and has taught them the art of singing."
    So the herald handed the meat to brave Demodocus,
Who took it with keen delight, and they all began feasting
On the good food spread out before them. But when they
        had eaten
And drunk as much as they wanted, ingenious Odysseus
Spoke to the bard:
    "Demodocus, I do indeed praise you
Above all other mortals. Either Zeus's daughter
The Muse or Apollo himself has taught you, so great
Is the art with which you sing the Achaeans' fate,
All that they did and suffered in the toils of war.
It's as though you had been there yourself, or heard the story
From someone who was. But now, if you will, pass over
All that, and sing the building of the wooden horse—
The horse Epeus made with the help of Athena,
That crafty ambuscade which my lord Odysseus managed
To introduce within the high walls of fortified Troy,
Having filled it with men who later sacked the city.
If you tell me this tale as it happened, I'll not hesitate
To declare, with all mankind for my audience, that God
Has graciously gifted you with heavenly song."
    He spoke, and the bard, by God inspired, took up
The tale where the Argives had set fire to their shelters
        and sailed off
In their well-decked ships, while famous Odysseus and his men
Were already sitting in the Trojans' place of assembly,

Concealed in the horse, for the Trojans themselves had dragged it
Within the high walls. Thus it stood there, while the people
Sat around it, endlessly talking, but unable
To reach a decision. They were of three different minds.
Some wanted to pierce the hollow wood with the ruthless
Bronze. Others were in favor of dragging it up
On the cliff and toppling it down the rocks. But still others
Insisted on letting it stand as a great and marvelous
Gift for the gods. And so they did, for it
Was their fate to die, now that their city contained
The great wooden horse, in which all the best Argives
      were sitting,
Loaded with death and destruction for Trojans. And he sang
How the sons of Achaeans poured out of that hollow horse,
Their ambush, and sacked the city, how this way and that
They managed to level the lofty town, and how
Odysseus went, like Ares himself, along with
King Menelaus to the house of Deïphobus, and there,
Sang the bard, Odysseus endured his most terrible fight,
Finally winning by the grace of great-hearted Athena.

    As the famous bard sang this song, the heart of Odysseus
Melted, and tears ran down his cheeks. He wept
Like a woman who wails and throws herself wildly upon
Her dear husband, who has fallen in front of his city, fighting
To ward off from his children and home the ruthless day.
She finds him there throttling and dying and pours herself
About him, frantically shrieking, while the enemy beat her
On the back and shoulders and lead her off in fetters,
Her face all drawn and shrunken with most pitiful grief,
To a life of misery and toil. So too from the eyes
Of Odysseus came pitiful tears. These he concealed
From the others, but Alcinous sat by him and heard his
      deep groaning,
And so could not help but notice. Then quickly he spoke

133

Among his sea-loving people:
    "Captains and counselors
Of the Phaeacians, your attention please, and let
Demodocus silence his melodious lyre, for all
Of us are not enjoying his song. Ever since
We started to eat and the sacred bard's inspiration
Moved him to sing, our guest has been moaning with misery,
Without ceasing, his heart weighed down with anguish.
        Come then,
Let the bard cease, that all of us, hosts
And guest alike, may enjoy ourselves. It will surely
Be better that way. After all, for this honored guest
Of ours, all of these things have been done, his convoy
Arranged and gifts of friendship given him out of
Our love. A stranger and suppliant is dear as a brother
To a man with any sense at all. Therefore,
My friend, be crafty no longer in answering these questions
Of mine. To be frank is much better. Tell me the name
You go by at home—what your mother and father and countrymen
Call you. For no one in the world is nameless, however
Mean or noble, since parents give names to all
The children they have. And tell me your country, people,
And city, that our ships, having minds of their own, may take you
There. For our ships are like no others, in that
The Phaeacians have no helmsmen or steering-oars. Our ships
Understand of themselves the thoughts and minds of men,
And they know the cities and farms all over the world.
Swiftly they cross the sea's great gulf, hidden
In mist and cloud, but with no fear at all of damage
Or ruin. Still, Nausithous, my father, would say
That Poseidon was angry at us for giving safe convoy
To all, and that someday, as a trim Phaeacian ship
Was homeward bound across the dim sea, returning
From a convoy, Poseidon, so said my father,

Would smite that ship and completely surround our city
With monstrous mountains. So spoke that old man,
        but whether
These things will happen or not remains up to God,
Who will do what pleases him most. So come now, tell me
Truly where you have wandered, to what countries
And what fine cities. Tell too of the people in them,
The cruel, unjust, and uncivilized, as well as those
Who love strangers and fear God in their hearts. And tell me why
You weep and grieve in spirit when hearing the doom
Of the Argive Danaans and Ilium. This was the work
Of the gods, who spun a web of destruction for men,
That people yet to be might have a song.
Can it be that one of your kinsmen by marriage fell
Before Troy, some splendid son- or father-in-law,
Even such as are most dear next to blood kin?
Or was it perhaps some comrade, your very soul-mate,
Some truly marvelous man? For an understanding friend
Is surely not less precious than a brother."

BOOK

IX

THE CICONES,
THE LOTUS-EATERS,
THE CYCLOPS

Then resourceful Odysseus replied: "King Alcinous,
Most famous of men, surely it is a good thing
To hear such a fine bard sing, for this man's voice
Is like that of a god. As for me, I know nothing
So completely delightful as a land where the people are filled
With good humor, and those that feast in the halls sit quietly
At tables covered with good things to eat and listen
To the songs of a poet, while the wine-bearer draws wine
            from the bowl
And fills the goblets of all. This seems to me
The finest thing in the world. But now you wish
To hear my woeful story, though I hardly think
My telling it will make me feel any better.
But where shall I begin and how much shall I tell?
For the heavenly gods have given me an almost
Boundless supply of woeful experiences. But first,
My name, that you may know who I am, for later,

When I have passed that ruthless day of doom
Toward which I move, I hope to be your host
In my distant home. I am Odysseus, the son
Of Laertes, and I am known among men and gods
For being able to use the mind I have.
My home is in Ithaca, where on any clear day
The leafy mountain Neriton may be seen for miles.
Ithaca lies well out in the sea toward the gloom
Of twilight, while the neighboring islands of Dulichium, Samos
And wooded Zacynthus lie nearer the rising sun.
My home is a rugged island, but a splendid place
For young men to grow up, and to me it is the sweetest
Place of all. The beautiful goddess Calypso
Did her best to keep me with her in her echoing caves
And make me her husband, as indeed did Circe too,
That tricky Aeaean lady, when I lived for a time
In her halls. But in neither instance could I be persuaded.
For no luxurious life in a foreign mansion
Can be so sweet as a man's own country and parents.
But enough. It's time for me to begin the story
Of the sad eventful return that Zeus decreed
For me as homeward I traveled from the land of Troy.
    "From Ilium the wind carried our ships to Ismarus,
Home of the Cicones. There, as I commanded,
We sacked the city and killed its defenders, dividing
Their wives and possessions as equally as possible among us.
Then I ordered my men to return to the ships with what
They had, but the fools did not obey me. There
On the shore they drank a great deal of wine and slaughtered
A great many sheep and lumbering long-horned cattle.
Meanwhile, word came to neighboring Cicones, an inland
People more numerous and valiant than those whom we first
Encountered. These men fought equally well from chariots
Or on foot when they had to, and in the misty dawn

They descended upon us as thick as the leaves and flowers
Of spring. Right then it was that we were overtaken
By the bitter fate that came from Zeus and caused
My unfortunate men and me so many sorrows.
The battle began beside the swift ships and soon
The air was full of spears well tipped with bronze
Flying in either direction. All morning we held
Our ground, though greatly outnumbered, but when the sun
Began to drop down the sky toward the time when oxen
Are relieved of the yoke, then the Cicones proved
Too much for the Achaeans, and of my well-greaved companions
Six from each ship left their bodies there on the beach.
That fate the rest of us were able to flee.
        "On we sailed, glad to be alive,
But grieving for our good friends no longer with us,
Nor would I allow the graceful ships to go
Any further before we had called three times on each
Of our unlucky comrades who had fallen before the Cicones
Back there on the beach. But now cloud-gathering Zeus
Aroused the North Wind and sent an incredible storm
Upon us, a blow so great that land and sea
Alike were blotted out as if night had suddenly
Rushed headlong from heaven. We lost all control of the ships,
And the sails were left in tatters by the violent wind.
Quickly we lowered the remains and stowed them away,
Lest we capsize and die, and we began with all
Our might to row for shore, where we lay for two days
And two nights with weariness and sorrow eating our hearts
Away, till finally Dawn of the lovely hair
Brought in a beautiful day. Having set up the masts
And raised the white sails, we all sat down to relax,
While the ship flew onward before a fair wind and the man
At the helm kept us straight on our course. And now I should
Have reached my home unharmed, but as I was rounding

Malea a rough sea and the North Wind beat me back
And drove me off my course beyond Cythera.

"For nine long days we were pounded by the howling gale
Through the teeming sea-water, but on the tenth we reached
The land of the Lotus-eaters, who feast on fruit.
We went ashore and found water and made a meal
Beside the swift ships. Then I chose two men and another
To act as their herald, and sent them to find what kind
Of men took their nourishment there. They went, but we got
No word from them, for the Lotus-eaters had received them
Kindly and served them the honeyed fruit of the lotus
To eat, a meal which deprived them of any desire
To return or send word. They were content to stay
With the Lotus-eaters, consuming the luscious fruit
And forgetful of home, but I brought them back to the ships
By force, three weeping men, tied them up
And dragged them beneath the benches low in the hull.
Quickly I ordered the rest of my trusty friends
To board the swift ships, lest someone else should happen
To eat of the lotus and forget about home. Soon aboard,
They took their seats, and all together they struck
The gray sea with their oars.

"From there we sailed on with hearts
Full of sorrow till we came to the land of the Cyclopes,
        those proud
And lawless creatures who neither plow nor plant,
Being willing to leave all that to the immortal gods.
And the Zeus-sent rain does indeed produce for them
A bountiful harvest of wheat, barley, and rich clusters
Of wine. They have no assemblies for counsel and no
Established laws, but live on high mountain peaks
In echoing caves, and each is sole master of his own
Children and wives. None of them cares anything

139

At all about his neighbors.
    "Now right outside
The harbor of the Cyclopes' country, lies a long and wooded
Island. There the wild goats have multiplied immensely,
For the tread of man never startles anything there.
No men who endure the hardships of woods and high mountains
For the sake of game come to molest them. No plow
Goes through that soil. No seed is sown. The fields
Feed flocks of bleating goats no shepherds tend.
For the Cyclopes have no ships with scarlet prows.
They have, in fact, no artisans able to build
Seaworthy vessels with which they might establish
Some adequate commerce with cities across the sea,
Making visits as other men do. Such builders of ships
Would long since have made Goat Island a populous place.
For in that soil almost anything would grow
In its proper season. There beside the gray sea
Are grassy, well-watered meadows, where vineyards would thrive,
And open arable land with soil so rich
That reaping at harvest time would always be bountiful.
We also found a splendid harbor there,
So safe that one needs no moorings, neither rope nor anchor,
But simply runs his ship up on the beach
Where it will remain until the wind stands fair
And the sailors decide to shove off. On the shore of this bay
A spring of bright water bubbles at the mouth of a cave
In a grove of poplars. Toward this we sailed, guided
By a god, for the moon was covered with clouds and the fog
All about us. Indeed not one of us saw that island
At all, or the long high waves rolling ashore,
Until we ran our well-rowed ships aground.
Then we pulled them up on the sand, lowered the sails,
And lying down on the beach we slept, awaiting

Bright Dawn.

"As soon as that rosy sweet lass appeared,
We roamed the island, marveling at what we saw,
Till the nymphs, daughters of Zeus who bears the aegis,
Aroused the mountain goats, that my companions
Might have something to eat. Quickly we took from the ships
Our bent bows and long spears and set out in three groups
        to hunt them,
And God soon gave us all the game we needed.
Of our twelve ships, eleven got nine goats apiece,
While ten were allotted to mine.

"Then all day long,
Till the sun went down, we sat and feasted well
On that abundant meat and good sweet wine.
For we still had jars of red wine stored in the ships,
Part of the plentiful supply we had taken from the sacred
Citadel of the Cicones. And as we ate
We could see the smoke rising from the fires of the Cyclopes,
So close that across the still bay water we could hear
Their voices and the bleating of their sheep and goats. When night
Had come, only the sound of the surf remained,
And we lay down on the beach to sleep. But when
The first pink light of Dawn appeared, I got
The men together and spoke to all of them thus:

" 'The rest of you, my very good friends, wait here,
While my crew and I go to find out what we can
Of the men who live over there on the mainland, whether just
Or unjust, insolent and uncivilized men or god-fearing
And friendly to strangers.'

"With this I went aboard
And called my comrades to follow and cast off, which they did.
Then taking their seats at the oars, all together they churned
The gray sea. We soon arrived, and just off the beach
We saw a huge cave, shaded with laurels, at night

141

The shelter of many sheep and goats. Around it
Was a high palisade of stones set deep in the ground
Along with great oaks and tall pines. That was the home
Of a monstrous and lawless man, who lived by himself
And tended his flocks alone. He was indeed
A remarkable monster, not at all like a bread-eating mortal,
Rather more like some lofty mountain whose wooded peak
Stands out alone, apart from the rest of the range.

"A number of my trusted companions I told to stay
And guard the ship, but I chose twelve of the best
To go with me. I took along a goatskin
Of the dark sweet wine which Maron, son of Euanthes,
Had given me. Maron was the priest of Apollo,
The god to whom the Cicones looked for protection,
And he had given me the wine for sparing
Him, his child, and his wife, which we did out of reverence,
Since he lived in a grove sacred to Phoebus Apollo.
Splendid indeed were the gifts he gave to me:
Seven talents of highly wrought gold, a mixing-bowl
Of solid silver, and twelve jars of that divine wine,
The pure and delectable. Not a single slave or housemaid
Of his knew anything at all about it. That secret
He shared only with his dear wife and the woman
In charge of supplies, and whenever they wanted to drink
Of that red wine, as delicious as honey, he would fill
One goblet and pour it into twenty measures of water,
Whereupon an aroma so incredibly sweet would arise
From the mixing-bowl that rare indeed is the man
Who would abstain. Besides a large skin of this wine,
I took with me a leather bag of provisions,
For in my stout heart I already suspected that soon
I would meet a man both powerful and wild, a savage
Utterly without regard for customs or decrees.

"Quickly we reached the cave and found that its owner

Was not within. He was out in the fields
With his fat flocks. So in we went and at once
Were struck with delight at what we saw. For there
Were crates heavy with cheeses and crowded pens
Of lambs and kids, these in three groups, according
To age, and there were his sturdy milking buckets and tubs
Running over with whey. My men tried hard to persuade me
That we should take what cheeses we could and come back
For the lambs and kids, drive them aboard our swift ships,
And sail off over the brine. But I would not listen,
For which, very soon, I was sorry. I wanted to see
The man himself and whether he would give me gifts
Befitting a guest. Unfortunately, as it turned out,
His coming was not much fun for my companions.
  "We built a fire and made a burnt-offering there.
Then we ate some of the cheeses ourselves and sat down
In the cave, where we waited till he and his flocks appeared.
He was carrying a great bundle of dry wood for his evening fire,
And he threw it down inside the cave with such
A crash that we scurried as far back in the dark as we could.
Then he drove all those that he milked into the great cavern
And left the he-goats and rams in the spacious yard.
The great door-stone he lifted high in the air
And set it in place, a truly tremendous boulder
That twenty-two four-wheeled wagons, the strongest there are,
Could not have begun to support. Now he sat down
And milked the ewes and bleating goats, and all
The new lambs and kids he placed beneath their mothers.
Quickly he curdled half the white milk, scooped it
Into wicker baskets, and stored them away. The rest
He left standing out that he might have it to drink
With his supper. When he had finished these chores, he rekindled
The fire. Then at last he saw us and began to ask questions:
  " 'Who are you, strangers? Where are you from? Is it

On business that you sail the ocean paths, or do you
Wander recklessly over the sea as buccaneers,
Risking your own lives and damaging those of others?'

"So terribly did the gruff voice of this monstrous man
Crash in the air that our hearts were shattered with fear,
But even so I managed to answer him thus:
'We—and I speak the truth—are Achaeans, homeward
Bound from Troy, but driven by all the winds
Far off our course and all over the sea's great gulf.
We've traveled a devious route indeed, but such
Was the will of Zeus. We are the men of Agamemnon,
Son of Atreus, he whose fame is now greatest
On earth, so mighty was the city he sacked, so many
The people he slew. But to you we have come as suppliants,
Have come to your knees in hope of warm hospitality,
Or some gift, perhaps, some customary gift to strangers.
At any rate, O man of might, reverence
The gods and remember that we are your suppliants, for Zeus
Is the god of strangers, the avenger of suppliants, the guardian,
I say, of sacred strangers.'

"Then the ruthless answer:
'Stranger, your telling me to fear or avoid
The gods means either that you're the most childish of fools
Or that you come from so far away that you
Know nothing of the Cyclopes. For we care nothing at all
For aegis-bearing Zeus, nor for any of the blessed gods,
Since we are far stronger than they are. Why I wouldn't think
Of sparing either you or your comrades simply to avoid
The wrath of Zeus, though I might do so merely
To please myself. But tell me, where did you leave
Your well-built ship, nearby or some distance from here?'

"But into that trap my quick wit kept me from falling,
And I did my best to misinform him: 'My ship

Was destroyed by earth-shaking Poseidon, who brought her
      in close
To shore with the sea-wind behind us and broke her up
On the rocks, where my men and I escaped sheer ruin.'
    "Such was my story, but this time his ruthless heart
Made no reply. Lunging at us, he snatched up
Two of my comrades as if they were puppies and dashed them
Down at his feet where their brains ran out on the ground.
Then he cut them up and prepared his evening meal,
Which he ate like a mountain lion—meat, bones,
Entrails and all. Watching this abominable feast,
We were all but dead with fear, able only to wail
And hold up our hands to Zeus. But when the Cyclops
Had filled his monstrous belly with human flesh
And fresh milk, he stretched out to sleep on the floor of his cave
Among the sheep. By then my dauntless wits
Had returned, and I thought how I might approach him now
With my drawn sword in hand, feel for the spot
Just over the liver, and run him through. But then
I thought again, for we all would have died with the monster,
Since we could not have budged that tremendous rock
He used for a door. So we groaned and waited for morning.
    "When young and blushing Dawn finally came,
The Cyclops rekindled the fire, milked his fine flock,
And placed each new lamb and kid beneath its mother.
With these chores done, again he snatched up two
Of my men and prepared them for breakfast. Having eaten,
      he removed
With ease the massive door-stone and drove his fat flock
From the cave, then replaced the stone, as one of us
Might put the lid on a quiver. So off to the mountain
He went, whistling like the wind when it roars, and driving
His flocks before him. I was left in the cave,
Brooding evil in the darker cave of my heart, hatching

Revenge, if only Athena would grant me that glory.
    "Here then is the plan that seemed to my mind the best.
There by one of the sheep-pens lay a great club
Of green olive, which the Cyclops had cut to cure and carry
With him. To us it seemed as long and thick
As the mast of a broad-beamed black merchant ship, a vessel
Of twenty oars that crosses the sea's great gulf.
From this I cut a log about the length of a fathom
And gave it to my comrades, asking that they dress it down
And bring it to a point, which they did, and I myself
Finished the point and thrust it in the blazing fire
To harden. Then with all care I hid it beneath
A pile of manure, of which that cave had its share.
And I asked my men to cast lots to determine which ones
Should have the courage to help me lift the log
And plunge its point into the eye of the Cyclops
Sweetly sleeping. Four men were chosen by lot,
The very four that I myself would have picked.
    "At sunset he returned with those fat flocks
That bore such splendid wool and quickly drove all
Of them into the huge cave. Either from some
Foreboding or at the command of a god, he left
Not a single one outside in the great stockade.
Then he lifted the tremendous door-stone high in the air
And set it in place, sat down himself and milked
The ewes and bleating goats, and placed the lambs
And kids beneath their mothers. This done, once again
He snatched up two of my men and ate them for supper.
Then I approached and spoke to the Cyclops, with an ivy
Bowl of dark wine in my hands:
    " 'Cyclops, here,
Drink this bowl of wine, now that you've finished
Your meal of human flesh, that you may know
What kind of drink we had with us in our ship.

I was indeed bringing it to you as an offering,
Hoping that you would take pity and set me once more
On my homeward way, but you have made yourself
Unbearable to us. After such barbarous cruelty,
How can you expect any man ever to visit
You here again?'

"He took the bowl and drained it
At a gulp, and finding it sweet and greatly to his taste
He asked for more:

" 'Let me have another.
Offer it gladly, and tell me your name right now,
That I may give you a gift that will, I believe,
Delight you. Here the grain-giving earth and rain
From Zeus produce some winy rich clusters, but you
Have tapped the gods' own supply of ambrosial nectar.'

"So again I handed him the fiery bowl,
And then again, and thrice he foolishly drained it.
When he began to grow groggy, I spoke to him
In a pleasant voice:

" 'Cyclops, you ask my name,
A famous name, and I will tell it to you,
That you may give me the friendly gift you promised.
Nobody is my name. They all call me Nobody—
My mother, my father, and all the rest of my friends.'

"Then ruthless as ever, he answered: 'Nobody I'll eat
Last of all, and all the others I'll eat before Nobody.'

"With this he reeled and fell on his back, his thick neck
Bent to one side, and all-conquering sleep overcame him.
As he lay in that sodden coma, he began to vomit
And out came wine and chunks of human flesh.
I took the pole and thrust it deep beneath
The red-hot coals, and with cheerful words I encouraged
All my companions, that no man might flinch when
            the time came.

147

Soon that stake, though green, began to glow
A terrible red, as if it would blaze any moment.
I took it from the fire, and as my men gathered around me
A god inspired our hearts with tremendous courage.
Then they took that pointed pole of glowing green olive
And plunged it into his eye, while I bore down
On the shaft from above and spun it around. Like a man
With a drill who bores a ship's timber while those below
Keep the drill constantly spinning with the thong they hold
On either side, so we took that pole with the head
Of fire and spun it about in his eye, and the burning
Blood oozed out around it. As the eyeball sizzled
And its roots crackled, his lids fell completely away,
And his brow began to blister. As when a worker
In bronze dips a large ax or adze into cold water
To temper it and a great hissing is heard—
For iron at least is strengthened by dipping in water—
Even so his eye hissed around the green olive pole.
Horrible were the screams that rang from wall
To rocky wall, and we shrank back in terror.
He tore the stake from his eye, all dripping with blood,
And frantically hurled it away. Then, throwing himself
Wildly about, he shouted as loud as he could
To the neighboring Cyclopes, who lived out there in caves
Among the windy mountains. Hearing his cry, they came
From all sides, and standing around the cave they asked
What his trouble was:
      " 'What unbearable pain,
Polyphemus, makes you cry out and keep us awake
In this fair and peaceful night. Is somebody rustling
Your flocks or actually killing you by force
Or some trick?'
      "Then from the cave came the voice of powerful
Polyphemus: 'O friends, Nobody is killing me

By a trick, not force!'
  "And they answered with winged words:
'If you are alone and nobody is hurting you,
You must be sick, and sickness you cannot escape
Since it comes from almighty Zeus. You had best pray
To Poseidon, our lordly father.'
  "They had their say
And left, and in my heart I laughed to think
What a sharp trick Nobody had pulled with an improper name.
  "The Cyclops, groaning in agony, groped for the door-stone,
Removed it, and sat there himself with his arms extended
Lest anyone try to get out with the sheep, so stupid
He apparently thought me. But I was searching my brain
For a plan, that my men and I might escape that death.
Many were the schemes I considered, as anyone would,
In the face of that great evil, and here is the plan
I preferred. There in the cave were woolly fat rams,
Great beautiful beasts with fleece as dark as the violet.
I tied them side by side in groups of three
With pliant branches that the lawless monster used
For a pallet. Beneath each middle sheep rode one of my comrades
With a beast on either side for added protection.
As for me, I chose the very best ram in the flock,
And grabbing two handfuls of hair I curled myself up
Beneath his shaggy belly, where I clung in dead earnest,
Holding on for dear life, my face in his marvelous fleece.
Thus with many groans we waited for morning.
  "As soon as rosy young Dawn arrived, the rams
Made for the pasture, while the females, their udders bursting,
Bleated unmilked about the pens. Their ailing
Master ran his hands over the backs of the rams
As they passed before him, but foolishly failed to check
Beneath the woolly beasts where my men were riding.
The ram I had chosen started out last of all,

Bearing his weight of wool and my anxious self,
And powerful Polyphemus felt along his back
And spoke to him thus:
    " 'Tell me, old fellow, why you
Are the last one out of the cave. It's not like you
To lag behind. You were always the first
To reach the tender grass, practically galloping,
And always the first to reach the running streams,
And always at evening you were the most eager to return
To our home. But now you're the very last one. I believe
You are grieving for the eye of your master, blinded by a horrible
Man and his despicable friends, by Nobody,
Who plied me with wine, and who, believe me, has not yet
Escaped death at my hands! If only you could understand
And talk, you could tell me where he is hiding. Then
I would scatter his brains all over the floor of this cave,
And so relieve my heart of the weight of woe
That no-good Nobody has caused me.'
    "With this he let
The ram go, and when we had got just a little outside
The enclosure in front of the cave I first freed myself
From under the ram and then untied my friends.
Fast as we could and often looking behind us,
We drove those sheep, fat but nimble on their slender
Legs, until we reached the ship. We
Were a welcome sight to our good friends there, but for those
Who didn't return they began to weep and lament.
This I ended with a frown and ordered them
To shove those fleecy sheep aboard as quick
As they could and to strike off from shore through the salt
        sea-water.
They obeyed at once, and taking their seats at the oars
They churned the gray sea. Then, before we got out
Of shouting distance, I yelled this taunt to the Cyclops:

" 'I say, Cyclops, that seems to have been a pretty
Capable fellow whose comrades you ate, like the brute
You are, in your desolate cave. Such horrors were bound
To come home to the wretch who in his own house would actually
Eat his guests. So Zeus and the other gods
Have revenged themselves on you!'
    "This made the monster
More frenzied than ever, and he broke off the stony top
Of a lofty mountain and heaved it in our direction.
It struck beyond the dark blue bow of our ship,
And the great backwash from the stone as it fell in the water,
Like a tidal wave from the open sea, carried
Our ship swiftly shoreward and drove it up on the beach.
But seizing a long pole, I shoved us off the sand
And with a toss of my head I urged my comrades to row,
That we might escape the imminent evil—and they rowed!
But when we had gone about twice as far as before,
Once again I felt an urge to shout at the Cyclops,
Though around me my comrades tried hard to change my mind:
    " 'Why, O reckless man, will you further provoke
That ruthless savage, whose boulder just moments ago
Drove our ship clear back to the shore, where all of us
Nearly died. Had he heard one word or so much as a sound
From one of us there, he would have hurled another
Jagged crag and crushed both us and our ship,
His aim is so good!'
    "They tried, but could not change
My daring mind, and angrily I yelled again:
'Cyclops, if anyone ever asks you about
The disgraceful blinding of your eye, say
That Odysseus, sacker of cities, put it out
With a pole—I, the son of Laertes, from Ithaca!'
    "He groaned and replied: 'Ah me, an old prophecy
Has been fulfilled. A soothsayer used to live here,

Telemus, son of Eurymus, a great and good man,
Who lived and died among the Cyclopes and had
No peer as a prophet. He told me that all these things
Would happen, that Odysseus would surely blind my eye.
But always I thought some great and important man
Would come, somebody clad in tremendous power,
When who should appear but the merest puny, a weakling,
A very nothing, who laid me low with wine
And then put out my eye! But come here, Odysseus,
That I may give you gifts befitting a stranger
And that the glorious creator of earthquakes may see you
Safely home. For I am his son, a fact
He proudly admits. If he wishes, he will restore
My eye, something no other god or man
Can do.'
        "He spoke, and this was my reply:
'I only wish that I were as able to end
Your life and send you packing to the house of Hades
As I am sure that not even the Earthshaker himself
Can help that eye of yours!'
        "Then, holding both hands
To the stars, he prayed to kingly Poseidon: 'O god
That embraces the earth, god with the blue-black hair,
If I am really your son and you aren't ashamed
To admit it, hear my prayer: grant that Odysseus,
Sacker of cities and son of Laertes, he
Who hails from Ithaca—grant that he never get home.
But if it should be his fate to reach his own land
And well-built house and see his friends again,
Then may his coming be late and hard, after losing
All of his comrades. Let him come, O god, in somebody
Else's ship, and may he find troubles enough
At home.'
        "He prayed, and the blue-haired god Poseidon

Heard his prayer. Then he picked up a boulder
Even larger than the one before, and swinging it around
He slung it with incredible force. It struck just behind
Our blue-bowed ship, barely missing the steering-oar,
And the mighty surge that arose where the great rock fell
Drove our ship all the way to the island.
    "There lay the rest
Of our excellent ships and around them our friends, in a state
Of constant expectation, sat weeping. We ran
Our ship on the sand and stepped out on the beach. Then
We took the sheep of the Cyclops from the hollow ship
And insofar as I could I divided them equally.
But the ram I had ridden my well-greaved companions gave only
To me, a special gift, and there I sacrificed
Him to the son of Cronos and god of storms,
Almighty Zeus, and there I burnt the thighs
To him. He, however, paid no attention
To my devotions, but even then was planning
How all my well-rowed ships and trusted friends
Would be destroyed.
    "Then, till the sun went down,
We sat and feasted on the plentiful meat and sweet wine,
And when it grew dark we lay down to sleep on the shore
Of the sea. But as soon as early Dawn, that rosy
Sweet lass, appeared, I got the men up and sent them
Aboard with orders to loose the ropes and cast off
From the stern. This they did, and taking their seats
At the oars they churned the gray sea. From there we sailed on
With grief in our hearts, glad to be still alive,
But mourning still for the loss of our dear dead friends.

BOOK

X

AEOLUS,
THE LAESTRYGONIANS,
CIRCE

"Next we came to the floating Aeolian island,
Home of Aeolus, son of Hippotas, whom
The immortal gods hold dear. All around it runs
A wall of unbreakable bronze, to which the rock rises
Straight from the sea. Aeolus has in his halls
Twelve children, six daughters and six strong sons, and he
Has given his daughters in marriage to his sons. There
In the palace with boundless refreshments before them, they sit
With their dear father and excellent mother, feasting
Continually. All day the house is filled with the fragrance
Of food and resounds throughout with the piping of flutes,
And at night in blankets on corded beds they sleep
With their cherished wives. To this their lovely home
And citadel we came, and for one full month Aeolus
Entertained me, asking of Ilium, the Argives' ships,
And the Achaeans' return, and I told him the tale as it happened.
When I, in my turn, asked him if I might continue

My journey with assistance from him, he did all he could
To help me. He gave me a leather bag, made
From the hide of an ox of nine years, and in it he bound
The winds, howling in all directions, for Zeus
Has made him their keeper, able to still or stir up
Whichever one he wishes. And in my hollow ship
He tied the bag tight with a strong bright silver cord,
That not even the smallest breath of a breeze might escape.
But to help me on my way, he sent the West Wind
Forth, that it might blow and bear us and our ships
On our course. But in this he did not completely succeed,
For through our own folly we failed.
  "For nine days we sailed on,
Day and night, till on the tenth our homeland
Appeared, and we were so close we could see men minding
The watch-fires. Then sweet sleep overcame me, for I
Was worn out from handling the sheet of the ship all the way,
Yielding to none, that we might the sooner return.
Now my comrades conversed and accused me of bringing home,
For myself, gifts of gold and silver from Aeolus,
The great-hearted son of Hippotas. Thus one, with a glance
At his neighbor, would say:
  " 'Just see how all men love
And honor this man, no matter what city or country
He comes to. He is carrying from Troy much splendid treasure,
While we, who have run the same road, come home
    empty-handed.
And now Aeolus has freely given to him these gifts
Of friendship. But come, let's take a quick look and see
Just how much gold and silver is in that bag.'
  "So spoke my comrades, and this baneful plan of theirs
Won out. But when they opened the bag, the whole jostle
Of winds rushed forth, and quickly a great squall broke
And swept my weeping comrades out to sea

Away from their homeland. I awoke and my goodly spirit
Was torn as to whether I should throw myself from the ship
And die in the sea, or suffer on in silence
Among the living. Drawing my cloak up over
My head, I lay down in the ship, stayed where I was,
And endured, while that malevolent storm bore all
The ships, and in them my groaning comrades, back
To the island of Aeolus.

   "There we went ashore,
And after renewing our water supply my comrades
Took their meal beside the swift ships. When we
Had eaten and drunk, I took a herald and one oarsman
And proceeded to the palace of Aeolus, where I found him feasting
With his wife and children. We went in and sat down
On the threshold by the posts of the door, and they, astounded,
Questioned us thus:

   " 'How did you get here, Odysseus?
What evil demon's to blame? Surely we sent you
On your way with all you needed to get
To your country and home and anywhere else you wished.'

   "So they, and I with a heart full of sorrow replied:
'Evil companions and wretched sleep undid me.
But help me, heal me, my friends, for with you lies the power.'

   "With such soft words I addressed them, but they
     said nothing
At all. Then their father spoke in reply: 'Get off
This island as fast as you can—you the most shameful
Creature alive! I cannot rightly help
Or further that man's journey whom the happy gods hate.
Go, for surely you come here as such
A man.'

   "So saying, he sent me, sadly protesting,
Out of the house. From there we went on in our grief,
The men worn-out and discouraged by the painful rowing,

For because of our folly no breath of breeze appeared
To help us on our way. So for six days
And six nights we journeyed, till on the seventh we came
To the towering town of King Lamus, the Laestrygonian
Citadel of Telepylus, where shepherds passing
Hail each other, one driving in his flocks,
The other driving his out. For twilight and dawn
Come so close together that there a man who could go
Without sleeping might earn double wages, as herdsman of cattle,
Then shepherd of silvery white sheep. When we reached
   the fine harbor,
About which high reefs of sheer rock run out on both sides
While opposing headlands jut in at the narrow mouth,
All the others steered their curving ships
Into this hollow haven and moored them together,
Right side by side, for the water there is never
Rough, no waves at all, but everywhere bright calm.
Only I tied up outside of that excellent harbor,
Making my black ship fast to a rock on the headland.
Then I climbed the rough cliff to get my bearings,
But from the top no works of oxen or men
Could be seen. We did, however, see smoke curling up
From the land. So I sent some comrades of mine—a herald
And two oarsmen—to find out what bread-eating mortals
   these were.
Ashore, they followed a road which wagons had worn
Bringing wood to the city down from the lofty mountains.
Outside the city they met a girl drawing water,
The strapping daughter of Laestrygonian Antiphates,
Who had come down to the burbling spring Artacia
From which the town got its water. They approached and asked
Who was king of her people and what people they were
   whom he ruled,
And she pointed to the lofty roof of her father's house.

Soon they were in the glorious palace and face
To face with Antiphates' wife, huge as the peak
Of a mountain, repulsive and horrifying. Quickly she called
Her eminent husband from the place of assembly, and he came
With a mind full of murder. Right away he snatched up a comrade
Of mine and prepared him for supper, but the other two
Shot out and fled to the ships. At this he gave
A great shout through the town, and the monstrous
      Laestrygonians—
More giants than men—heard it and came in unnumbered
Throngs from all directions. From the cliffs they hurled
Huge rocks at us, huge as a man could lift,
And throughout the fleet the horrible screams of the dying
Could be heard above the splintering and crashing of timbers.
Then spearing the dead like so many fish, they carried them
Home for a loathsome supper. Now while they were slaughtering
Those within the deep cove, I drew my sharp sword
From my hip and slashed the hawsers of my dark-prowed ship,
Urgently bidding my comrades row, that we
Might escape this danger. And they, in fear of death,
Beat the brine with their oar-blades, speeding us on
With relief away from those beetling cliffs and so out
To sea—my ship alone, the others all lost.
    "From there we sailed on in our grief, glad that we
Escaped death, but mourning our dear dead comrades. Thus
We came to the island Aeaea, home of fair-haired
Circe, dire goddess with the voice of a woman, own sister
To evil Aeëtes—both of whom are the children
Of light-giving Helios and Perse their mother, whom great
Oceanus sired. Quietly, here we put in
To the rocky shore, and found, with the help of some god,
A safe harbor. Once out of the ship, we lay there two days
And two nights with exhaustion and woe consuming our hearts.
But when Dawn with fair tresses brought in the third day, I took

My spear and sharp sword and briskly started the climb
From the ship to a high and rugged point, where I hoped
I might see the works and hear the voices of men.
Taking my stand at the top, I saw smoke curling up
From the much-traveled earth, rising from the halls of Circe
Through the dense scrub oak and tall trees. The sight of
    that smoke
Left me debating in mind and in heart, uncertain
Whether or not I should go and investigate. Pondering
I found the best plan—to go first to the beach and swift ship,
Give my comrades a meal, and send them out
To explore. But when I drew near the curved ship, some god
Took pity on me in my desolation and sent
A great high-antlered stag right into my path.
Oppressed by the sun, he had left his woodland pasture
And was on his way down to the river to drink. As he entered
The path, I struck him square in the middle of the back,
And the spear's bronze head went all the way through him. He fell
In the dust with a cry, and his spirit took flight. Putting
A foot on the carcass, I drew the keen spear from the wound
And laid it down on the ground. Then I pulled some twigs
And supple branches and twisted a rope of about
One fathom in length, plaiting it well all the way.
With this I tied the great beast's feet together,
Got him across my back, and continued on
To the black ship, supporting myself with my spear.
I couldn't have held him with just one shoulder and hand,
So huge a beast he was. I flung him down
In front of the ship and made the rounds of my friends,
With kind and gentle words arousing them:

   " 'Come, my friends, we'll not go down to Hades'
House just yet, surely not before our time comes,
Wretched though we may be. While food and drink
Remain in our swift ship, let's not forget

To eat. Then at least we won't starve.'
    "Right away they revived
At my words, and uncovering their heads they stared
        in amazement
At the stag, that monstrous beast, there on the shore
Of the desolate sea. But when they had sated themselves
With gazing, they washed their hands and prepared a glorious
Feast. Thus all day long till sundown, we sat
And feasted on the plentiful meat and sweet wine. Then,
When the sun was gone and darkness had come, we lay down
On the beach to sleep. I awoke at the very first touch
Of young Dawn's rosy fingers, called all my men
Together, and spoke to them thus:
    " 'In spite of your misery,
Comrades, pay heed to my words. Here, my friends,
We're ignorant of east and west alike. We do not
Know where the light-giving Sun goes down beneath
The earth, nor where he rises. But let us consider
Right now if there's any way out of this trouble—not
That I think there is. For I climbed to a high rocky point
For a look at the island, which is set, low-lying, in a boundless
Crown of deep sea, and from the midst of the island
I saw smoke curling up through the dense scrub oak
And tall trees.'
    "At these words their spirits were broken, for they
Remembered the crimes of Laestrygonian Antiphates
And the arrogant violence of the man-eating Cyclops. They wailed
And wept and the big tears fell, but their wailing and weeping
Got nothing done.
    "So I split them up in two groups,
Those well-greaved comrades of mine, and for each I appointed
A leader. I myself took charge of one, of the other
Godlike Eurylochus. Then without more delay we shook lots
In a helmet of bronze, and out leaped the lot of great-hearted

Eurylochus. So he and twenty-two weeping comrades
Set out, leaving us behind, likewise lamenting.
Deep in the forest in a spacious glade they found
The polished-stone palace of Circe, and roaming around it
Mountain wolves and lions, victims bewitched
By the evil drugs of the goddess. But instead of attacking
My men, they reared up upon them and fawningly wagged
Their long tails, like hounds that fawn on their master,
     as he comes
From a feast, for the soothing bits of food he always
Brings them. Even so friendly and playful were the great-clawed
Wolves and lions, but my men were filled with fear
At the sight of such dread beasts. As they stood at the gates
Of the fair-haired goddess, they could hear her beautiful voice,
As Circe, sweetly singing, moved back and forth
Before an immortal great web, exquisite, delicate,
Dazzling, such as goddesses weave. Then able Polites,
Whom of all my comrades I liked and trusted most,
Spoke thus:
    " 'In there, my friends, someone goes back
And forth before a great web, beautifully singing,
And the whole floor echoes her song. Some goddess or woman,
But quickly, let's call to her.'
    "He spoke, they called,
And she came out at once, opened the gleaming gates,
And invited them in. And they, like fools, all followed—
All, that is, but Eurylochus, who suspected a trick.
Inside she sat them on chairs, both reclining and straight,
And fixed them a potion of Pramnian wine, in which
She mixed grated cheese, barley meal, yellow honey, and a dose
Of her miserable drugs, that they might completely forget
Their own country. When she had served them the potion
    and they
Had downed it, Circe, without more ado, smote them

161

All with her wand and penned them up in the pig-sties.
And sure enough they had the heads and bodies,
Bristles and voices of swine, but their minds were as human
As ever. So there they were, penned up and weeping,
And Circe flung them some mast, acorns, and fruit
Of the cornel tree, such stuff as wallowing pigs
Are fond of.

      "Eurylochus quickly returned to the swift
Black ship to report the miserable fate of his comrades.
But his heart was so stricken with anguish, that all he could do,
Despite his desire, was weep and lament. Then,
As we in amazement asked him about the others,
He told us this story concerning the fate of his friends:

      " 'We went, as you bade, most noble Odysseus, through
The thick forest, and there in a spacious glade we found
A fine palace of polished stone. Someone inside,
Either goddess or woman, was going back and forth
Before a great web, singing in a clear sweet voice.
The men called to her, and she came out at once,
Opened the gleaming gates, and invited them in.
And they, like fools, all followed—all but myself,
For I suspected a trick. All vanished together,
And not one reappeared, though I sat and watched a long time.'

      "At these words I slung my great bronze sword, silver-hilted,
About my shoulders and my bow across my back
And bade him take me there by the very same path.
But he clasped my knees with both arms and frantically pleaded
In these winged words:

      " 'O nurtured of Zeus, don't make me
Go there against my will, but let me stay here,
For I'm certain you won't come back, nor will you recover
Any of your comrades. But come, with the men that are left,
Let us flee as fast as we can, for we may yet

Escape this day of destruction.'

"And I answered him thus:
'Eurylochus, stay where you are, eating and drinking
Here by the hollow black ship, but I will go,
Since I very strongly feel that I must.'

"Then I left
The ship and the sea and took off through the hallowed glades
Of the forest, but when I had almost reached the great house
Of the sorceress Circe whom should I meet but Hermes,
God of the golden wand! He appeared in the form
Of a handsome young man with the first fine down on his lip,
At that age when youth is most charming. Taking my hand,
He spoke:

" 'Where now, unhappy man, do you go
Through the hills alone, ignorant as you are of this island,
While yonder in Circe's house your comrades are penned up
Like swine in the crowded sties? And have you come
To free them? Indeed—I say that you yourself
Shall not return, but remain right there with the rest.
But come, I have protection and a sure way out
For you. Here is a marvelous herb. Take it with you
To the palace of Circe, and from your head it shall
Ward off the day of destruction. Now I'll tell you all
Her pernicious wiles. She will mix you a potion—drugs
Included—but still she will be unable to charm you
By virtue of the marvelous herb I'll provide. Now listen,
I'll tell you all. When Circe gives you a blow
With her long wand, then draw your sharp sword from beside
Your thigh and rush upon her, eager, as it were,
For the kill. And she will become very frightened and invite you
To bed. Nor should you refuse her favors, if you want her
To free your friends and entertain you like a guest.
But first have her swear a great oath by the blissful gods
That she will try no more of her baneful tricks

163

On you, for when she has stripped you she may try to unman you
And take your courage away.'
    "So the slayer of Argus
Pulled an herb from the earth and gave it to me, explaining
Its special power. A plant with black root and a flower
Like milk, the gods call it Moly, and hard it is
For mortal men to dig, but the gods are almighty.
Then Hermes went off through the wooded island and from there
To lofty Olympus, while I continued on
To the house of Circe, my heart darkly seething with many
Emotions. Now I stood at the gates of the fair-haired goddess,
Stood there and hailed her. She heard me and came out at once,
Opened the gleaming gates, and invited me in.
With many misgivings, I went inside with her
And took the chair she offered, a lovely chair,
All richly wrought and studded with silver, with a rest
Below for the feet. Then, by way of refreshment,
She fixed a potion for me in a golden cup,
And in it, with evil intent in her heart, she put
A drug. She served it and I drank it down, but was not
Bewitched. Then she gave me a blow with her wand, and said:
'Now go to the sty and wallow with friends of yours there!'
    "So Circe, but I drew my sharp sword from beside my thigh
And rushed upon her, eager, as it were, for the kill.
With a scream she ducked underneath, and clasping my knees
She spoke, between wails, these winged words:
    " 'Who are you?
Where from? Your city, your parents, where are they? I'm amazed
That you have drunk this potion and remain unenchanted.
No other man—but no one!—has ever been able
To resist this charm once it passed the barrier
Of his teeth. Your mind refuses to be
Enchanted. Surely, you must be that versatile man
Odysseus, who the slayer of Argus, god of the golden

Wand, has always said would stop off here
As he returned from Troy in his swift black ship.
But come, put your sword in its sheath, and let's both get
In my bed, that we may make love together and come
To trust each other.'
    "So she, and I answered her thus:
'Now Circe, how can you bid me be gentle with you,
When here in your halls you've turned my friends into pigs
And now hold me here while you, with a mind full of malice,
Entice me into your bedroom and into your bed
So that when you have stripped me you may unman me and take
My courage away? Don't think I'll ever want
To get in the same bed with you, my goddess, unless
You can bring yourself to swear a great oath that you'll try
No more of your baneful tricks on me.'
    "I spoke,
And she, without hesitation, did as I said
And swore to do me no damage. Then, when she
Had ended the oath, Circe and I went up
To her beautiful bed.
    "Meanwhile, the four nymphs who take care
Of the palace for Circe were busily stirring about
In the halls. They are the daughters of the springs and groves
And sacred sea-flowing rivers. One spread linen covers
On the chairs and threw rich purple robes on top.
Another drew tables of silver up to the chairs
And set them with golden baskets. The third mixed sweet wine,
Honey-hearted, in a silver bowl and placed golden goblets
Around, while the fourth brought water and renewed the fire
Beneath a large cauldron, wherein the water grew warm.
When it boiled within the bright bronze, she sat me down
In a bath and bathed me with water, mixed to my liking,
From out the great cauldron, pouring it over my head
And shoulders till it took the soul-sapping fatigue from my limbs.

165

Having bathed me, she rubbed me richly with oil and helped me
Put on a fine tunic and mantle. Then bringing me into
The hall, she seated me on a lovely chair,
All richly wrought and studded with silver, with a rest
Below for the feet. Now a maid brought water in a golden
Pitcher and poured it out above a silver basin,
That I might wash my hands, and she drew up before me
A polished table. On this the respected housekeeper
Put gracious helpings of bread and other good things
To eat. And she asked me to help myself, but I had
No appetite at all. There I sat, completely
Dejected and filled with foreboding.

   "When Circe saw
How I sat without eating, so deeply depressed, she came over
To me with these winged words: 'Odysseus, why
Are you sitting here like one of the dumb, eating
Your heart, but not so much as touching either food
Or drink? Are you still afraid of some trick? You needn't
Be, for already I've sworn a great oath not to harm you.'

   "To this I replied: 'But Circe, what right-thinking man
Could endure the taste of food or drink before
He had freed his friends and seen them once again
With his own eyes? If you really want me to eat
And drink with pleasure, release them and allow me to see
My loyal companions.'

   "At these words, Circe, wand
In hand, strode out of the hall, and opening the gates
Of the sty she drove out a herd of nine-year-old pigs—
My comrades, who stood there while she went among them
    applying
One of her ointments. This caused the bristles to fall
From their limbs, as the first confounded drug of mighty
Circe had caused them to come. And now once again

They were men, but younger, more handsome and tall,
      than they had been
Before. They recognized me, and each man there
Clung to my hands, while the walls re-echoed the sound
Of our joyful sobbing—so moving that even the goddess
Was touched.
     "Then beautiful Circe drew nearer and spoke:
'Zeus-sprung son of Laertes, resourceful Odysseus,
Go back right now to your swift ship and the shore
Of the sea. There, first of all, drag your ship well up
On the beach and store away in caves your goods
And your rigging. Then come back yourself and bring your
      good friends.'
     "She spoke, and to this my proud heart agreed. I made
The trip back to my graceful ship and the shore of the sea.
There I found my good comrades, pitifully moaning
And weeping big tears. As when calves on a farm cut capers
Round droves of cows that have had their fill of grazing
And so to the yards are returning—all together
They burst from the pens to sport and gambol before them,
Constantly lowing and frisking about their mothers:
Even so those men about me, weeping as though
They had made it to their own native land and the very city
Where they had been born and raised in rugged Ithaca.
And thus through their wailing they spoke these winged words:
    " 'We're as glad to see you, O god-nurtured man, as we
Would be glad to get back to Ithaca, our own native land.
But come, tell us what end has befallen the others,
Our comrades.'
     "So they spoke, and I answered them softly:
'First let's drag the ship well up on the beach
And store away in caves our goods and our rigging.
Then all of you step lively and come with me
To see your friends in the hallowed halls of Circe,

Where they are eating and drinking of a boundless supply.'
    "Quickly they did as I said, all but Eurylochus,
Who tried to restrain my comrades, as he spoke to them all
With these winged words:
    " 'Ah, pitiful wretches, now where
Are we going? Can it be that you're really so fond of these horrors
As to enter the great hall of Circe, who will surely change us
To pigs, or wolves, or lions, and force us to guard
Her great palace? You know what the Cyclops did when
        our comrades
Visited him with this reckless Odysseus. It was through
This man's blind folly that those men lost their lives!'
    "At this I had half a mind to draw my sharp sword
From beside my stout thigh and send his head rolling down
In the dust, though he was by marriage a near kinsman of mine.
But the rest of my comrades gently restrained me, saying:
    " 'O descended of Zeus, if it be your will, let us leave
This man behind as a guard for the ship, but as
For the rest of us—lead on to the hallowed halls
Of Circe.'
    "So we left the ship and the sea, but we did not
Leave Eurylochus there by the hollow ship.
He chose to go with us, afraid of my harsh reprimand.
    "Meanwhile, back in the palace, Circe bathed
My other comrades, rubbed them richly with oil,
And clothed them in tunics and fleecy warm cloaks. We found
        them
All together, royally feasting. But when
The men met and knew one another, they wept and cried out,
While the house re-echoed their sobbing. Then the lovely goddess
Stood near me and spoke:
    " 'Please don't do anything
To prolong this bout of lamenting. I know very well
Just what you've been through on the teeming deep and all

The wrongs cruel men have done you ashore. But come now,
Eat meat and drink wine, till again your breasts are full
Of such spirit as surely was yours when first you left
Your own rugged Ithaca. For now you're all worn-out
And despondent, and always thinking of your painful roaming,
Nor do you ever feel real joy, so great
Your sufferings have been.'
        "With this our manhood agreed,
And there for one full year we remained, feasting daily
On the plentiful meat and sweet wine. But as the seasons
Turned and the waning months brought back the long days,
My dependable comrades called me out for a word:
        " 'Unpredictable man! if it be God's will that you
Should be saved and arrive once more at your high-roofed home,
It is now high time that you thought of Ithaca again.'
        "My proud heart agreed. So all that day till sundown
We sat and feasted on the plentiful meat and sweet wine,
But when the sun set and darkness arrived, my men
Lay down to sleep throughout the shadowy halls,
While I went up to Circe's beautiful bed,
Clasped her knees, and spoke these winged words
To the listening goddess:
        " 'O Circe, make good the promise
You gave to send me home. I'm eager to go,
And all of my men are too. They wear my heart out
With their constant complaining, whenever you're not around.'
        "Then without hesitation the beautiful goddess replied:
'Zeus-sprung son of Laertes, resourceful Odysseus,
In my house stay no longer against your will,
But before I can send you home, there's another journey
You must make, to the halls of Hades and dread
Persephone, to hear the truth from Theban Tiresias,
The blind seer, whose mind remains quite steadfast.
To him even in death Persephone has given

Insight and understanding—vision to him alone.
The others there are mere shadows flitting about.'
    "These words crushed my spirit completely. I sat
On the bed, weeping and wanting to die, with no wish
At all to see the sunlight again. But when
I had had enough of weeping and writhing, I said:
'But Circe, who will show us the way? No man
Has ever yet gone to Hades in a black ship.'
    "To this the beautiful goddess answered at once:
'Zeus-sprung son of Laertes, resourceful Odysseus,
When you get to your ship, don't trouble yourself for a pilot,
But set up the mast, spread the white sail, and sit down,
While the North Wind carries her on. But when you have crossed
The stream of Oceanus, you'll come to a level shore
And the groves of Persephone—great poplars and
               fruit-dropping willows.
Draw your ship up on the beach by swirling Oceanus
And proceed to the moldering house of Hades. There
The River of Flaming Fire and the River of Wailing,
A branch of the waters of Styx, meet round a rock
And go thundering on into the waters of Acheron.
This is the spot, my lord, that I bid you find.
Then dig a pit something less than two feet on a side
And pour to every ghost a libation around it,
With milk and honey first, then with sweet wine,
And finally with water, sprinkling grains of white barley on all.
Then earnestly, fervently pray to the feeble dead,
Vowing that when you reach Ithaca, in the halls of home
You will sacrifice the best of your barren heifers and heap
The altar high with many good things, and that
To Tiresias alone you will offer a solid black ram,
The most outstanding ram in the flock. After
These promises and prayers to the ghostly nation, sacrifice
A ram and black ewe, holding their heads toward Erebus,

170

But your own in the other direction toward the stream of Oceanus.
Then many ghosts of those who are gone will come thronging.
Call to your men to flay and burn the sheep
That lie there victims of the ruthless bronze, and to pray
For all they are worth, especially to powerful Hades
And dread Persephone. As for you, draw your sharp sword
From beside your thigh and sit there, and do not allow
The strengthless dead any nearer the blood until
You have talked with Tiresias. That seer, O leader of men,
Will soon appear and tell you the way of return
And how far you have to go on the fish-full sea.'

"So she spoke, and shortly thereafter came Dawn
Of the golden throne. Then Circe gave me a tunic
And cloak to put on, while she slipped into a shimmering
White gown—long, lovely, and very sheer.
Round her waist she put an exquisite golden sash
And arranged a veil high up on her head. I went
Through the palace and gently aroused my men, saying
To each of them:

" 'Enough of sweet sleep. It is time
To get up and go. For at last my lady Circe
Has given the word.'

"Their manly hearts were quite willing,
But not even from there could I lead my men without mishap.
The youngest man among us, Elpenor, a lad
Not any too brave or bright, had gone apart
From his friends in the hallowed halls of Circe, seeking
Fresh air. Heavy with wine, he went to sleep.
Then hearing the noise and bustle of his comrades stirring
About, he sprang up, but forgot the long ladder by which
He came up and proceeded to fall headlong from the roof,
Breaking his neck. His soul went down to Hades.

"On our way to the ship, I spoke these words to my men:
'You think, I know, that you're going to your own dear country,

But Circe decrees quite another journey for us—
This one to the halls of Hades and dread Persephone,
To hear the truth from Theban Tiresias.'
    "At this
Their spirits collapsed, and right there they sat down, weeping
And tearing their hair, which they might just as well not
        have done
For the good it did us.
    "Now while we were on our way
To the beach and our swift ship there, greatly grieving
And weeping away, Circe had tethered beside
The black ship a ram and black ewe. With no trouble at all
She had gone by us, for who can lay eyes on a god,
If it be against a god's will, whether coming or going?

BOOK

XI

THE KINGDOM
OF THE DEAD

"Once on the beach together, we dragged the ship down
To the shimmering sea, and in her black hull we mounted
The mast, raised the sail, and took the sheep
On board. Ready at last, we pushed off from shore
Deeply lamenting and shedding great copious tears.
In the wake of our blue-prowed ship a sail-filling wind
Sprang up, a splendid companion, sent us by Circe,
Dread goddess with the voice of a woman. When we had readied
The rigging and made everything fast, we sat down,
                   while the wind
And the man at the helm kept us true to our course straight ahead.
All day long our sail was taut as we
Went skimming over the sea. Then the sun went down
And the sea-lanes grew dark.
          "So we came to the circling stream
Of distant deep Oceanus, where the gloomy Cimmerians
Live enveloped in fog. On them the bright Sun
Throws never so much as a beam as he rises and sets,
And dreadful night is endless for the wretches there.

We ran our ship ashore and led out the sheep.
Then we walked by the waves of Oceanus till we came
        to the place
Of which Circe had spoken.
    "Now Perimedes and Eurylochus
Held the sheep while I dug a pit something less
Than two feet on a side and poured to every ghost
A libation around it, with milk and honey first,
Then with sweet wine, and finally with water, sprinkling grains
Of white barley on all. And I earnestly, fervently prayed
To the feeble dead, vowing that when I reached Ithaca
I would sacrifice in my halls the best of my barren heifers
And heap the altar high with many good things,
And that to Tiresias alone I would offer a solid
Black ram, the most outstanding ram in the flock.
After these promises and prayers to the ghostly nation,
I took the sheep and slaughtered them over the pit,
Into which the dark blood ran. Then the souls of the dead
Came thronging up from Erebus, young brides and bachelors
And worn-out old men, innocent girls to whom sorrow
Was yet a stranger, and many who had died by the spearhead's
Deadly bronze, soldiers in bloody armor.
All these and more came crowding about the pit
Of blood with the weirdest of wails and shrieks, and I turned
A ghastly pale olive with fear. Then above the din
I shouted to my men to flay and burn the sheep
That lay there victims of the ruthless bronze, and to pray
As hard as they could, especially to powerful Hades
And dread Persephone. As for me, I drew my sharp sword
From beside my thigh and sat there, and would not allow
The strengthless dead any nearer the blood until I
Had talked with Tiresias.
    "The first to approach was the soul
Of my comrade Elpenor, who had not yet been buried

In the much-traveled earth. We had left his body behind
In the palace of Circe, unwept and unburied, so urgent
Our journey had been. Seeing him now, I wept,
My heart pierced with pity, and spoke to him with what
Compassion I could:
    " 'Elpenor, how did you come
Into the gloom of this dark kingdom? Though you
Were on foot and I in my black ship, you
Got here before me.'
    "Here I stopped, while he groaned
And answered me thus: 'Zeus-sprung son of Laertes,
Resourceful Odysseus, some god's fatal curse
And that god only knows how many drinks
Were my undoing. When I woke up in the house
Of Circe, I did not remember that long ladder
By which I came up and proceeded to fall headlong
From the roof, fatally breaking my neck. Right then
It was that my soul unhappily got that head start
For Hades. Now I have something to ask in the name
Of those at home, your wife and the father that raised you
And your only son Telemachus, for I'm sure that after
You leave this kingdom you'll stop for a while at that
Aeaean island with your excellent ship. There,
O King, I beg you, remember me. Do not
Leave me behind unwept and unburied, for then
You'll surely have me to haunt you. But take me with all
My armor on and burn me with all I own.
Then, on the shore of the gray sea, make a mound
For me, in memory of a most unfortunate man,
That those as yet unborn may learn of Elpenor.
Do this for me, and upon the mound for monument
Set up the oar with which in life I labored
Among my companions.'
    "To these words I replied: 'All

175

'That you ask, O man of misfortune, I will do in every
Detail.'

"So in sad conversation we sat, I
On one side of the pit, guarding the blood with my blade,
My friend on the other, freely telling his story.

"Next to emerge was the soul of my dead mother,
Anticleia, the daughter of bold Autolycus, mere shade
Of the woman whom I had left alive long ago
When I sailed for sacred Troy. One look at her
Brought tears, and fierce compassion filled my soul,
But still, though my grief was great, I could not let her
Approach the blood until I had talked with Tiresias.

"He was the next to come forth, the Theban seer
With staff of gold. When he had recognized me,
He began to speak: 'Zeus-sprung son of Laertes,
Resourceful Odysseus, what curse compels you, unlucky
Man, to leave the sunlight behind and enter
This mirthless kingdom of death? But since you are here,
Stand back, and lower your sword, that I may drink
Of the blood and tell you the truth you seek.'

"I gave way
And sheathed my silver-mounted sword, and then, having drunk
Of the dark blood deeply, that peerless prophet spoke
These words to me: 'Renowned Odysseus, you want
To know the details of your return which looms
So honey-sweet ahead, but which a god is determined
To make very hard for you, and so he will,
The god that shakes the earth, since in his heart
He nurses red wrath against you for blinding the eye
Of his own dear son. But even so you may still
Reach Ithaca, having suffered much, if only you have
Sufficient control of yourself and comrades when you
In your excellent ship escape from the violet sea
At the island Thrinacia, where you will find grazing the cattle

And woolly fat sheep of Helios, the god to whom
All sights and sounds are known. If these you leave
As safe as you found them and concentrate on your return,
Then truly, though suffering much, you may return.
But if one hair you harm, I foretell utter
Destruction for your ship and crew, and should you yourself
Escape, your return will be lonely, late, and unhappy,
For you will come home without friends in a ship not your own
To a house full of trouble—full of arrogant men, swollen
With pride and consuming your substance and wooing with gifts
Your wife, a woman worthy of heaven. You
Will have to punish their presumption and violence, by trickery
Or your bold keen blade. Then you must go a journey,
Taking a graceful oar along, and continuing
Inland until you meet men who know nothing at all
Of the sea, men who eat their food without salt
And are completely ignorant of red-cheeked ships
And wing-like, shapely oars. And now I will tell you
A sign you cannot miss. When you meet a man
Who asks why you carry a winnowing-fan on your shoulder,
Then plant that shapely oar in the earth and there
Most fitly sacrifice to mighty Poseidon a ram,
A bull, and a sow-mounting boar. Then return to your home
And sacrifice holy hecatombs to each of the immortal
Gods that rule the wide sky. And to you will come
An easy death from the sea, a peaceful death
In your comfortable calm old age with your people happy
And thriving around you. All this will come to pass.'
    "Thus he foretold, and I answered him thus: 'Tiresias,
Surely the very gods have spun the thread
Of destiny. But tell me this. Over there I see
The soul of my dead mother. Silently she sits
Near the blood and will not look at her own son,
Nor will she speak to him. Tell me, O prince

Of prophets, how she may know that I am he.'
    "Then quickly the seer: 'The answer is easy. Whoever
Of these the long-lost dead that you allow
To drink of the blood will speak the truth to you,
But those whom you refuse will have to go back
Again.'
    "With this the lordly spirit of Tiresias
Re-entered the house of Hades, his prophecy complete,
But I stayed still by the pit and watched as my mother
Approached and drank of the cloud-black blood. She took
One look at me and then in tears she spoke
These words so winged with woe:
    " 'My child, how did you
Find your way while still alive to this
Dark kingdom of gloom? It is not easy for the living
To see these things, for between your world and ours
Lie mighty rivers and terrible torrents: Oceanus
First, which no man can wade. Truly yours must be
An excellent ship. Have you and your friends been wandering
All this time? Do you come here from Troy
Without having reached your home in Ithaca, and haven't you
Seen your wife in all these years?'
    "And I answered:
'Mother, this journey I had to make, down
To the house of Hades to hear the truth from Theban
Tiresias. For as yet I haven't come near the land
Of Achaea, nor have I set foot on my own island.
But ever since that day when I with glorious
Agamemnon left for Troy to fight the Trojans
I have been woefully wandering. But tell me truly,
What fate of dateless death brought you so low?
Was it some lingering illness, or were you slain
By the painless arrows of Artemis the archer? And tell me
Of those I left behind, my father and my son.

Do they or some other man receive the honor
That used to be mine, and do they say that I
Shall never return? Tell me too of how
My wife has managed and what she intends to do.
Has she stayed with her son and kept unceasing watch,
Or has already the best of the Achaeans made her
His wife?'

    "To this my mother's ghost replied:
'I assure you that her patient heart remains
Within your palace, where pitifully she weeps, as the days
And nights waste slowly away. But the high esteem
That you enjoyed has been given to no one else,
Though Telemachus is undisputed lord of the lands
You own and is invited to feasts by all men
As an equal of any, which is as it should be for one
Who gives the law. Your father, however, lives
Out in the country and never comes to the city.
He has no bed with sheets and soft bright blankets,
But all winter long he sleeps, as would a slave,
In ashes by the fire and clothes himself in rags.
When summer comes and the teeming autumn, his beds
Of fallen leaves are scattered everywhere throughout
His fruitful vineyard. There on the slope he lies
In sorrow, and the grief in his heart is great and growing
As he yearns for your return. His is a heavy
Old age. Even so, death came at last for me.
For the painless arrows of the keen-eyed archer goddess
Were not my fate, nor was my strength, as is
The common lot, destroyed by disease. But longing
For you, for your quick mind and gentle heart—
That surely took my honey-sweet life away.'

    "When she had finished, my hesitant heart made me long
To embrace her, and thrice I went toward the ghost of my
Dead mother with outstretched arms, and thrice she flitted

Through them like a shadow or a dream. The pain in my heart
Grew increasingly keener, and, when I spoke, my words
Came winged with anguish:
    " 'My mother, why don't you wait
For me, since I am so eager to hold you close,
That even here in the house of Hades we two
Might embrace and give full vent to our cold lamenting?
Are you a mere image that mighty Persephone has sent
To mock me and make me lament and groan all the more?'

    "Soon then she answered: 'Alas, my child, unluckiest
Of men, Persephone, daughter of Zeus, does not
Deceive you, but this is the way it is when one
Is dead. For the nerves no longer knit the flesh
And bones together, since the heat of blazing fire
Consumes the body as soon as the white bones are lifeless,
And the soul takes flight like a dream. Now quick as you can
Go back to the light, and remember all these things,
That someday you may tell them to your wife.'

    "As we sat talking there, queenly Persephone
Sent forth a crowd of women, all wives and daughters
Of high-ranking men. These came thronging about
The dark blood, and soon I thought of a way to speak
With them one at a time. I drew my long sword
From beside my strong thigh and would not allow them to drink
Of the blood until one by one they came up. Then each
Said who she was, and so I talked with them all.

    "The first I saw was high-born Tyro, who said
That her father was good Salmoneus and that she was the wife
Of Cretheus, the son of Aeolus. She fell in love
With a river, divine Enipeus, by far the loveliest
River on earth, and it was her delight to wander
Where that fair water flowed. But the god that covers
And shakes the earth took the river's form and lay
With her where the eddying river flows into the sea.

180

And the purple waves stood up like mountains about them
And arched above them, thus insuring their privacy.
He undid the maiden's belt and lulled her to sleep.
But when the god had finished his work of love,
He took her hand and spoke:
      " 'Woman, rejoice
In our love, and as the year grows old you shall bear
Wonderful children and know what it is to sleep
With a god. These you will care for and raise, but now
Go to your house and tell our secret to no one.
You have known Poseidon, creator of earthquakes!'

      "With that he plunged beneath the billows of the sea,
And Tyro conceived and gave birth to twins, Pelias
And Neleus, both of whom did yeoman duty
For almighty Zeus. Pelias came to live
In broad Iolcus, where good pasture is plentiful,
And he became rich in flocks. Neleus went
To live in Sandy Pylos. Her other children,
Aeson, Pheres, and Amythaon, lover of chariots,
This queen of women bore to Cretheus.

      "Then I saw
Antiope, Asopus' daughter, proud that she
Had slept in the arms of Zeus. She bore him two boys,
Amphion and Zethus, who founded seven-gated Thebes
And walled it in, for without protection they could not
Live in that large city, no matter how strong
They were.

      "Alcmene was next, Amphitryon's wife,
Who also had mingled in love with mighty Zeus.
Their son was Heracles, whose enduring heart was stout
As the heart of a lion. There too I saw the daughter
Of haughty Creon, Megara, who married the strong
And tireless son of Amphitryon.

      "And there I saw

Lovely Epicasta, the mother of Oedipus, who
In the dark of ignorance unknowingly became the wife
Of him she bore, who had already slain his own father.
These monstrous things the gods made known to men.
Then Oedipus lived on in beautiful Thebes as King
Of the Cadmeans and suffered much from the fatal will
Of the gods, but she journeyed down to the house of Hades,
The strongest gate-guarder of all. Wild with grief,
She fastened a noose to a lofty beam and left him
With all the woes that the Furies can bring to avenge
A mother.
      "And there I saw the comely Chloris,
Whom Neleus courted with countless gifts and married
Because of her beauty, Chloris the youngest daughter
Of Iasus' son Amphion, who once was King
Of the Minyae and ruled with might in Orchomenus. She
Was the Queen of Pylos, and splendid were the offspring she bore
To her husband: Nestor, Chromius, and brave Periclymenus.
Glamorous Pero was her daughter, whom all men
Thereabouts adored and wished to marry. But Neleus
Would give her to none but the man who from Phylace
Should drive the unruly herd of mighty Iphicles,
Those long-horned cattle so sleek and broad of brow
And so hard to herd. Only one man, a gallant
Seer, undertook the task, and he was himself
Overtaken by fickle fate in the form of crude cowboys
And ropes that cut. He remained their prisoner as season
Followed season and the year grew old. By that time
He had prophesied enough for mighty Iphicles
And he released him, fulfilling the will of Zeus.
      "Leda was next, the wife of Tyndareus, who bore
To him two stalwart sons, horse-mastering Castor
And Pollux, good in a fist-fight. These two are buried
Alive in the life-giving earth, but even in the nether

World Zeus honors them. They live and die
On alternate days, one dead while the other lives,
And equal to that of the gods is the honor they share.
  "Then I saw Iphimedeia, the wife of Aloeus,
Who claimed she had lain with Poseidon. Her sons were two:
Otus and famed Ephialtes, who both died young,
Though next to renowned Orion they were the tallest,
Best-looking men that the grain-giving earth ever nourished.
At the age of nine they were nineteen feet through the shoulders
And towered some fifty-nine feet in the air. They
Were the boys who threatened to raise a rebellion and wage
Chaotic war against the Olympian gods.
Their plan was to pile Mount Ossa on top of Olympus,
And Pelion on top of Mount Ossa, that they might ascend
To heaven itself. And this they would have done
Had they been fully grown, but the son of Zeus
And lovely-haired Leto destroyed them both before the down
On their chins had blossomed into beard.
  "Phaedra and Procris
Were there and the daughter of crafty Minos, the bewitching
Ariadne, whom Theseus wished to carry from Crete
To sacred Athenian soil. But he never enjoyed her,
For before there was time Dionysus told Artemis all,
And Artemis slew her in Dia surrounded by the sea.
  "And I saw Maera and Clymene and despicable Eriphyle,
Who sold for seductive gold the life of her lord.
But if I try to name and tell of all
The heroes' wives and daughters that I saw,
We'll be here till immortal night grows thin,
And already it is time to retire. Now whether I return
To my swift ship and crew or spend the night here
Is up to the gods and you."
      Thus he ended,
And throughout the halls, where the flickering torches burned,

183

The listeners sat silent and still as though in a trance.
Arete, with the lovely white arms, was the first to speak:
"What do you think, Phaeacians, of a man so remarkable
For splendid physique, good looks, and a balanced mind?
Like all of you, he is my honored guest.
Be not, therefore, in a hurry to send him away,
Nor should you stint in your gifts to one whose need
Is so great, for the treasures are many that lie in your halls
By grace of the gods."
     Then the venerable Echeneus spoke,
He who was grown before most of those present were born:
"Truly, my friends, the words of our Queen are wise
And do but echo the thoughts in all of our hearts.
Do as she says, providing that Alcinous here
Approves, for word and deed depend on him."
     And Alcinous replied: "Her word shall prevail as surely
As I am alive and King of the seagoing Phaeacians.
I'm sure our guest, despite his great longing for home,
Will stay until tomorrow, that I may show him
How generous a king can be. Meanwhile, his departure
Shall be the concern of all, but especially mine,
For I am the one with whom the decisions rest."
     Resourceful Odysseus replied: "Lord Alcinous,
Most famous of men, if you really wished me to stay
For even so much as a year, to prepare me for
My return with your glorious gifts, then surely I would stay,
For think how much better it would be for me to reach
My beloved Ithaca with so many splendid presents.
No doubt I would win more respect and affection from all
I should meet in that dear land on my return."
     Then Alcinous spoke again: "Odysseus, we know
That you are no cheating dissembler like so many men
The black earth breeds and scatters all over the world,
Men who can make up lies out of nothing at all.

But you have verbal grace and a heart full of wisdom,
And you've told your story with art, like the poet you are,
Told us of the Argives' woeful afflictions and of
Your own troubles. But don't stop now. Tell me truly if there
In Hades you saw anything of the godlike companions
Who went with you to Ilium, where they were destined
To die. The night is long and lies before us,
Indescribably long, nor is it yet time to retire.
Continue then, if you will, your account of these thrilling
Adventures. Truly, I could sit right here
In the hall until bright morning, if you were willing
To go on telling this marvelous tale of your woes."
      Then that obliging man made this reply:
"Lord Alcinous, of greatest renown, there is
A time for talk and a time for sleep, but if
You really wish to hear more, I'll continue my story,
Though now of things that are even more wretchedly pitiful,
Of my unhappy friends who finally escaped
The terrible Trojans and their bloodcurdling cries of battle
Only to die at home as the fatal result
Of an evil woman's will.
      "When sacred Persephone
Had completely scattered those phantoms so feminine still,
There emerged the grieving ghost of Agamemnon, son
Of Atreus, and with him the spirits of those who were fated
To die with him in the house of Aegisthus. He
No sooner drank the black blood than he knew me and sobbed,
The tears streaming down his face. He reached out, frantic
To touch me, and I saw that the steadiness and strength were gone
From those limbs that had once been so supple. At this I wept
And my words came winged with compassion:
      " 'Most honored son
Of Atreus, Agamemnon, king of men, by what fate
Of dateless death were you undone? Did Poseidon

Stir up a storm in the deep and sink your ships,
Or were you slain by enemies while rustling their cattle
And fair flocks of sheep or fighting to win their city
And women?'
    "He answered without hesitation: 'God-sprung
Son of Laertes, resourceful Odysseus, Poseidon
Stirred up no storm in the deep to sink my ships,
Nor was I slain by battle-foes ashore. Aegisthus
Laid the plans for my dark death and doom,
And with the help of my own accursed wife he slew me!
Having asked me to a feast at his house, he slew me, as one
Would slaughter an ox at the manger. Thus I died
A most miserable death, and around me my comrades were slain
Like so many hogs when their white tusks run with blood
And they're slaughtered in the house of a rich and powerful man
For a wedding feast or sumptuous banquet or perhaps
A joint barbecue. You have seen many men die,
In single combat and in the midst of battle,
But your heart would have felt more compassion than ever before
Had you seen how we lay in death on that bloody floor,
All strewn about the wine-bowl mid the laden tables.
But the most pitiful voice I heard was that
Of Priam's daughter Cassandra, whom treacherous Clytemnestra
Murdered almost within my reach. I
Was already dying, transfixed with a sword, but my last
Act was to raise my hands against her. She,
The shameless bitch, merely turned her back and left me
To Hades, nor had the decency to close my eyes
And mouth! Surely there is no beast more horrible
And shameless than a woman who harbors such deeds in
        her heart,
As she most monstrously plotted the death of her husband.
Truly I thought to receive warm welcome from my children
And slaves, but found in her such villainous degradation

186

That women yet unborn shall not escape
Its taint, even truly feminine women whose lives
Are good.'
    "And I to him: 'Shameful indeed,
But surely farsighted Zeus has from the beginning
Shown through willful women a terrible hatred
For the house of Atreus. For Helen we died by the score,
While at home Clytemnestra was deceitfully plotting against you.'
    "He answered at once: 'Then let me be a warning
To you. Never be too softhearted, even
To your wife. By no means should you tell her all
You know, but just enough, keeping the rest
To yourself. But no woman, Odysseus, will ever be
The death of you, for unusually prudent and wise
Is the heart of thoughtful Penelope, daughter of Icarius.
When we left for the war, she was scarcely more than a bride
With a baby boy at her breast, who now, I dare say,
Sits among men as an equal, looking forward to the day
Of his father's return and thinking how he will greet him.
So it should be with father and son, but I,
Because of my wife, had no such joy in the eyes
Of my son, for she, as you know, killed even me,
Her own husband, before there was time for much rejoicing.
And something else there is for you to remember.
Come in your ship quietly and secretly home
To your dear island, for no longer can women be trusted.
But enough. Tell me what you know, if anything,
About my son. It may be you have heard
Of him alive in Orchomenus or sandy Pylos
Or perhaps with Menelaus in the spacious town of Sparta.
For I know that my Orestes is still alive
On earth.'
    "I answered him thus: 'Why, O son
Of Atreus, do you ask me this? I have no knowledge

Of him at all, either living or dead, and surely
Windy words do no one any good.'
     "Thus we stood in sad conversation, weeping
Together. Then up came the ghost of Peleus' son
Achilles, and with him Patroclus, matchless Antilochus,
And Ajax, who next to the peerless son of Peleus
Had, of all the Danaans, the most manly bearing.
The ghost of Achilles knew me and wept, and his words
Came winged with woe:
     " 'Zeus-sprung son of Laertes,
Resourceful Odysseus, you are daring indeed!
What greater thing than this will your heart devise?
How could you be so bold as to come down here
To Hades mid the senseless dead, mere shadows of men
Outworn?'
     "So spoke the wraith of Achilles, and I answered
Him thus: 'Achilles, son of Peleus, I came
To talk with Tiresias in hope of some word from him
As to how and when I might reach my rocky home.
For not yet have I approached the Achaean shore
Or set one foot on my own soil. Bad luck
Is my constant companion, but you, Achilles, no man
Was ever so blessed as you were when alive,
Nor shall any man ever be in time to come.
We Argives heaped honor upon you equal to that
Of the gods, and now that you're here your rule is mighty
Among the missing. Then do not sorrow so
That you are dead, Achilles.'
     "And he to me:
'Keen Odysseus, do not try to make me
Welcome death. I would rather live on earth
As a hireling of one who was but poor himself
Than to be king of all the ghosts there are!
But come, tell me what you know of my son,

That splendid youth who may have become a leader
In the war. And what have you heard of noble Peleus?
Is he still honored among the Myrmidon host,
Or has old age deprived him of his glory
Throughout all Hellas and Phthia? For I no longer
Live up there in the sunlight where I might be
Some help to him with strength such as was mine
At the broad city of Troy where I, in defense
Of the Argives, slew the best men the Trojans had.
If I might come again to my father's house
For even a little while with strength such as I
Had then, you may be sure that those who do him
Wrong and dishonor him would have good reason
To remember that strength and my invincible hands!'
        "I answered: 'Of Peleus I know nothing at all,
But I can tell you much of your dear son
Neoptolemus. I myself brought him from Scyros
In my well-balanced ship to join the ranks
Of the well-greaved Achaeans. And whenever around the city
Of Troy we met for counsel, he was always
The first to speak, nor was he ever at a loss
For winning words. Godly Nestor and I
Were the only men who spoke any better than he.
And when we battled with bronze on the Trojan plain,
He was never one to lag behind
In the crowd, but always charged ahead, yielding
To none. Many were the men he slew, so many
That now I couldn't begin to describe or even
Name them all, but I cannot leave unmentioned
One mighty Prince who fell beneath his sword,
Eurypylus, the son of Telephus, and many of his comrades
Among the Ceteians fell with him there, who but
For his mother's love of trinkets would not have been
In the war at all. With the exception of magnificent Memnon,

189

Eurypylus was truly the handsomest man that I
Have ever seen. Then again, when the pick of the Argives
And I went down into the horse Epeus
Made and all the charge was mine for closing
The door and for saying when it should be opened again,
Then the other Danaan leaders wiped tears from their eyes
And could not keep from shaking, but never once
Did I see his handsome face grow pale, nor did
He weep, but earnestly he begged me to let him out
Of the horse, so impatient was he to shed the blood
Of Trojans, so eager that he could not keep his hands
Away from his sword and spear made heavy with bronze.
Then after we had sacked Priam's high city,
He boarded his ship with his due share of the spoil
And a splendid prize to boot, but what was most
Remarkable is that he had not got a scratch
From spear or sword, which happens to very few men
In the course of a war, for Ares without a doubt
Is the god of chaos.'

    "So I spoke, and the ghost
Of swift Achilles, grandson of Aeacus, stalked joyfully
Away through the field of asphodel, made glad by what
I had said about his son.

    "Other souls of those
Who from this world are gone forever stood about me
Grieving, and each inquired of those most dear
To him. Only the ghost of Telamonian Ajax
Kept at a distance, still seething with wrathful resentment
For the victory I won over him when there by the ships
We strove for the arms of Achilles, whose queenly mother
Had set them for a prize. The judges were Pallas Athena
And sons of the Trojans. But now I wish that I
Had never won in such a contest, since the earth,
Because of those arms, soon closed above the head

Of him who lost, the powerful Ajax, who
In form and fighting surpassed us all except
The peerless son of Peleus. I spoke to him
As gently as I could:
      " 'Ajax, son
Of matchless Telamon, can it be that you still harbor
Wrath against me because of those baneful arms?
The gods have made them a curse to the Argives. For in **you**
We lost a citadel of valor, and for you the Achaeans
Grieve unceasingly, no less than they grieve for the loss
Of Peleus' son Achilles. Zeus alone
Is to blame for your death, he who bore such terrible hatred
Against the Danaan spearmen. Only he
Could have brought this doom on you. But now come here,
My lord, and let me tell you my story. Get a grip
On your proud spirit and try to control your anger.'

    "Without a word of reply he left for Erebus
Along with other souls of the long-lost dead.
I pressed that bitter ghost no further, for I
Was eager to see the souls of others who are
No longer among us.

    "I saw King Minos there,
The illustrious son of Zeus, on a throne with his scepter
Of gold, giving judgment to the dead, while throughout the house
Of Hades with its great gates the spirits were gathered
Around him, some sitting, some standing, and all asking him
To judge them.

    "Next I saw huge Orion pursuing
In the asphodel meadow all the wild beasts that he
Had killed on earth in the lonely hills, and he bore
In his hands a club of solid unbreakable bronze.

    "Tityos too was there, son of glorious Gaea,
Stretched out on the ground for what seemed a thousand feet
With a vulture on either side tearing at his liver

191

And plunging their beaks into his bowels, and his hands
Were quite unable to beat those horrors off.
Thus he suffered, for he had assaulted Leto,
The marvelous mistress of Zeus himself, as she traveled
To Pytho through the lovely dancing-lawns of Panopeus.

    "Yes, and I saw Tantalus in terrible torment,
Standing in a pool with the water almost to his chin.
He seemed to have a thirst he could not quench,
For whenever that eager old man bent over to drink
Some god would cause the ground to swallow the water
Until black earth appeared at the old one's feet.
And just above his head hung lovely fruit
From lofty, leafy trees, pears and pomegranates,
Gorgeous apples, sweet figs, and luscious olives.
But no sooner would the starving man reach up to clutch them
Than the wind would toss them away toward the lowering sky.

    "And there was Sisyphus in agony, laboring with all
His might to raise a monstrous boulder. Bracing
His hands and feet, he would roll the stone toward the top
Of a hill, but as he was about to heave it over
The crest, the weight would win and the ruthless stone
Would go rolling and bouncing on down to the plain again.
So time after time he would strain and fall, with the sweat
Streaming down his limbs and a cloud of dust rising high
Above his head.

    "Of mighty Heracles too
I saw the dim shade, but he himself is feasting
With the immortal gods, and his wife is trim-ankled Hebe,
The daughter of Zeus and Hera of the golden sandals.
Around him arose a din from the dead like the clamor
Of frantic birds that beat themselves wildly about
In terrified abandon. Like black night he crouched,
Glaring fiercely around with his bow bare and on

The string an arrow which he seemed always on the verge
Of shooting. Across his chest was a fearful belt
Of gold on which, wonderfully wrought, were bears,
Wild boars, and lions with fiery eyes, battles
And ambuscades, murders and dying men, and various
Other degrees of homicide. I hope that the man
Who made it made only one and that he will never
Make another one like it. He soon knew who I was
And weeping he spoke these winged words:
    " 'Zeus-sprung
Son of Laertes, resourceful Odysseus, but now,
It seems, a most unhappy man. Is your lot
As wretched as mine was when I lived up there in the sunlight?
Zeus is the son of Cronos and I am the son
Of Zeus, but I suffered immeasurable hardship and misery.
For I was the slave of a man in every way worse
Than I, and he laid hard labors upon me. Once
He sent me here to fetch the hound of Hades,
Since he couldn't think of any task more difficult
Or dangerous. But I, with the help of bright-eyed Athena
And Hermes, led that dog from Hades' halls
And carried him off.'
    "With this he re-entered the gloom,
But I stood fast, hoping to see still another
Of those tall men who died so long ago.
And such I would have seen, men like Theseus
And Peirithous, the gods' own glorious children, but before
There was time the dead came thronging up in hordes
With the weirdest of wails and shrieks, and pale fear gripped me
Hard, lest Queen Persephone send up from Hades
The Gorgon's monstrous head.
    "Quickly I returned
To the ship and ordered my companions to go aboard

193

And cast off. This they did, and took their seats
At the oars as the current carried the ship well out
In the stream of Oceanus. Here we began to row
And continued so till the welcome wind arose.

BOOK

XII

THE SIRENS, SCYLLA
AND CHARYBDIS,
THE CATTLE OF
THE SUN

"Leaving the stream of Oceanus, we sailed through waves
Of the wide, much-traveled sea till we reached Aeaea,
The island home of early Dawn. Here
Are the greens whereon she dances and here the Sun rises.
We ran our ship well up on the beach and stepped out
On the sand. Then we lay down and slept, awaiting
Bright Dawn.

"No sooner had that rosy-fingered young goddess
Arrived than off to Circe's house I sent
My comrades, to bring back the body of dead Elpenor.
Quickly we cut some wood, and on a high headland
Jutting out in the sea performed the last rites, shedding
Great tears in our grief. When the corpse and armor
       were consumed

By the blaze, we built a barrow and hauled up rocks
For a pillar. Then on top of the mound we planted
His shapely oar.

  "While we were busy performing
The funeral rites, Circe, not at all unaware
That we had returned from Hades' house, adorned
Herself and came down with her maids, who brought bread,
   much meat,
And sparkling red wine. Then the lovely goddess stood among us
And spoke:

  " 'Brave but wretched men! you
Have gone down alive to the house of Hades, and so,
Alone among mortals, the rest of whom only die once,
You are destined to make that journey twice.
But come now, for the rest of this day I want you to stay
Right here and help yourselves to this food and wine,
But at Dawn's first light you shall sail, and I'll plot the course
For you and give instructions, that you may not
Suffer woes from evils unforeseen.'

  "To this
Our proud hearts agreed. So all that day till sundown
We sat and feasted on the plentiful meat and sweet wine,
And when the sun set and darkness arrived, my men
Lay down to sleep by the hawsers at the stern of the ship.
But Circe, taking my hand, led me apart
From my friends, sat me down, and lay down beside me.
Then, in answer to questions from her, I recounted
All we had done, to which my lady Circe
Replied:

  " 'So all these things are finished, but now
Pay attention to what I shall tell you, and God himself
Will help you remember. First you'll come to the Sirens,
Enchanters of men. Whoever in ignorance comes near them
And hears their song, never again returns

196

To rejoice at home with a welcoming wife and small children.
With the clear liquid tones of their song, the Sirens bewitch him,
As they sit in a meadow mid the moldering bones of men,
Great heaps of them, round which the skin is still shriveling.
Here knead some sweet wax, stop up the ears of your comrades,
And row by, that none of your friends may hear that singing.
But if you yourself want to listen, have them tie you,
Hand and foot, upright on the thwart supporting
The mast and lash you securely to the mast itself,
That you may enjoy the dulcet song of the Sirens.
And if you implore and command your friends to release you,
They must tie you still tighter with even more ropes.
      " 'Now when your men have rowed by them, you'll reach
         a place
Where you'll have to think for yourself and make a decision.
All I can do is describe the two possible ways.
On one side you'll see tall beetling rocks, against which
Roar the big breakers of dark-eyed Amphitrite. The blessed
Gods call these the Wandering Rocks, and not even
Wings are sufficient to pass them safely by.
No, for even the fearful doves, birds
That bear ambrosia to Father Zeus, fall prey
To this sheer rock, though the Father himself, whenever
One falls, sends another out to replace it. From there
No merely mortal ship has ever escaped,
But the timbers of ships and bodies of men are soon
Confounded together by waves of the sea and blasts
Of deadly fire. One vessel alone has gone by,
The *Argo,* of interest to all, from Aeëtes returning,
And even she would quickly have broken up
Against the huge rocks if Hera had not helped her by
Because of her love for Jason.
      " 'On the other side
Are two cliffs, and the sharp peak of one is so high that it hits

The wide sky, where a dark unmelting cloud surrounds it,
And that peak is always enshrouded even in summer
And harvest time. No mortal could scale or climb down it,
Though he had ten times the usual number of hands
And feet, for every inch of the rock is as smooth
As polished stone. About half way up is a cave,
A gloomy cavern facing the West and Erebus,
And beneath this cave, my gallant Odysseus, you
Must steer your ship. It will be so high above you
That not even the strongest man could reach it with an arrow
Shot from the deck of his hollow ship below.
In it lives Scylla, yelping terribly, with a voice
That sounds no stronger than that of a puppy just born.
But she herself is an evil monster that no one
Would be glad to see, not though a god should meet her.
She has twelve feet in all, horribly dangling,
And six necks, tremendously long, on each of which
Is a terrible head with teeth in triple tiers,
Close set and chocked with black death. From her waist down
The deep cave hides her, but her heads sway out from the awful
Abyss, and with them, around the rock, she avidly
Fishes for dolphin and dog-fish and what greater beast
She may catch of the countless creatures that Amphitrite,
Deeply moaning, feeds. Never yet have sailors
Been able to boast that they got by her unscathed
In their ship, for with each of her heads she snaps up a man
From the dark-prowed ship.
　　　　" 'Now the other cliff, as you
Will see, Odysseus, is lower, and the distance between
The two is not great—you could shoot an arrow from one
To the other. On this lower cliff is a huge fig tree,
Covered with rich green leaves, beneath which the demon
Charybdis sucks down the black water. Three times a day
She belches it back and three times sucks it down,

Most horribly! May you not be there when she does so, for no one
Could bring you safely to the surface again, not even
The Earthshaker himself. But head in close to the cliff
Of Scylla, and row your ship by with all speed, for it's better
To mourn for six of your men than to lose the whole crew.'
        "So she spoke, and I answered her thus: 'Goddess,
I beg of you, tell me truly if I in some way
Might escape from deadly Charybdis and also ward
Dread Scylla off when she tries to seize my companions.'
        "And lovely Circe replied: 'O foolishly valiant,
Now again you would put your trust in force, fighting,
And toil. Can it be that you will not yield, even
To the immortal gods? There's nothing mortal about Scylla.
Her evil is deathless, terrible, dire, and ferocious—
Truly invincible! Against her there is no defense.
To flee her is bravest and best. For if you stay
To arm yourself by the cliff, I fear she will rush out
At you with as many heads as before and seize
As many men. Row by her, then, with all
Your strength, and call to Crataeis, Scylla's mother,
Who bore her a bane to mortals. She will prevent
A second attack.'
        " 'Next you will reach the island
Thrinacia. There you'll find grazing the cattle and woolly
Fat sheep of Helios, seven herds of cattle and seven
Fair flocks of sheep, with fifty head in each.
These bear no young, nor were they born themselves,
Nor will they ever die. Their shepherds are goddesses,
Those radiant nymphs with the beautiful braids, Phaëthusa
And Lampetia, whom lovely Neaera bore to Helios
Hyperion. Having brought them up, their queenly mother
Sent them to live far away on the island Thrinacia,
To watch over their father's flocks and sleek cattle. If these
You leave as safe as you found them and concentrate on returning,

Then truly, though suffering much, you may return.
But if one hair you harm, I foretell utter
Destruction for your ship and crew, and should you yourself
Escape, your return will be lonely, late, and unhappy.'
 "So she spoke, and shortly thereafter came Dawn
Of the golden throne. Then lovely Circe left me
And made her way inland, while I went to the ship, aroused
My comrades, and sent them on board to loose the hawsers.
Quickly they did so, and taking their seats on the benches
They churned the gray sea with their oars. Then, in the wake
Of our blue-prowed ship, a sail-filling wind sprang up,
A splendid companion, sent us by Circe, dread goddess
With the voice of a woman. So when we had readied the rigging
And made everything fast, we sat down, while the wind and he
At the helm kept us true to our course straight ahead.
 "Then I,
Heavy-hearted, spoke thus to my comrades: 'Friends, it's not right
That only one or two of us should know
The divine predictions that the beautiful goddess Circe
Made known to me. I'm going to tell all of you,
That thus informed we may die, or escape this fate
And live on. First she bade me avoid the song
Of the Sirens, who sing so divinely in their flowery meadow.
I alone, she said, might hear their voices,
But you must bind me fast with ropes so tight
They cut, upright on the thwart supporting the mast
And lash me securely to the mast itself, and if
I implore and command you to release me, tie me
Still tighter with even more ropes.'
 "While I was repeating
What Circe had told me, our sturdy ship, rapidly
Running before the fine breeze, bore down on the island
Where the two Sirens live. Soon the wind died down
To a calm, and the waves were lulled by a god. My comrades

Got up, furled the sail, and stowed it away
In the hollow ship. Then they sat down at their oars
Of polished fir and churned the water white,
While I took a large round of wax and with my sharp sword
Cut it up in small pieces. These I kneaded with my powerful
Hands, and soon the wax grew warm, what with
The kneading and the rays of that ruler, Hyperion the Sun.
So with it I plugged the ears of all my comrades,
And they bound me hand and foot in the ship, upright
On the thwart supporting the mast and lashed me securely
To the mast itself. Then, sitting down at their oars,
They smote the gray sea. But no sooner were we within call
Of the island, moving on at a goodly clip, than the Sirens
Saw the swift ship approaching and began their sweet song:
    " 'Here on your way, O great glory of all the Achaeans,
Most famous Odysseus, linger awhile. Stay your ship
And listen as we two blend our voices. Never yet
Has any man rowed his black ship by this spot without hearing
The honeyed tones of our song. Such listeners enjoy
What they hear and go on all the wiser. For we know all
The suffering and hardship that Argives and Trojans endured
By will of the gods at wide Troy, and we know all
That will happen on the bountiful earth.'
    "Thus they sang
With their beautiful voices, and I, more than willing to do
As they wished, ordered my men to release me, frowning
And nodding my head. But they bent to their oars and rowed on,
And soon Perimedes and Eurylochus got up and drew
My bonds tighter and added still more. But when they had rowed
By the Sirens far enough not to hear their singing, my loyal
Companions took out the wax I had put in their ears
And untied the ropes that held me.
    "We had scarcely left
That island behind than I saw smoke and great waves

And heard the roar and booming of surf. The oars flew
From the hands of my terrified men and dragged in the water,
While the ship stood still now that none of them pulled
          on the tapering
Keen blades. But I went through the ship and cheered each
          of them up
With gentle words of encouragement, saying:
          " 'Friends,
Surely we have not been at all unaccustomed
To hardship and danger, nor is this evil confronting
Us now any worse than that we knew when the Cyclops
Penned us up by brute strength in his cave. But even
From there we escaped, through my valor and counsel
          and presence
Of mind, and I'm sure that someday we'll look back on these
Dangers too. But come now, do as I say, and let's all
Follow instructions. Stay on the benches and beat
The deep surf of the sea with your oars, for it may well be
That Zeus will grant us deliverance from this destruction.
And to you at the helm I give these instructions, that you must
At all costs remember, for the steering-oar of this hollow
Ship is in your charge. Keep clear of that smoke
And those breakers and feel your way by at the base of the cliff.
One thoughtless moment, the ship swerving to the other side,
And you'll surely wreck us completely!'
          "They obeyed me at once,
But I said nothing of Scylla, that curse without cure,
Since I didn't want my men too frightened to row
And scrambling for cover in the hold. As for me, I forgot
The irksome command of Circe not to arm myself.
I put on my splendid armor, and with two long spears
In hand I took my stand on the deck at the bow
Of the ship, since I figured that cliff-dwelling Scylla could first
Be spotted from there, she who brought such ruin

On my friends. But she was nowhere in sight, and my eyes
Grew tired of straining toward the misty wall of rock.
  "On up the strait we sailed, groaning with fear,
For on one side Scylla was lurking, while on the other
Demonic Charybdis terribly sucked down the briny
Sea-water, and whenever she belched it back she would be
All boiling and foaming like a cauldron on a roaring fire,
And the spray would shoot high in the air and wet the peaks
Of both cliffs. Each time she sucked the brine down,
            with an awful
Roar round the rock, we could see the swirling turmoil
Within the great vortex and the sand dark blue at the bottom.
  "As we watched, my companions turned olive pale, aghast
In the face of death, and then it was that Scylla
Seized six of my men from the hollow ship, the six best
And strongest men I had. I looked back at the ship
And my crew just in time to see their ascending feet
And hands dangling above me. They shrieked out to me
In their anguish, for the last time calling my name. As a fisherman
Out on a point of rock, with a long pole casting
His baits for what he can catch, lets down his line
And leader of ox-horn, hooks a fish and flings it
Flapping ashore, so they were snatched up toward the cliff,
Convulsively writhing. Then, in the mouth of her cave,
She devoured them, screaming and reaching their hands toward me
In their horrible throes. Of all the sights I suffered
While searching the sea-lanes, this was the most heart-rending.
  "Escaping the Rocks and Scylla and dire Charybdis,
We soon arrived at the excellent island of Helios,
God of the sun. Here were his beautiful broad-browed
Cattle and many fair flocks of sheep. While
The black ship was still out at sea, I could hear the lowing
Of cattle being penned for the night, and the bleating of sheep.
And right then I remembered the words of the blind Theban seer

Tiresias and those of Aeaean Circe, who had urgently
Warned me away from the island of Helios, bringer
Of joy. So I spoke these words to my unhappy crew:
  " 'Hear me, comrades, pay heed in your misery, that I
May tell you the word of Tiresias and that of Aeaean
Circe. They urgently warned me away from the island
Of Helios, the comfort of mortals, for there, said Circe,
Lies the worst of all evils for us! So come now, and row
On out from this island and leave it astern.'
  "At this
Their spirits collapsed, but quickly Eurylochus answered
With these despicable words: 'You're a tough one, all right,
Odysseus, stronger than other men, and tireless.
Now, in fact, it seems you're made of iron,
Solid throughout, since you won't allow your friends,
Exhausted with toil and lack of sleep, to set foot
Ashore on this sea-girt island, where we might enjoy
A good meal. No, you want us to go roving on
Through the fast-falling night, driven away from this island
And over the misty deep. The worst winds come up
At night, shipwrecking winds. How could we avoid
Disaster, if a sudden blustering squall came out
Of the South or West, winds that frequently shatter
Vessels at sea, with no regard at all
For the sovereign gods? But now, this time let's yield
To black night and prepare our supper beside the swift ship.
Then in the morning we'll board her again and head out
To the open sea.'
  "When the rest of them heartily praised
This speech, I felt very certain that a god was plotting
Some evil against us, and answered in these winged words:
'I'm one against many, Eurylochus, and forced to agree.
But all of you come now and swear a great oath to me,
That if we should happen upon a herd of cattle

Or large flock of sheep, no man will be so blindly foolish
As to slaughter so much as one head, but all will eat only
The food that immortal Circe gave us.'
        "Then
They did as I said and swore they would do them no harm,
And when they had ended the oath we moored our stout ship
In a sheltered cove, close to fresh water, and my men
Went ashore and skillfully fixed our supper. But when
They had eaten and drunk as much as they wished,
                they remembered
Their dear dead comrades whom Scylla had snatched from
                the ship
And made a meal on—they remembered, and wept themselves
To sleep, a most welcome relief. That night, however,
When the third watch came and the stars were already setting,
Cloud-gathering Zeus aroused against us a gale
Of incredible force, a blow so great that land
And sea alike were blotted out, as darkness
Rushed suddenly down to envelope the world. So as soon
As the first rosy tints of young Dawn appeared, we dragged
Our ship up the beach and tied her securely in a spacious
Cave, a meeting place of the nymphs, with fine floors
For dancing. Then I called my men around me, and said:
        " 'My friends, since in our swift ship we have both meat
And drink, let us leave the livestock strictly alone,
Protecting ourselves. For the cattle and fat sheep here
Belong to an awesome god, Helios himself,
Who oversees and overhears everything in the world.'
        "To this their proud hearts agreed. Then the South Wind
                blew
Without ceasing for one full month, and no other wind
Came up except one from the East. My men, so long
As the bread and red wine held out, left the livestock alone,
For they too wanted to live. But when our stores

In the ship were completely exhausted, and hunger pinching
Their bellies reduced the men to roaming about
With barbed hooks searching for game, fish or birds
Or whatever they were able to catch, I went off alone
In the island to pray to the gods, hoping that one
Of them would show me the way I should go. Having gone
Through the island some distance away from my friends, I washed
My hands in a spot well protected from wind, and prayed
To all the gods that live on Olympus. But they merely
Shed sweet sleep on my lids, while Eurylochus had already
Started to give this baneful advice to my crew:

" 'You, my long-suffering friends, hear now what I
Have to say. To miserable mortals no form of death
Is less than hateful, but none is so pitifully wretched
As death by starvation! So come, let us round up the best
Of the Sun-god's cattle and offer them up in sacrifice
To the immortal gods who rule the wide sky. And if
We ever do get home to Ithaca again,
We'll build a rich temple to Helios, god of the sun,
And in it we'll put all sorts of splendid things
Most precious to him. If, however, he does
Get angry with us on account of his straight-horned cattle
And chooses, with the other gods' consent, to wreck
Our ship, why then I would surely prefer to gulp
At a wave and give up the ghost all at once, than have life
Leak out drop by drop on a desolate island!'

"Thus Eurylochus, and all the rest of my comrades
Felt the same way. So quickly they rounded up
The best cattle of Helios, for the beautiful beeves, so sleek
And broad of brow, were grazing not far away
From our blue-prowed ship. Then they stood in a circle
                    around them
And prayed to the gods, taking some tender leaves
From a lofty oak for use in the rites, since they had

No white barley on board the well-decked ship. When the prayers
Were completed, they cut the throats of the cattle, flayed them,
And sliced out the thigh-pieces. These they wrapped in two layers
Of fat and on them laid still more raw meat.
They had no wine to pour on this blazing gift
To the gods, so they made libations with water and roasted
All the innards. Now when the thigh-pieces were wholly
Consumed by the flames and they had all tasted of the vital
Parts, they cut up the rest in small pieces and put them
On spits. Just about then, sweet sleep deserted
My lids, and I started back to the ship and the shore
Of the sea. But when I drew near the curved ship, I was met
With the hot sweet smell of burning fat, whereat
I groaned with grief and cried out to the immortal gods:

      " 'Father Zeus and you other eternally happy
Gods, truly that sleep was ruthless, a costly
Oblivion indeed, for meanwhile the men I left
Have committed a horrible crime!'

      "Long-robed Lampetia
Lost no time on her way to tell Hyperion,
God of the sun, that we had killed his cattle.
And he, without delay, spoke thus in his wrath
Amid the immortals:

      " 'Father Zeus and you other
Eternally happy gods, revenge me now
On the friends of Odysseus, son of Laertes, who have
In their thoughtless presumption killed cattle of mine, wherein
I daily rejoiced as I rose toward a sky full of stars
And again in my descent from heaven to earth.
If I don't get satisfaction from them for those
Dead cattle, I'll go down to Hades and shine for the dead!'

      "And Zeus, the cloud gatherer, answered: 'Sun, you keep
On shining among the immortals and for living men

207

On the grain-giving earth. As for the offenders, I'll soon
Strike their swift ship with a bolt of dazzling fire
And shiver its timbers in the midst of the wine-blue sea.'

"This part of the story I heard from fair-haired Calypso,
Who said that the messenger Hermes had told it to her.

"When I reached the ship and the sea, I one by one
Berated the men, but nothing could do any good,
Since the cattle were already dead. And the gods were already
Causing omens to appear. The hides began
To crawl, and the meat, both roasted and raw, bellowed
And moaned on the spits with a sound like the lowing of cattle.

"So, for six days, my trusty companions feasted
On the Sun-god's stolen cattle. Then Zeus, the son
Of Cronos, brought the seventh day in, and the gale subsided.
Quickly we boarded the ship and raised the mast,
Hauled up the white sail and headed for the open sea.

"When that island was far in our wake and no land at all
In sight, just sea and sky, then sure enough
Cronos' son caused a black cloud to form
Right over our hollow ship, while beneath it the sea too
Grew dark. We didn't get far after that, for soon
The West Wind came shrieking upon us, a blow of hurricane
Force that snapped both forestays of the mast, toppling
It backwards, with the rigging tangled up in the bilge, and falling
It struck the head of our pilot at the stern of the ship
And bashed in his skull, so that he, like a diver, flipped
From the deck, and his proud spirit took leave of his bones.
Then, with a great clap of thunder, Zeus hurled his bolt
At the ship, and struck by the lightning of Zeus, she shuddered
From stem to stern and was filled with the fumes of brimstone.
My comrades fell overboard and tossed on the waves
Around the black ship like so many gulls. Thus
God took their returning from them. But I kept scrambling
Around in the ship till the battering waves beat the sides

From the keel and carried what little was left of her on.
The mast snapped off at the keel and became entangled
With one of the ox-hide backstays. With this I lashed
The keel and mast together, and aboard these two
I was driven on by the havocking winds.
   "Then the West Wind's
Gale of hurricane force died down, but swiftly
The South Wind replaced it, much to my sorrow, since I feared
I would have to retravel the way to deadly Charybdis.
All night long I was borne on the surge, and when
The sun rose I had reached the high rock of Scylla and the pool
Of dire Charybdis. But just as she sucked down
The salt sea-water, I sprang up and caught the huge fig tree
And clung to its bark like a bat. I couldn't begin
To find a firm foothold or climb into the tree,
For its roots spread out far below me, while tremendous branches
Stretched far out of reach above, shading Charybdis.
So I fairly grew to the bark as I waited for her
To disgorge the mast and keel, which at last reappeared
As I had so earnestly hoped they would. It was just
At that hour when a judge, one who decides the numerous
Quarrels of litigious men, leaves the court for his supper.
At that very time those timbers came out of Charybdis,
And I let go with my hands and feet and plunged down
In the pool some distance beyond them. Once on them, I rowed
Along with my hands. And the Father of gods and men
Did not allow Scylla to spot me again, which would surely
Have been the end right there.
   "I drifted on
For nine days, till on the tenth night the gods washed me ashore
On Ogygia, the island home of that dread goddess
With the voice of a woman, Calypso of the beautiful braids.
She took me in and kindly cared for me.

But why am I telling you this? Just yesterday I told
This part of my story to you and your gracious wife
In this very hall, and I strongly dislike repeating
What I've already said as well as I know how to say it."

BOOK

XIII

THE RETURN
TO ITHACA

This was his story, and throughout the shadowy halls
His listeners sat in silence as if enchanted,
Till finally Alcinous found his voice: "Since you,
Odysseus, have made it this far and are sitting here
With me in my high-roofed home with floors of bronze,
Having won through many woes, I do not think
That anything now will keep you from your home.
And to all of you that gather in my halls
To drink the sparkling wine of aldermen and hear
The moving songs the poet sings, I give
This charge: garments for our guest lie stored
In a polished chest along with highly wrought gold
And other gifts brought here by the wise Phaeacian
Elders. But come, let each of us give to Odysseus
A fine big tripod and cauldron of brightest bronze,
And we in turn will pay ourselves back from the people,
Since you can't expect a man to give so freely
Without some reasonable hope of remuneration."
    So spoke Alcinous, pleasing them all, and now

Each man went home and to bed. But as soon as Dawn,
That rosy sweet lass, appeared they quickly carried
Their gifts of enriching bronze down to the ship,
And the mighty Alcinous himself went through the ship
And stowed the gifts with care beneath the benches,
That they might not get in the way when the sailors were
   laboring
Hot at their oars. Then they all went home with Alcinous
And prepared a feast.
  And for them Alcinous, their strong
And sacred King, sacrificed a bull to Zeus,
The god of stormy skies and almighty ruler
Of all. After the burnt-offering they merrily fell
To feasting, and among them the sacred bard Demodocus,
Honored by everyone, sang to his lyre. But Odysseus,
So anxious was he to start for home, kept looking
At the sun, as eager for it to set as a man
Who all day long has plowed a yoke of red oxen
Through fallow land and toward evening grows hungry and tired
And longs for the setting sun. So gladly Odysseus
Watched as night came on. Then he spoke to Alcinous
And the other sea-loving Phaeacians:
  "King Alcinous,
Most famous of men, pour wine to the almighty gods
And send me on my way to Ithaca in peace.
And to all of you, farewell. For you've already
Given me all I desired: a ship, a crew,
And gifts of friendship. May the gods in heaven bless them
And my use of them, and when I arrive may I find
In my house my matchless wife with those I love
Unharmed. And may you remaining here make happy
Your wives and children, and may the immortal gods
Give goodness to you of every kind, and may

No evil come, O King, among your people."
    So he spoke, and they all had praise for his words
And favored his sending, since he had spoken so wisely.
Then great Alcinous spoke thus to his herald: "Pontonous,
Mix a bowl and serve out wine to everyone
Here, that we may pray to Father Zeus
And send Odysseus home to Ithaca."
    And now
Pontonous mixed the winsome wine and served
Them all, and some of it they poured to the fortunate
Sky-ruling gods. Then thoughtful Odysseus stood up
And handing his cup to Arete he spoke to her
With tenderness and reverence: "Farewell, O Queen, forever.
I must go, but may you live long and well
In this house and take great joy in your children, your people,
And noble Alcinous the King."
    Then gentle Odysseus
Left the banquet hall and with him mighty
Alcinous sent a herald to show him the way
Down to the shore of the sea where lay the swift ship,
And Arete sent some of her women with the sturdy chest,
A fresh cloak and tunic, bread and red wine.
    When they reached
The ship and the sea, right away the noble young men
Of the crew took all of these things and stowed them away
Aboard ship. On the deck at the stern they prepared a soft pallet
With linen sheet on which Odysseus was
To sleep. Then he came aboard and lay down in silence.
They cast off from the bored-stone mooring and sat down
       in their places
To row. And with the first flash of brine from their oarblades
A sweet sleep fell on the eyes of Odysseus, a most
Delicious deep sleep like nothing so much as death.
And as on a plain four stallions yoked to a car

Leap forward under the lash and quickly complete
The course, so sprang the ship through the dark blue waves
Of the crashing sea, and the water boiled in her wake.
With perfect ease she cut through the deep dark water,
And not even the circling hawk, the fastest of fowls,
Could have kept up with her. Safely aboard
Was a man godlike in wisdom whose heart had suffered
Countless woes in passing through wars and the waves.
But now the man slept a deep, deep sleep, oblivious
To all that pain.
      Now, as the brightest of stars
Arose to herald the coming of early Dawn,
The seaworthy Phaeacian ship approached the island.
      There is in the land of Ithaca a harbor dear
To Phorcys, that briny old man of the sea, a bay
Protected on either side by cliffs that extend
Far out in the deep. So well do these walls resist
The walloping waves that the splendid ships within
Lie completely unmoored and safe where the sailors leave them.
Within near the water is a long-leafed olive tree
And near it a cool, shadowy cave, sacred
To the nymphs called Naiads. Inside are mixing-bowls
And stony urns and hives for the honeybee
As well as the broad looms of stone where the busy nymphs
Weave wonderful cloth of a blue as deep as the sea,
And also inside are springs whose waters well
Unceasingly. Entrances are two, one
On the side where the North Wind strikes, through which
         mortals descend,
The other on the side where the South Wind blows, a sacred
Way through which pass none but immortal feet.
      Into this well-known harbor they pulled, so hard
That the ship was beached by half her length when they landed.
Then from the tightly built ship they stepped out on the sand

And proceeded to lift Odysseus from the deck
And lay him on the shore, still sound asleep
In his soft bright blanket and linen sheet. Next
They set on the beach the gifts those fine Phaeacians
Had given him as he left for home with the blessing
Of the thoughtful goddess Athena. All these they set
By the trunk of the olive tree, out of the path,
So that no passer-by might happen upon them
And help himself before Odysseus awoke.
Then they set out for home. But earth-shaking Poseidon
Had not forgotten the threats which he had uttered
Against Odysseus years ago, and now
He asked to know God's will.

      "Father Zeus,
Gone is my reputation mid the deathless gods,
Since mortals now respect me not at all,
Nor even the Phaeacians, who, as you know, are my kinsmen.
For I but lately decreed that Odysseus should suffer
Many evils before he got home, though I did not
Completely deprive him of his return once you
Had given your word and your nod that he would get home.
Now, with him asleep, these sailing men
Have carried him over the sea in their swift ship
And left him in Ithaca, along with countless gifts,
Great heaps of splendid bronze and garments and gold,
More indeed than Odysseus would ever have won
For himself at Troy if he had come back untouched
With his just part of the plunder."

      Then cloud-assembling
Zeus replied: "For shame! you that cause
The very earth to tremble, you whose power
Is as wide as the world, what are you saying! The gods
Have done nothing for you to resent. How could we fail
To respect our oldest and best? And if a man

215

Should trust in his own strength to the point of irreverence
To you in any way, you always have
The right to make him pay whatever price
Your heart most deeply desires."
    And earth-shaking Poseidon
Replied: "I would, O god of gales, already
Have done as you suggest if I had been sure
That you would suggest it. Now indeed I will shatter
That shapely Phaeacian ship as she returns
On the misty deep, and to insure that hereafter
Their people will never again conduct another
Over the sea, I'll fling some monstrous mountains
Around their city!"
    Then Zeus, collector of clouds:
"O hesitant one, here now is what I advise.
When all have come out to watch the swift ship arrive,
As she nears the shore turn her to solid rock
Before their eyes, that they all may be stricken with wonder.
Then go ahead and fling your mountains around them."
    Now earth-shaking Poseidon was satisfied, and he left
For Scheria, where the Phaeacians live, to wait
For the swift seaworthy ship. Then, as it neared
The shore, the Earthshaker struck, and with a single blow
Turned her to stone and anchored her fast to the bottom,
After which he vanished.
    On shore the Phaeacians, so renowned
For their ships and long oars, spoke in trembling amazement
To one another: "O fearful! who could have fixed
Our swift home-coming ship stone-still on the water?
Who could have stopped her so, and she in full view
Of home?"
    Thus one man would say to another, for they
Didn't know what was to be. Then Alcinous spoke:
"Truly, those evils my father foretold are coming

To pass. He always said that Poseidon was angry
With us for safely conducting strangers over
The deep. It was his prediction that some day, as a fine
Phaeacian ship, after such a convoy, was heading
For home across the foggy sea, Poseidon
Would surely strike her, then fling some monstrous mountains
Around our city. So said that ancient man,
And now I know that his voice was truly prophetic.
But quickly, my people, obey me! Stop this transporting
Of strangers over the misty deep and sacrifice
With me to Poseidon twelve of our best bulls,
And earnestly pray that he will change his mind
And not fling those monstrous mountains about our city."
     In terror they sacrificed the bulls, while the Phaeacian leaders
Stood praying about the altar. But now Odysseus
Awoke in his own native land after so long away
And failed to see where he was, for Zeus-born Athena
Had shrouded the King in a mist, that she might make plans
With him and change his appearance, thus rendering him
Unknown to his wife and friends and people till the wooers
Had paid in full for their every act of cruelty
And pride. Hence everything seemed strange to the King himself,
The winding paths and sheltered bays, the craggy
Cliffs and trees luxuriant with leaves and flowers.
He sprang to his feet and looked about him, looked
On his native land, but groaning he let his arms fall
And began to lament:
     "O not again! among
What manner of mortals can I be now? Will they
Be cruel, unjust, uncivilized, or god-fearing men
And kind to strangers? Where shall I put all this treasure,
And where shall I go from here? Now truly I wish
I had left this wealth among the Phaeacians and gone on
To some other great king, some powerful ruler and generous

217

Man who would surely have entertained me and sent me
Safely homeward. But where can I leave this treasure?
I'll not leave it here, since I don't want it stolen—that's sure.
Confound it! I'm not at all sure the wise Phaeacians
Knew what they were doing when they brought me here
To this strange land. They said they would take me to Ithaca,
Sunny and clear, but where in the world am I now?
May Zeus, who cares for all and punishes sin,
Hear my prayer and even the score. But now
Let me count these gifts and examine them closely, to make sure
Those false Phaeacians didn't take some of their presents
Back home with them in their hollow ship."
      So he counted
The lovely tripods, the urns, the gold, and the beautifully
Woven garments, and everything was there. Then,
As homesick and weeping he walked up and down on the shore
Of the crashing sea, Athena approached in the form
Of a handsome young shepherd, a youth as delicate and tender
As the son of a king. Twice folded about her shoulders
She wore a well-wrought mantle, sandals were on
Her shining feet, and in her hand a spear.
Odysseus was more than glad to see her, and as he
Rapidly lessened the distance between them, he spoke
These winged words:
      "My friend, you're the first I have met
In this country. All joy to you, and may you be a man
Of good will. For I come to your dear knees in prayer,
As to a god, beseeching you to save
This treasure and me. And tell me, if you will,
What land this is and who the people are
That live here. Is this some island that one may see
From afar across the water, or is this the shore
Of the fertile mainland where it slopes down to the sea?"
      And the goddess, her blue eyes sparkling, made this reply:

"If you don't know what land this is, then you're either
A fool or a stranger indeed, for here we have
A name and everybody knows it. All those who live
Between the sunny East and gloomy West
Have heard the name of this rugged island. For though
It's narrow and a very poor place for driving horses,
It's not altogether poor. The land is golden
With grain and flowing with wine, since there's always plenty
Of rain and enriching dew, and also plenty
Of grazing land for goats and cattle, all sorts
Of timber, and a water supply that one can depend on.
And so it is, strange sir, that even in Troy
They have heard the name of Ithaca, and Troy, they say,
Is very far from this Achaean country."
      When he heard these words from the daughter of
             aegis-bearing Zeus,
The godly, long-suffering Odysseus was truly glad,
And inwardly he rejoiced in the land of his fathers.
But since he had no intention of revealing himself
Just yet, he answered with winged words as wily
As he could make them:
      "I have heard of Ithaca, even
In the ample island of Crete far over the sea,
And now I have come here myself, and with me this treasure.
Leaving as much again at home with my children,
I fled our spacious land, for I had killed
The own dear son of Idomeneus, swift Orsilochus,
Who in broad Crete was the fleetest of toiling mortals.
Because at Troy I commanded men of my own
Instead of serving as his father's squire, Orsilochus
Wanted to rob me of all that Trojan booty,
For which I had suffered sorely in cleaving my way
Through warring men and the painful, punishing waves.
So one dark night I lay by the road in wait

219

With one of my men, and as he came home from the field
I struck him down with my bronze-headed spear, and no man
Saw us there. Thus the keen bronze killed him.
Then with all speed I went to a ship and besought
The Phoenician owners to take me aboard. I gave them
Booty sufficient to quiet their qualms and asked
To be set ashore at Pylos, or at Elis,
That splendid land where Epeans rule. But the might
Of the wind drove that honest crew, who meant me
No harm, far from our destination, until
One night, completely lost, we approached this shore.
Eagerly rowing we entered the harbor and landed.
Then, though very hungry, we lay down on the sand
To rest. Sweet sleep came on my weary self,
And while I slept the Phoenicians took my treasure
From the ship and placed it beside me on the sand.
Then they went aboard and set sail for populous Sidon,
Leaving me here with a heavy heartful of trouble."
　　At this the bright-eyed goddess smiled and gave him
A little pat with her hand, then changed herself
Into a beautiful woman, tall and talented, who spoke
These winged words to him: "The cunning rogue
That hopes to outdo you in the art of deception
Will have to be cunning indeed, or, for that matter,
So would a god. Wretch! even here in your very own
Country you refuse to abandon that repertory of tricks
And artful tales that you're so fond of. But enough
Of this. We are both deeply learned in craft, I am sure.
Just as you surpass all men in planning and speaking,
So I am famous among all the gods for wisdom
And cunning. After all, you didn't know that I
Was Pallas Athena, daughter of Zeus, the goddess
Who always looks out for you regardless of the trouble
You're in. It was I, you know, who made those Phaeacians

So fond of you. Now I have come to weave
A plan with you and to help hide all that treasure
That the gracious Phaeacians gave in accord with my will
And advice when you left their country for home, and finally
I am here to tell of the suffering fate has in store
For you in that fine house of yours. But you
Must be strong and silently endure your many afflictions.
Tell no man or woman your wanderings have ended, but humbly
Suffer the violence of men."
    Then wily Odysseus
Replied: "It's very hard, O goddess, for a mere man
To recognize you when you appear, regardless
Of how much he knows, for you take whatever form
You wish. But of this I'm sure, that you were very kind
To me when some years ago at Troy we sons
Of Achaeans were fighting a bloody war, but since
That time where have you been? For after we sacked
The high city of Priam and went away in our ships
And were scattered abroad by a god—never since then,
O daughter of Zeus, have I seen you coming to help me
On ship or shore. But always I wandered on,
My heart cloven with sorrow, till at last the gods
Delivered me from evil. Not until then,
In the wealthy land of the Phaeacians, did you appear.
There you restored my courage with your cheerful words
And led me to their city. But now I beseech you
In the name of your Father—for I am by no means sure
That this really is brave Ithaca: I rather think
I'm lost in some other land and that you have spoken
To mock and befuddle me—I implore you, then,
To tell me in all good faith if I have indeed reached
My own dear country."
    Then blue-eyed Athena replied:
"How truly typical that is of the way you think,

Which is why I cannot leave you in your misery, for you
Are gentle, intelligent, and discreet. Had any other man
Returned from wanderings such as yours, can't you just see him
Eagerly running to greet his wife and children
At home? But you can rest content till you've further
Tried your wife, who let me assure you remains
As ever in your palace, where pitifully she weeps
While the days and nights waste slowly away. As for me,
I always knew in my heart that you would return
After losing all your companions. But as you can imagine,
I had no wish to antagonize Uncle Poseidon,
Who was furious at you for blinding the only eye
Of a favorite son. But enough, look about you now
And be persuaded. This harbor belongs to Phorcys,
That briny old man of the sea, and here is the long-leafed
Olive tree and near it the cool dim cave
Sacred to the nymphs called Naiads, the same vaulted cave,
As surely you must remember, where you to the nymphs
Have sacrificed many a perfect offering. And there
Is Mount Neriton in its cloak of trees."

     So saying,
The goddess scattered the mist and once again
Godly Odysseus saw his own native land.
His patient heart was filled with joy as he kissed
The grain-giving earth and lifted his hands in prayer
To the sacred Naiads:

     "O nymphs, daughters of Zeus,
I never thought to see you again, but now
With joy and loving prayers I greet you, and if
Athena, the booty-bringing daughter of Zeus, will grant me
Grace to live and see my son a man,
Then as of old I'll sacrifice richly to you."

     And again the bright-eyed goddess: "Cheer up, and try not
To worry. Come, let's quickly hide this treasure

As far back as we can in this marvelous cave, where it
Will be safe, and then let's decide what is best to do."
        With this the goddess went into the shadowy cave
In search of a good hiding-place, and Odysseus brought all
The treasure in, the gold, the stubborn bronze,
And the lovely clothes the Phaeacians had given him.
These he carefully stowed, and Pallas Athena,
Daughter of aegis-great Zeus, blocked the cave's mouth
With a boulder. Then they sat down in the shade of the sacred
Olive tree and pondered some means to destroy
The arrogant wooers. Athena's blue eyes blazed
As she broke the silence:
        "Zeus-descended son
Of Laertes, resourceful Odysseus, consider how you
May lay hands on these unscrupulous men who have
For three years been lording it here in your palace
            with presumption
And riot, wooing your wonderful wife and offering her
Gifts. And she, sorrowfully waiting for you
To appear, sends messages of hope and promise to all
Of them, though her heart is elsewhere."
        Then keen Odysseus:
"The horrible fate of Agamemnon, son of Atreus,
Would surely have been mine, if you, O goddess,
Had not thus timely told me how things are.
But come, weave me a plan by which I may
Repay them for all they've done, and stay with me
That I may not flinch when the hour arrives, and that we
May be as we were when we reduced bright Troy
To a heap of dusty rubble. If, O goddess
With the blazing blue eyes, you would stand by me, as willing
And eager to help as you were then, I would not
Hesitate to go against three hundred men!"
        And the bright-eyed goddess Athena replied: "But I will

Be with you in that trying hour, nor will I forget you,
And many a man who now makes free with your goods
Shall then bespatter your hall's great floor with his blood
And brains. But come, I will change your looks completely,
That no one may know who you are. First I will shrivel
The healthy skin on your supple limbs and ruin
Your auburn hair, then dress you in rags so filthy
That seeing you men will shudder. Finally, I'll blear
Your beautiful eyes, that are now so bright, that you
May seem contemptible and unimportant to wooers,
Wife, and son. Then go to your keeper of swine,
For he still cares for you and loves both your son
And prudent wife. You will find him tending your swine
By Raven's Rock at the spring Arethusa, where his charges
Wax fat on the plentiful acorns and cool dark water.
There I want you to stay, finding out all
You can from him, while I go to Sparta, where the glamorous
Women are, and call Telemachus home,
Your own dear son, Odysseus, who went to Menelaus
In wide Lacedaemon, hoping to hear that you
Were still alive."
    Then wary Odysseus replied:
"But why, since you know everything—why didn't
You tell him what he wanted to know? Surely it wasn't
Your will that he too should suffer a wanderer's woes
On the restless sea while others devoured his belongings!"
    And the flashing-eyed goddess replied: "Concerning him
You've no cause for care. I took him there myself,
That men might think well of him for going, and now
He sits at ease in the palace of King Menelaus
With all good things before him. It is true
That in a black ship young men lie waiting to kill him
Before he can reach his home. I don't think they
Will succeed, but before very long black earth will lie over

Not a few of those who now consume what is yours."
    She spoke, and touched him with her wand, and the flesh
So firm was withered on his supple limbs, his head
Made bald, as he became suddenly old. And she bleared
His beautiful eyes, that before had been so bright,
And dressed him in filthy rags begrimed with soot.
About him she threw the hairless old hide of a deer,
Gave him a staff, and hanging from a piece of rope
Across one shoulder. a worn-out leather pouch.
    Having thus made plans together, at last they parted,
And now the goddess went straight to sacred Lacedaemon,
That she might bring the son of Odysseus home.

BOOK

XIV

EUMAEUS THE SWINEHERD

Leaving the harbor, Odysseus took the rough path
Through the wooded hills to the spot where Athena had said
He would find the faithful swineherd, who cared more about
His master's well-being than did any of the other servants.

He found him sitting in the porch in front of his lodge
In a fine large yard set up on a lofty rise
And enclosed with a wall of huge stones. This the herdsman
Had built for the swine of his absent master, without bothering
His mistress or the old man Laertes about it, and on top
Of the wall was a thorny hedge of wild pear. Outside,
He had driven tall stakes, split from the black heart of oak,
Close-set, and running the whole length of the wall. Inside,
For bedding down swine, he had built twelve sties right next
To each other, and in each he had penned fifty wallowing sows
For breeding, while the boars were kept outside in the yard.
These weren't nearly so numerous, for the constant feasting
Of the high-born wooers daily decreased their number,
And the herdsman was forced to send them the best he had.

There were still three hundred and sixty boars left,
        and beside them
Slept four dogs, ferocious as any wild beast,
All trained by the master swineherd himself. Just then
He was cutting a rich brown piece of leather and fitting
His feet with sandals, while the men who helped him were out
Here and there with droves of swine—or rather three of them
Were, for the fourth he had sent into town with a hog
For the bloated wooers, that they might kill it and stuff
Themselves with pork.
        All at once the loud-baying hounds
Saw Odysseus approaching and charged down upon him, barking
At the top of their lungs. Odysseus had the sense to sit down
And drop his staff, but still, even on his own farm,
He would have suffered severely had the swineherd not dropped
The work he was doing and rushed after the dogs through the gate,
Loudly calling to them and driving them off
With a constant raining of rocks. Then he spoke thus
To his King:
        "Truly, old fellow, the dogs might have torn you
To pieces, and that very quickly. Then I would have gotten
The blame, though surely the gods have already given me
Plenty to grieve and groan about. I sit here
Mourning for a marvelous master, fattening hogs
For others to eat, while he, like as not, is hungry
And wandering around in some city or land where the language
Is strange to him—if indeed he's still alive
And sees the sunlight at all. But come, old man,
Let's go inside the lodge, that when you have eaten
And drunk to your heart's content, you may tell me where
You are from and the trials you've endured."
        Then the faithful herdsman
Showed him in and gave him a seat, heaping up
A thick pile of brushwood and covering it over with the skin

227

Of a shaggy wild goat so large and so soft that the swineherd
Used it to sleep on. Odysseus was pleased to be
So received, and spoke to him thus:
 "My good man, may Zeus
And the other immortal gods give you what most
You desire for this most generous welcome that I
Have received from you."
 Then, Eumaeus, you said:
"It would not be right, my friend, for me to slight
A stranger, even though a man much meaner than you
Should come, for all strangers and beggars are surely from Zeus,
And a gift from such as we, though small, is well meant
And welcome. Servants, you know, can hardly do more,
So long as they live in constant fear of tyrannical
Masters—that is to say, these new young masters
Of ours. For he whose return the gods have prevented
Would surely have showered his loving kindness on me.
He would have given me things of my own—a house,
A piece of land, an attractive wife—all
Such things as a right-minded master gives to a servant
Who has labored a great deal for him and whose labor God
Has made prosper, as this work prospers that I do here.
Indeed my master would have rewarded me richly,
Had he stayed here and grown old at home. But he died—
As I heartily wish all the people of Helen had done
In utter exhaustion, since many brave men sank down
In the dust on her account. So too, my master,
For Agamemnon's sake, journeyed to Ilium, land
Of fine horses, that he might do battle with Trojans."
 So saying,
He quickly tucked his tunic up under his belt
And went out to the pens where he kept the young porkers. Having
 picked out
A couple, he brought them in, singed and slew them

Both, then cut up the meat and put it on spits.
When all was roasted, he carried it over, hot
On the spits, set it in front of Odysseus, and sprinkled
It with white barley. Then in an ivy bowl
He mixed the honey-sweet wine, took a seat across
From Odysseus, and urged him to eat:
     "Fall to, my friend,
For such is the food we servants are able to offer—
Young porkers. All the fat hogs are consumed by the wooers,
Who have no fear of God's wrath and no pity at all.
The blissful gods care not for such behavior,
But continue to honor decorum and sweet moderation.
Even cruel buccaneers that go raiding abroad
And load their ships with loot Zeus allows them to steal—
Even on those hard hearts, as homeward they go,
Falls an awful fear of God's wrath. So it must be that these men
Know something, perhaps by some word from a god, concerning
The disastrous death of my master, for they go right on
With their indecent wooing and won't return to their homes.
They loll around in their insolent way and waste
What they can. Zeus sends no day or night that they
Don't slaughter our livestock—and not just one or two victims,
And they draw much wine and likewise sinfully waste it.
For believe me, my master's possessions were unspeakably great.
No lord on the loamy mainland or in Ithaca either
Has nearly so much—in fact, no twenty men have!
Just listen. On the mainland he has twelve herds of cattle,
Twelve flocks of sheep, twelve droves of swine, and as many
Herds of wide-roaming goats—and herdsmen, both hirelings
And men of his own, to pasture them. Here,
All around the edges of the island, scattered herds
Of goats are grazing, eleven in all, and trustworthy
Men watch over them. Every day, though,
Each man drives up for the wooers the sleekest goat,

The choicest in his herd, while I select
And send them, from these swine I keep and protect, the best
Of the boars."

    As he spoke, Odysseus, silent, preoccupied,
Bolted the meat and drank the wine, and all
The time he was busy sowing seeds of evil
For the arrogant wooers. When he felt refreshed, having eaten
Enough, he filled the cup brimful of wine
And handed it to his host, who took it with pleasure.
Then Odysseus spoke these winged words:
    "My friend,
Who is this man who bought and paid for you
And whom you describe as so very wealthy and strong?
You said he died for Agamemnon's sake. But tell me
His name. It might just be that I know him. Only Zeus
And the other immortals know whether I've met him
        and can tell you
About him, but surely I've seen a good bit of the world
In my travels."

    Then the noble swineherd replied: "Old fellow,
No traveling man that came here telling of him
Could ever convince his wife and dear son. Tramps
In need of refreshment are notorious liars and have no
Regard at all for the truth. But when these vagrants
Come to Ithaca and go to my mistress with their clever
Lies, she welcomes them in and questions them closely,
Weeping like any woman who loses her husband
Abroad. And you too, old man, would make up a story
Quickly enough if you thought it would get you a cloak
And a tunic. But Odysseus is dead, his spirit gone,
And right now the dogs and swift birds have probably cleaned
The flesh from his bones. Either that, or the fish in the sea
Have devoured him and his bones lie up on some beach
        buried deep

In the sand. So somewhere out there he died, and the days
To come hold grief for all of his friends, but especially
For me, since I'll never find another master
So gentle and kind, no matter how far I go,
Though I come again to the house of my father and mother
Where I was born and where they brought me up.
But I do not mourn for them so much, keen
As I am to see them and be in my own land again.
O no, the one I miss most is Odysseus. Even now,
My friend, gone though he is, I speak his name
With awe and tender affection, for he loved me deeply
And thoughtfully cared for me. He's no longer here,
But he's still very precious to me."

    And Odysseus, patient
As ever, answered him thus: "My friend, since you have
No faith at all that he will come again,
I'll not just tell you so, I'll swear it. Nor do
I want a reward for this good news, until
He arrives at his home. Then will be time enough
To give me a new cloak and tunic. Meanwhile, no matter
How great my need, I'll accept nothing at all.
For the gates of Hades are not more hateful to me
Than a man who surrenders to need, and lies for a living.
And now by Zeus, the first among gods, by this
Hospitable board and the hearth of noble Odysseus
Which I am approaching, I swear that all I have said
Shall happen. In this very month, in the dark of the moon,
Odysseus shall be here, and returning he'll make them
All pay for the sins committed against his wife
And wonderful son."

    Then, Eumaeus, you said:
"That reward for good news, old man, I won't have to pay.
Odysseus will never return. But relax and drink
Your wine. Meanwhile let's talk about something else,

231

For any mention of my most thoughtful lord
Is grievous to me. As for that oath of yours,
We'll let it pass, though I wish with all my heart
That Odysseus would come, as do Penelope, and old
Laertes, and godlike Telemachus. But now I grieve
All the time for Telemachus, the son of Odysseus. For when
He had grown by grace of the gods like a sturdy young tree
And I thought that he among men would be just as fine
As his father, marvelous in form and feature, then one
Of the gods unbalanced his splendid mind, or perhaps
Some mortal did it, and he took off for sacred
Pylos, seeking news of his father. And now
The illustrious wooers are lying in wait for him
As he returns, hoping to destroy in Ithaca
The line of godlike Arceisius and root out the name.
But whether they get him or he gets away remains
To be seen. May God's own hand guide and protect him.
But come, old fellow, tell me your troubles, and tell me
Truly. I'd like to know all about you. Who are you
And where are you from? What kind of ship did you come in,
And who were the sailors who brought you? Now don't tell me
You walked."
      And Odysseus, careful and cunning, replied:
"I'll give you a frank account of all these things,
But if we had a full year to sit here in your lodge
And talk, with plenty of food and sweet wine to enjoy,
While the rest of the world went on about its business,
Even then I couldn't begin to finish the story
Of the troubles my spirit has known, so many are the trials
I've suffered by will of the gods.
      "I come from broad Crete,
Where I got my start as a rich man's son. Many other
Sons were born and brought up in his halls, all
Legitimate offspring, but my mother was bought, a concubine.

Even so, the man who begot me—his name was Castor,
Son of Hylax—treated me just as well
As the true-born sons. At that time the people of Crete
Respected him like a god for his rich and happy
Estate and his glorious sons. But he died, and the fates
Bore him to Hades. By lot his haughty sons
Divided his wealth among them. To me they gave
A mere pittance, along with a place to live. But I,
By valor alone, won me a wife from a family
As wealthy as any, for I was no fool, nor was I
Disposed to run from a fight. Now all that prowess
Has left me. Still, I think you can tell from the stubble
What the harvest grain was like. Needless to say,
I've had my share of trouble since then. In those days,
However, I had from Ares and Athena the kind
Of daring and strength that bears all human things
Before it. Whenever I picked the best men and planned
An ambush, not once did any foreboding of death
Unman my proud spirit. I was always the very first man
To spring out with my spear and transfix anyone failing
To flee. When it came to war, I was that kind
Of man. But farming and domestic economy, on which
Fine children thrive, I cared not for. All
My love was ever for well-oared ships and fighting,
For gleaming spears and arrows—horrible things
That give cold chills to other folks. I guess
I liked them because God made me that way, and each
To his own, I say. Before the sons of Achaeans
Had set one foot on the Trojan shore, I
Had already led nine expeditions against
Our foreign foes, nine swift fleets, filled
With warriors, and great was the spoil I came by. From it
I took what I wanted, and later by lot I got
Much more. Thus my estate quickly increased,

233

And among the Cretans I came to be feared and respected.
   "But when all-seeing Zeus contrived that lòathsome journey
Which loosened the limbs of so very many brave men,
The people demanded that I and renowned Idomeneus
Should lead the ships to Ilium, nor was there any
Way out, so great was the force of public opinion.
There we sons of Achaeans fought on for nine years.
Then in the tenth we sacked the city of Priam
And left in our ships for home, only for God
To scatter us far and wide. But Zeus, always
Inventive, had planned worse woes than that for me,
Poor wretch that I was. I had been home no more
Than a month, enjoying my family and wealthy estate,
When the spirit urged me to fit out some ships and set sail
For Egypt, along with my godlike comrades. Nine ships
In all were readied, and quickly the great crew gathered.
For six days I furnished the food for my loyal companions,
That they to the gods might sacrifice and prepare a feast
For themselves. On the seventh day we boarded our ships
And sailed from broad Crete, with the North Wind blowing
            so fresh
And so fair that we ran on before it as if we were headed
Down stream. Not a single ship was harmed, and we sat there
Safe and sound while the wind and the men at the helms
Kept us straight on our course.
         "On the fifth day we came to the great
Egyptian river, and there in that fair-flowing stream
We moored our ships. Then I told my trusty companions
To stay by the ships and guard them, and I sent some scouts
To high vantage points to get the lay of the land.
But the crews gave in to their own wanton violence, and carried
Away by their strength they began to pillage and plunder
The fine Egyptian farms. They abducted the women
And children and murdered the men. But their cries were heard

In the city, and at dawn the whole plain was full of foot soldiers
And chariots and the flashing of bronze. Then Zeus, the hurler
Of lightning, filled my men with ignoble panic,
And such were the dangers that pressed from all sides, that not
One man had the courage to stay where he was and fight.
Thus, with keen bronze, their men cut us down by the dozen,
And they led up others to their city as slaves. But I
Had a timely idea from Zeus himself—though I wish
I had died right there and met my fate in Egypt,
For even then sorrow was waiting to make me
Her own. I doffed my fine helmet, let the shield fall
From my shoulder, dropped my spear, and made for the royal
Chariot. Embracing the King's knees, I kissed them,
        and he saved me
From harm. Out of pity he gave me a seat in his chariot
And took me weeping home, though his angry subjects
Pressed from all sides, lusting to shed my blood
With their ashen spears. But he kept them off, duly
Respecting the wrath of Zeus, the protector of strangers,
For he most of all exacts due payment for evil.
    "So there I remained for seven years, and grew wealthy
Among the Egyptians, who were all more than generous to me.
But when the eighth year rolled around, I met a low fellow
Indeed, a guileful, greedy Phoenician, who had already
Caused mankind his share of trouble. He took
Me in with his cunning and got me as far as Phoenicia
Where he had a house and estate. I stayed a whole year.
Then as days became months and the seasons began to roll by
He put me aboard a merchantman headed for Libya.
His lying pretext was that I should help with the cargo,
But all the time he was planning to sell me there
For a very large sum. I went on board with him,
Apprehensive enough, but I had no choice. Then the ship
Ran on before a splendid wind from the North,

Well out to sea and windward of Crete. But Zeus
Had planned their destruction. When Crete was far in our wake
And no land at all in sight, just sea and sky,
Then the son of Cronos caused a black cloud to form
Right over our hollow ship, while beneath it the sea too
Grew dark. Then, with a great clap of thunder, Zeus hurled
His bolt at the ship, and struck by the lightning of Zeus
She shuddered from stem to stern and was filled with the fumes
Of brimstone. My comrades fell overboard and tossed
On the waves around the black ship like so many gulls.
Thus God took their returning from them. As for me,
When my heart was riddled with woe, Zeus himself
Brought the great tossing mast of our blue-prowed ship to where
I could reach it, that I might be saved. Clinging to this,
I was borne by the raging winds for nine days. Then at last,
On the tenth black night, a huge roller washed me ashore
In Thesprotia. Pheidon, the Thesprotians' lordly King,
Treated me kindly and asked nothing at all in return,
For his own dear son had found me, half dead with cold
And fatigue, had helped me up by the hand, taken me
Home to his father's palace, and given me a cloak
And tunic to wear.
     "It was there I learned of Odysseus.
The King said he'd taken him in and befriended him
On his way home, and he showed me the tremendous treasure
Odysseus had amassed in bronze, and gold, and iron
Highly wrought with much labor. Truly, it would have sufficed
To keep both him and his heirs to the tenth generation,
So great was the wealth stored there for him in the halls
Of the King. But Odysseus, he said, had gone to learn
The will of Zeus from his lofty-leaved oak in Dodona,
Hoping to hear just how to return, after being
So long away, to his own rich home in Ithaca,
Whether incognito or not. And in my presence

236

He swore, as he poured libations there in his house,
That a ship was launched and a crew standing by for the sole
Purpose of taking Odysseus home. But I left
Before he returned, since a Thesprotian ship
Chanced to be leaving for wheat-rich Dulichium. The
        King ordered
The crew to take me there, with all the comfort
They could, to King Acastus. But yielding to malice,
They turned against me and tried to complete my ruin.
No sooner had the seagoing vessel got well out from land
Than they began to make a slave of me.
Stripping off my clothes, my cloak and tunic, they threw me
Some filthy rags to put on, the same ones I'm wearing
Now. Then just as the sun was setting on the fields
Of far-seen Ithaca, we reached your island. Tightly
They tied me with rope in the well-decked ship and went
Ashore for a hasty meal on the beach. But the gods
Undid my bonds with the greatest of ease, and covering
My head with this rag I have on, I slid down the smooth
Steering-oar, breasted the water, and struck out, swimming
For all I was worth. Soon I was far enough
From the seamen to leave the water and go into the woods,
Where crouching low I hid in a fragrant thicket.
They hunted all over the place, shouting and cursing
As loud as they could, but unable to find me they finally
Got discouraged, gave up the search and reboarded
Their hollow ship. Thus the gods easily hid me
And led me on to the lodge of a very wise man.
So it seems that my lot, as of now, is to go on living."
      Then, Eumaeus, this was your response:
"Poor man, you have moved my heart deeply with this tale
        of your woes
And your wanderings. But regarding Odysseus you have not
        spoken well,

Nor shall you ever convince me. Why should you,
In the fix you're in, tell such a useless lie?
What there is to know of my lord's return,
I already know very well—that the gods all hated him
Utterly, else they would have slain him among the Trojans,
Or let him die in the arms of a friend, when he
Had wound up his career in the war. Then all the Achaeans
Would have made him a tomb, and his story in days to come
Would have won great glory for both him and his son, but now
Some fiendish storm has swept him ingloriously away
And left no clues at all. So here with swine
I live apart and never go into town,
Except when wise Penelope asks me in
Because someone has come to her with news.
Then they all sit around and probe him with questions, both those
Who sincerely mourn their long-lost King and those
Who stuff themselves at his expense. But I've lost
All desire to ask such questions since I fell for the story
Of a wandering Aetolian. He'd killed a man and roamed
All over the world before finally coming to my house.
I welcomed him warmly, and he told me a tale of Odysseus—
How he had seen him in Crete at the house of Idomeneus,
Where Odysseus was staying while his storm-battered ships
       were repaired.
He said my lord would return, either that summer
Or the following fall, with his godlike companions and
       much treasure.
But you, old man of many sorrows, don't try
To deceive me or win my favor with lies. They'll make you
No more respected by me, nor any dearer.
I act as I do in awe of mighty Zeus,
The god of strangers, and because I pity you."

     Then wily Odysseus replied: "Surely yours is a skeptical
Heart, not even by an oath to be won or persuaded.

But come now, let's make a pact between us, with the gods
Of Olympus as witnesses from this moment on. If your lord
Returns to this house, give me a cloak and tunic
To wear and send me on to Dulichium, my heart's
Destination. But if your lord does not come back
As I say, have your men seize me and throw me down
From a great rocky cliff, that another tramp may think twice
Before he starts lying!"
    And the noble swineherd replied:
"Ah, my friend, then indeed I should make a fine name
For myself among men once and for all, if I
Who invited you into my home and entertained you
Should turn right around and take your precious life.
After that, I'd surely be earnest and eager in my prayers
To Zeus, the son of Cronos. But it's suppertime now,
And I hope my men will soon be here, so that we
Can prepare a good meal."
    While they were talking, the herdsmen
Arrived with the swine and penned them up for the night
In their sties. Then above the unspeakable grunting and squealing,
Eumaeus called out to his comrades:
    "Bring in the best boar
We've got. I want to slaughter him for this guest
Who comes to us from so far away, and we too
Will enjoy a good meal—we who have labored so long
In our painstaking care of these porkers, while others live off
Our labor and go without payment."
    So saying, he took
The unfeeling bronze and split some wood, and the others
Brought in a fat boar of five years and stood him by the hearth.
Nor did the swineherd, who was surely a right-thinking man,
Forget the immortals. He began the sacrifice by throwing
A tuft of bristles from the head of the white-tusked boar
Into the fire, and he prayed to all the gods

239

That thoughtful Odysseus might come home again.
Then he raised an unsplit piece of oak and struck
The boar a fatal blow. His men cut the throat
Of the victim, singed and rapidly quartered him.
Eumaeus took pieces from the various cuts, and laying them
On the rich fat he sprinkled it all with barley meal
And threw it in the fire. The rest they cut up
And put on spits, carefully roasted it all,
Drew it off, and piled it on platters. The swineherd,
Who well knew what was right and fair, stood up to carve
And divided the meat seven ways. One portion he prayerfully
Saved for the nymphs and Maia's son Hermes, and to each
Person there he gave one. Odysseus he especially honored
With the lengthy chine of the white-tusked boar, thus
Delighting the heart of his quick-witted master, who spoke
To him thus:

"Eumaeus, God love you. May you be as dear
To Father Zeus as you are to me, for honoring
A man in my condition with so splendid a portion."

Then, Eumaeus, you answered him thus: "Eat,
My unhappy friend, and enjoy what there is to enjoy.
God gives and God takes away as he sees fit,
And there's nothing that he can't do."

So saying, he made
A burnt-offering of the portion set aside for the immortal gods,
And then, having poured a libation of the sparkling wine,
He handed the cup to Odysseus, sacker of cities,
And sat down before his own share of the pork. Bread
Was served by Mesaulius, whom the swineherd had bought
            from the Taphians
In his master's absence, with goods of his own and without
Bothering his mistress or the old man Laertes.
Then they all fell to and enjoyed the good things before them.
When they had eaten and drunk as much as they wanted,

240

Mesaulius cleared away what was left, and they all,
Having had their fill of bread and meat, began
To feel drowsy and ready for bed.
     Night came on
In the dark of the moon and with it bad weather. Zeus rained
All night and the wet West Wind blew hard. Now Odysseus
Decided to see how far the herdsman would go
In his care for a guest—in fact, to see whether he would give him
The cloak off his back, or at least off the back of one
Of his comrades:
     "Listen, Eumaeus, and you men of his, too.
I've a story to tell, a wishful story that the wine
Wants told, crazy wine, that takes even a very wise man
And sets him to singing and giggling, makes him get up
And dance, and say things he shouldn't, but now that I've started
This babbling, I might as well go on—O
How I wish that I were as young and as strong as I was
When we got that ambush ready and led it up under
The walls of Troy! Odysseus and Atreus' son
Menelaus had asked me to join them as third in command.
When we reached the high wall, we lay round the city
      in the tangled
Growth of a reedy swamp, crouching low beneath
Our shields, which soon were covered with ice. For as night
Came on, the North Wind dropped, freezing weather set in,
And snow began falling, bitter cold as any frost.
Now all the others had cloaks and tunics and slept
Well enough, with their shields drawn over their shoulders.
     But I
Had foolishly left my cloak behind, sure
That I wouldn't be cold, and had come off with nothing
     but my shield
And bright tunic. So that night, when the third watch had come
     and the stars

Were already setting, I spoke to Odysseus, who was right
Beside me, giving him a nudge with my elbow that instantly
Got his attention:
    " 'Zeus-sprung son of Laertes,
Resourceful Odysseus, I'm truly not long for this world!
I don't have a cloak and I'm freezing to death. Some demon
Saw to it that I went off with nothing on
But a tunic, and now there's no way out.'
    "So I,
But he was a thinking, as well as a fighting, man,
And knew what to do. He whispered: 'Quiet now, somebody
Might hear you.'
    "Then propping his head on his elbow, he spoke:
'Friends, wake up! I've just had a dream from the gods.
We've come a long way from the ships, and I want a man
To go back and tell our commander-in-chief Agamemnon.
He may be able to send more men from the ships.'
    "He'd scarcely finished when Thoas, son of Andraemon,
Leaped up, threw down his purple cloak, and took off
At a run for the ships. So I blissfully lay in his cloak
Until Dawn of the golden-throne appeared—O
How I wish that I were as young and as strong as I was
In those days! Then one of these herdsmen here would give me
A cloak out of real respect and affection for a valiant
Man. But now they see these filthy rags
And make fun of me."
    Then, Eumaeus, this
Was your response: "Old fellow, you picked a good story,
And you'll be rewarded accordingly, with clothes and whatever
Else a wayworn wanderer should have when he comes
As a suppliant—but just for tonight. In the morning you'll have to
Flutter about in the rags you've got on, since these men
Have no extra clothing, just one cloak and tunic apiece.
But when the dear son of Odysseus gets back, he'll give you

A cloak and tunic to wear and send you wherever
Your heart and soul most want to go."
    So saying,
He was quick to get up and prepare a bed for Odysseus.
He placed it there by the fire and covered it well
With the skins of sheep and goats. Then Odysseus lay down
And the swineherd threw over his guest a heavy huge cloak,
One he kept ready to wear whenever a cold storm
Came.
    There slept Odysseus, with the young men beside him.
But the swineherd was loath to lie down so far from the boars,
So he got himself ready to spend the night outside.
And Odysseus was glad to see how careful he was
Of all that belonged to his absent master. Eumaeus
Proceeded to sling a sharp sword from his powerful shoulders
And put on a cloak thick enough to ward off the wind.
Then, he picked up the large fleece of a well-fed goat,
Took a sharp javelin to protect against dogs and men,
And went out in the night to sleep with the white-tusked boars
Beneath a jutting crag where the North Wind never blew.

BOOK

XV

THE RETURN OF
TELEMACHUS

Now Pallas Athena had journeyed to wide Lacedaemon
To remind great-hearted Odysseus' noble son
Of his return and get him started. She found
Telemachus and the glorious son of Nestor sleeping
In the portico of famous Menelaus. At any rate, Nestor's
Son was fast asleep, but to Telemachus
Sweet sleep had not come, since all through the immortal
Night he lay there anxiously thinking about
His father. Blue-eyed Athena stood by him and spoke:
    "Telemachus, it isn't good for you to be
So far fom home any longer, what with a houseful
Of insolent men who might very well divide
And devour all that you own, thus rendering your trip
Quite useless. So hurry and urge your helpful host
Menelaus to send you on your way, that your matchless
Mother may still be at home when you get there. For already
She is under considerable pressure from her father and brothers
To marry Eurymachus, who far outdoes all the other
Wooers in his presents to her and now in his gifts

To her father is more lavish than ever. And she might carry off
Some precious thing you would not willingly part with.
You know how women are. A wife will do
What she can to increase the estate of her lord, but she gives
No thought to a former husband, once he is dead,
And she no longer inquires about her children by him.
So go, and until the gods see fit to show you
A bride sufficiently glorious, turn over the management
Of all your possessions to the serving woman you think
Is most able. And here's something else for you to remember.
The best men of the wooers are waiting to ambush you
In the strait between Ithaca and craggy Samos, panting
To kill you before you reach your own country. Not that
I think they will, though it is very likely that a number
Of those love-stricken household devourers will be
Both dead and buried before long. Even so, keep
Your sturdy ship well out from the islands and sail
By day and night too. The god whose special care
You are will keep a fine breeze at your back. At the first land
You touch in Ithaca, get off and send your ship
And crew on around to the city harbor. Then make
Your way at once to the faithful herdsman who keeps
Your swine and kindly looks out for you. Spend
The night there, but send him into town to tell
      thoughtful Penelope
That you have returned fom Pylos and she has you back safe."
    Then the goddess departed for the heights of Olympus,
      but Telemachus,
With a touch of his heel, woke Nestor's son from sweet sleep:
"Wake up, Peisistratus! Go fetch your eager-hoofed horses
And yoke them to the chariot, so that we can take to the road
Right away."
    And Peisistratus, son of Nestor, replied:
"But Telemachus, it's still pitch dark. We can't leave now,

No matter how much we may want to. But it will soon
Be light. So let's wait and give our spear-famous host,
Atreus' son Menelaus, a chance to put gifts
In the chariot and send us off with a friendly good-by.
No guest ever forgets a hospitable host."
    Soon after he spoke came Dawn of the golden throne,
And Menelaus, good host that he was, got up from beside
The lovely blonde Helen, and went out to see his guests.
When the princely son of Odysseus saw him approaching,
He quickly put on his bright tunic, threw a great cloak
Around his sturdy shoulders, and hurried to meet him.
Then the dear son of godly Odysseus spoke:
    "Zeus-fed Atrides, Menelaus, leader of many,
I want you to send me back now to my own dear country.
My heart is most eager to go."
    And Menelaus, quick
To be helpful, replied: "Telemachus, I certainly won't keep you
Here any longer when you want so much to return.
In fact, I blame any host who overdoes his esteem
Or disgust. Moderation is always best. It's just
As bad to detain a visitor eager to go
As it is to get rid of company that wants to stay
Awhile longer. One ought to make a willing guest want
To stay, and the guest who is ready to leave he should help
On his way. But wait till you see the exquisite things
I'll bring and put in your chariot, and I'm going to have
The women prepare, from the plenty within, a meal
In the palace. Such will be honor and glory to me,
And you'll be glad you waited, for a man should eat something
Before he starts over the broad and boundless earth.
And if you think you'd enjoy a tour through Hellas
And central Argos, I'll go along myself.
I'll hitch up my horses and show you all the big towns.
And nobody we visit will send us away empty-handed.

Each host will give us at least one gift—some splendid
Tripod or cauldron of bronze, or a pair of mules,
Or a golden chalice."
    Then thoughtful Telemachus answered:
"Zeus-fed son of Atreus, great Menelaus,
I think I'd rather go home at once, for I left
No one there to guard my belongings. In this effort to find
My godlike father, I don't want to lose my own life,
Nor do I wish to lose from my palace some noble
Treasure."
    When the warrior-host Menelaus saw how
His guest felt, he bade his wife and her maids to take
Of the plenty within and prepare a meal in the palace.
At that moment, his neighbor, Boëthous' son Eteoneus,
Who had just got out of his bed, came up, and Menelaus
Asked him to start a fire and roast some meat,
Which he wasn't unwilling to do. Meanwhile, Menelaus
Went down to the fragrant vault where his treasures were stored—
But not alone, for with him went Helen and Megapenthes.
Once there, the King picked up a two-handled cup
And told his son Megapenthes to bring a silver
Wine-bowl. Helen went to the chests where she kept
The richly embroidered gowns that she herself
Had carefully worked. Then that exquisite lady
Got out the most flowing and beautifully embroidered of all
And carried it with her. It lay beneath all the others,
But now like a star it glittered. Then they went back
Through the house to Telemachus, and tawny-haired Menelaus
Spoke to him thus:
    "Telemachus, about your return—
May Zeus, the thundering husband of Hera, bring
You home, just as you wish. And of all treasures
Here in my house, I'll give you the one most gorgeous
And precious. I'll give you a richly wrought wine-bowl, solid

Silver, with ribs and rim of gold, the work
Of Hephaestus, given to me by royal Phaedimus,
The Sidonians' King, when on my way home I stayed
At this house for a while. Now I want you to have it."
    So heroic Atrides placed the two-handled cup
In the hands of Telemachus, strong Megapenthes brought
The bright wine-bowl of silver and set it before him, and Helen,
So fair of face, came up with the gown in her hands,
And spoke:
    "I too have a present for you, dear child,
That you may remember Helen and the work of her hands.
It's for your bride to wear on the day of the marriage
You long for. Until then, let your dear mother keep it
For you in the palace. And now I wish you a joyful
Return to your own native land and firm-founded home."
    With this she placed the gown in the hands of Telemachus,
Who was greatly thrilled to accept it. Prince Peisistratus
Took the gifts and stowed them away in the chariot,
Marveling at them in his heart. Then their tawny-haired host
Showed them inside and offered them chairs both reclining
And straight. When the two young men had sat down, a maid
Brought water in a golden pitcher and poured it out
Above a silver basin, that they might wash their hands,
And she drew up before them a polished table, on which
The respected housekeeper put generous helpings of bread
And other good things to eat. Boëthous' son,
Close by, carved and divided the meat into helpings,
While the son of renowned Menelaus poured wine. They all
Enjoyed the good things spread out before them, but when
They had eaten and drunk as much as they wanted, Telemachus
And Nestor's glorious son harnessed the horses,
Stepped up in the carved and ornate car, and drove out
Through the gate and echoing columns. Atreus' son,
Tawny-haired Menelaus, walked after them, in his right hand

Holding a golden cup of honey-hearted wine,
That his guests might not leave without pouring
       libations. Standing
Beside the horses, he raised the cup and spoke:
    "Good-by, young men, and give my regards to Nestor,
Shepherd of the people, for truly he was as kind
As a father to me when we sons of Achaeans made war
In the land of Troy."
    And thoughtful Telemachus replied:
"We will surely tell him all this, O god-nourished King,
Just as you've told us to do. I only wish
That I were as sure of finding Odysseus at home
When I get to Ithaca, that I might tell him how I met
With everything gracious during my stay with you
And left loaded down with all these wonderful gifts."
    At that very moment a bird soared in from the right,
An eagle with talons embedded in a great white goose
From the yard, and a shouting crowd gave chase. The eagle
Flew straight for the chariot, then swiftly veered off to the right
In front of the horses. At this the hearts of host
And guest alike rejoiced and their spirits rose.
The first to speak was Nestor's son Peisistratus:
    "Decide, Menelaus, god-fostered leader of many,
And tell us for whom God shows this sign—for us
Or yourself?"
    He spoke, and Menelaus, the favorite of Ares,
Pondered the event and its meaning. But long-robed Helen
Spoke before he did: "Hear me, and I will tell you
The meaning put into my heart by the immortal gods,
The meaning that I believe future events
Will confirm. Just as this eagle came down from his native
Mountain and seized the tame and home-fed goose,
So shall Odysseus return to his home, after wandering
And suffering much, and exact from the wooers full payment,

Or else he is already home and sowing the seeds
Of evil for all of them!"
    Then thoughtful Telemachus:
"If the husband of Hera, loud-thundering Zeus, so wills,
Then there will I worship you like a goddess."
    He spoke,
And cracked the lash, and the horses took off through the town
At a gallop and ran briskly on to the plain. All day
They shook the yoke on their shoulders. Then, as the sun
Was setting and all the roads growing dark, they came
To Pherae and the house of Diocles, son of Ortilochus,
The son of Alpheus. There they stayed all night,
And he entertained them as guests should be entertained.
    But as soon as young Dawn touched the sky
        with her rosy fingers,
They harnessed the horses and mounted the colorful car.
Then out through the gates and echoing columns they drove.
Peisistratus cracked the lash and the horses sped on
Till soon they came to the tall towers of Pylos.
Then Telemachus spoke to the son of Nestor:
    "Peisistratus,
Will you do a favor for me? Because of our fathers'
Friendship, we also think of ourselves as old friends.
Then too, we're about the same age and this trip has brought us
Even closer together. So don't go by my ship,
My god-nourished Prince, but let me off there. For the old one
Wants so much to be gracious, he'll surely keep me
Whether I want to stay or not, and I must
Get started for home."
    He spoke, and the son of Nestor
Consulted his heart as to how to oblige his friend.
Having chosen the way that seemed best, he turned the horses
And drove down to the beach where the swift ship lay.
      There he took

The lovely gifts of Menelaus, the clothes and the gold,
And stored them away in the stern of the ship, then spoke
These winged words of advice to Telemachus:
        "Hurry up, now.
Go on board and order your crew aboard too,
Before I get home and have to tell the old man.
For I'm very sure that his spirit is too overbearing
To let you go. He'll come down here himself
And invite you up to the house, and believe me, he won't
Take no for an answer! In any event, he'll be more than
Annoyed."
        So saying, he drove his lovely-maned horses
Back to the city of Pylos and quickly came
To the palace. Meanwhile, Telemachus urgently called
To his comrades:
        "Get all the gear ready, men, and aboard
The black ship. Then let's go aboard ourselves and get started
For home."
        He spoke, and they eagerly did as he said.
Quickly they went aboard and took their seats
At the oars.
        Telemachus busied himself with all this,
And now at the stern of the ship he was praying and burning
A gift to Athena, when a stranger approached—a prophet,
But one who had killed a man and was fleeing from Argos.
This seer was descended from the line of Melampus, who was
At one time a very rich man in Pylos, mother
Of flocks. He had lived in a palace among the Pylians,
But great-hearted Neleus, the lordliest man alive,
Had forced him to leave his own country for a land of strangers,
And had taken much that was his and had held it for one
Full year. Meanwhile, Melampus lay painfully bound
In the house of Phylacus, suffering mighty woes
Because of the daughter of Neleus and the crushing blindness

251

Of soul that the furious goddess, home-wrecking Erinys,
Had inflicted upon him. Even so, he escaped that death
And drove the bellowing cattle from Phylace to Pylos.
There he avenged the cruelty of lordly Neleus
And brought home his daughter to be his own brother's wife.
But Melampus himself left home for a land of strangers,
Horse-pasturing Argos, where he was destined to live
And be King over many Argives. There he married,
Built a huge house, and begot two powerful sons,
Antiphates and Mantius. Antiphates begot great-hearted
Oïcles, and Oïcles man-marshaling Amphiaraus,
A man much loved and favored by aegis-bearing Zeus
As well as Apollo. Still, he failed to reach
So much as the threshold of old age, but died in Thebes,
The victim of a gift-loving wife, and left two sons,
Alcmaeon and Amphilochus. To Mantius were born Cleitus
And Polypheides. So remarkably handsome was Cleitus
That Dawn of the golden throne took him to live
Among the immortals. But Apollo made a prophet
Of gifted Polypheides, who was much the best man alive
After the death of Amphiaraus. Having quarreled
With his father, Polypheides left for Hyperesia, where he lived
And prophesied for all mortals.

      It was his son
Theoclymenus who now came up to Telemachus, whom he found
At prayer and libations by the swift black ship, and spoke to
With these winged words:

      "Friend, since I find you burning
An offering here, I beseech you by that burnt-offering
And the god it's for, and by your own life and the lives
Of the friends who are with you, be frank and answer my questions
Truly. Who are you and where are you from? Your city,
Your parents, where are they?"

      And thoughtful Telemachus answered:

"Sir, I'll tell you all this quite frankly. I was born
In Ithaca, and my father is Odysseus—if there ever was
An Odysseus. Now, though, he's come to some miserable end,
Which is why I have taken these men and this black ship
And come in search of some word concerning him,
My father, who has been away for so long."
        Then the sacred
Seer Theoclymenus: "I too have left my own country.
I killed one of my kinsmen, and horse-pasturing Argos
Is full of his brothers and cousins, a powerful clan
Who lord it among the Achaeans. It was to avoid
Death and black fate at their hands that I fled and became
A wanderer on the face of the earth. But since I have come
To you as a suppliant, put me aboard your ship.
If you don't, they'll surely make short work of me,
For they must be close on my trail."
        And thoughtful Telemachus:
"Then you may be sure I'll not turn one so desperate
Away from my ship. Come on, you're welcome to what
We have, such as it is."
        So saying, he took
The stranger's bronze spear and laid it at length on the deck
Of the well-balanced ship. Then aboard the seaworthy vessel
He went, took his seat in the stern, and sat Theoclymenus
Beside him. His men cast off from the stern, and Telemachus
Called out to them to man the tackling. Quickly
They did so, raising the mast of fir, setting
It firm in the socket, and binding it down with forestays.
With halyards of twisted ox-hide they hauled up the white sail,
And bright-eyed Athena sent a fast-following wind
That blew through the fair sky briskly and carried them swiftly
Over the salt sea-water toward their destination.
So they sailed on past Crouni and the beautiful streams
Of Chalcis.

As the sun went down and all the sea-lanes
Grew dark, the ship, still running on before
The god-sent wind, sailed close by Pheae and on past
Splendid Elis, where Epeans are powerful, and on past
Islands that flitted by in the dark, with Telemachus
Wondering whether he would get home alive, or be taken.

Meanwhile, Odysseus and the noble swineherd were having
Their supper in the lodge with the others. When they had eaten
And drunk all they wanted, Odysseus spoke, in an effort
To find out what he might expect of the swineherd, whether he
Would go on being gracious and ask him to stay at the farm,
Or whether he would send him on to the city:

"Now listen,
Eumaeus, and you other men, too. In the morning I want
To go into town and beg, before I make paupers
Of all of you. But I would appreciate your advice
And someone to show me the way. Once there, I'll have to
Make my way through the city alone, in hope
Of a handout, a cup of water and crust of bread.
And I'd like to go to the palace of sacred Odysseus
And give what news I have to wise Penelope.
In fact, in hope of a meal, I might even mix
With those insolent suitors, since they have such great plenty.
You can be sure I'd do both quickly and well
Any job they might have for me there, and believe me, by favor
Of the messenger Hermes, who gives both grace and glory
To the labors of all, no man alive can touch me
When it comes to serving—building up a fire, splitting
Dry wood, carving, cooking, pouring—I'm best
At all things humble men do for those above them."

This moved you deeply, Eumaeus, and you answered
          him thus:
"Ah, my guest, how can you have such a thought?
If you really want to join that mob of wooers,

Whose pride and violence reach the iron sky, then you must
Want to die in the process. Their servants are not your kind,
But all young and handsome, with fancy clothes and grease
On their hair, and they wait on gleaming tables, loaded down
With bread and meat and wine. So stay here with us.
You're no bother to anyone here, not to me
Or my men. Then, when the son of Odysseus comes home,
He'll give you a cloak and tunic to wear and send you
Wherever your heart and soul most want to be."

    And noble, long-suffering Odysseus replied: "I hope,
Eumaeus, that you may be as dear to Father
Zeus as you are to me for putting an end
To my wanderings and terrible hardships. No life is worse
Than that of a tramp, yet a man will endure much wandering
And misery and pain for the sake of his wretched belly.
But come, since you want me to stay and wait for your master,
Tell me about the mother of King Odysseus
And the father he left at home on the threshold of old age.
Can it be that the sun still shines on them, or are they
Already dead and in the halls of Hades?"

    Then the master herdsman answered: "Truly to you, sir,
I'll tell what I know. Laertes is still alive,
But he spends his time at home, praying to Zeus
That life may leave his limbs, so great is his grief
For the son he lost and that wise lady his wife,
Whose death it was that hurt him most of all
And brought him to raw old age before his time.
She wasted away with grief for her gallant son
And died a most miserable death—may no other friend
Of mine ever die as she did. But while that unhappy
Lady was living, I used to take pleasure in asking
How she was, for she raised me herself, along with
Ctimene of the flowing gowns, her own splendid daughter
And youngest child. We were brought up together,

255

And I was treated pretty much as one of the family.
When we two reached that yearned-for marriageable age,
They sent her to settle in Samos, and received in return
Bridal gifts beyond counting. But to me my lady gave
A handsome cloak and tunic and a pair of sandals
And sent me out to the farm, though in her heart
She loved me more than ever. Now I miss
All that, though the blessed gods have prospered my work here,
So that I've had enough to eat and drink
And give to sacred strangers. Still, nothing nice
Ever comes to me from my mistress, no word or deed,
Since on the house that plague of proud men fell.
And servants long to chat with their mistress and learn
What's going on, to eat and drink a bit
And afterwards take something home with them to the farm.
Such never fails to warm the heart of a servant."
    Then resourceful Odysseus answered: "But you were so little,
Eumaeus, to go so far from your home and your parents.
Tell me exactly what happened. Was some broad-wayed city
Sacked, in which your father and lady mother
Were living? Or did a crew of pirates catch you
Alone with your sheep or cattle and carry you off
In their ship to the house of this man you speak of, from whom
They got a good price?"
    And the master herdsman replied:
"Sir, since your interest in me seems real, sit
Where you are and quietly enjoy your wine. These nights
Are unspeakably long, so there's plenty of time both to sleep
And enjoy good stories. Anyway, too much sleep
Is no good for a man. You other men, if you'd rather,
Go out and sleep till dawn, then get some breakfast
And take out our master's swine. As for us, we'll sit here
Eating and drinking and recalling delightful old stories
Of our grievous misfortunes. It can be very sweet for a man

256

Whose wanderings and woes have been many to remember
      the hardships
He had in earlier days. So I'll start by answering
Your questions.
      "Perhaps you've heard of an island called Syria,
Far in the West beyond Ortygia where the Sun,
Going down, turns in his course. It's not any too full
Of people, but a fine land for all that, rich in cattle
And sheep, flowing with wine, and full of wheat.
Famine's unknown and no loathsome disease ever comes
To make folks wretched. When people grow old in the cities
There, silver-bowed Apollo comes with Artemis
And lays them low with his painless arrows. The cities
Are two, and everything there is divided between them.
Over all my father was King, Ormenus' son
Ctesius, a man, but like the immortals. To that island
Came swindling ship-famous Phoenicians, with a whole
      black boat-load
Of trinkets. In my father's house was a handsome woman
Of their race, tall and wonderfully skillful, but she
Was taken in by the slippery Phoenicians. First,
One of them made love to her, while she
Was supposed to be washing out clothes, and seduced her there
By the hollow ships, and such is enough to change
The mind of a woman, however well-intentioned. Then
He asked who she was and where she was from, and at once
She pointed to the high-roofed house of my father, and said:
      " 'I'm from Sidon, where bronze is so plentiful, and
      the daughter of Arybas,
A most affluent man. But coming in from the fields
One day, I was seized by Taphian pirates and carried off
To that house over there, where they sold me to him who owns it
And got a very good price.'
      "Then her seducer:

257

'So won't you go back with us to your home and see
The high-roofed house of your father and mother, see them,
In fact? For believe me, they're still alive and people say
Rich as ever.'

"And she answered: 'I might very well,
If you sailors will swear that you'll get me home safe and sound.'

"All of them swore the oath she required. Then again
The woman: 'Quiet now, and if any of you happen to meet me
On the street, or perhaps at the well, don't speak, for someone
Might go to the palace and tell the old King, who would probably
Get suspicious, put me in painful bonds,
And find some way of destroying you. So remember
My words, and exchange your freight for homeward cargo
As fast as you can. Then as soon as your ship is loaded,
Quickly send a message to me at the palace. I promise
To bring all the gold I can lay my hands on, to pay
For my passage, and something else besides. The King
Has a bright little boy, whom I look after at home
And take out to play. I'll fetch him along on the ship.
He'll bring a fine price, no matter in what foreign land
You sell him.'

"With this, she returned to the beautiful palace.
The traders stayed a full year and got many fine things
In their hollow ship. When it was full and ready
To go, they sent a man with word for the woman.
One of the sliest, he showed up at my father's house
With a golden necklace strung with amber. Then,
While the palace maids and my royal mother were handling
And admiring and bargaining for the necklace, he nodded
To the woman. This done, he left for the hollow ship,
And she took my hand and led me outdoors. In the front hall
She found some cups and tables of my father and his men,
Who had feasted before leaving for the public forum. Quickly
She hid in her bosom three goblets and went out, and I

Was foolish enough to follow. The sun was setting
And all the streets getting dark as we hurried down
To the excellent harbor, where the fast Phoenician ship
Was lying. They put us aboard and set out, sailing
The sea-lanes with a wind from Zeus for six days and six nights.
But when Zeus, son of Cronos, brought in the seventh
       day, Artemis
The archer struck the woman, and she dropped in the bilge
With a splash, like a gull in the sea. Then over the side
They heaved her, a lucky find for fish and the seals,
But I was left with a heart more wretched than ever.
Wind and wave bore them on and brought them to Ithaca
Where wealthy Laertes bought me. And that's how I got
My first sight of this country."
      Then Zeus-sprung Odysseus replied:
"Eumaeus, this story of the truly great woes your spirit
Has known moves me deeply. But surely for you
Zeus has matched the evil with good, for though
Your misery was much, you came to the house of a kindly
Man, who makes sure that you have enough to eat
And drink, and so you live very well. But I
Have come here after wandering through countless cities all over
The world."
      Thus they talked, till at last they lay down to sleep,
Though not for long, for Dawn of the beautiful throne
Came soon.
      Meanwhile, the comrades of Telemachus drew in
To shore, quickly took down the sail and the mast,
And rowed the ship to her moorings. They threw out
      the anchor-stones
And tied up to shore from the stern. Then they stepped out
On the surf-pounded beach, fixed their breakfast and mixed
The sparkling wine. When they had eaten and drunk

All they wanted, thoughtful Telemachus spoke first:
    "You men
Row the black ship around to the city. I'll see
How the farms and the herdsmen are doing and come into town
This evening after I've seen the estate. In the morning,
As a token of my thanks, I'll give you all a fine feast
Of meat and sweet wine."
    Then godlike Theoclymenus spoke:
"And where, dear child, shall I go, to the house of which prince
In rocky Ithaca? Or shall I go straight to the house
You share with your mother?"
    And thoughtful Telemachus answered:
"If things were different, I'd tell you to go to our house,
Where there's certainly no lack of entertainment. But now
      I'd be doing you
No favor, since I won't be there myself, and my mother
Won't see you. She seldom appears in the house where the wooers
Can see her, but stays upstairs at her loom, away
From them. I'll tell you, though, of another to whom
You may go, the brilliant son of fiery Polybus,
Eurymachus, to whom the Ithacans look as to
A god. He's quite the superior man and most anxious
To marry my mother and gain the prestige of Odysseus.
But only Olympian Zeus, whose house is the sky,
Knows which will be first—that marriage or doomsday
      for the wooers."
    As he was speaking, a bird flew by on the right,
A hawk, Apollo's swift messenger. His talons were deep
In a dove, from which the feathers fell in a path
Halfway between the ship and Telemachus. At this
Theoclymenus called the young Prince apart from his friends,
Clasped his hand warmly, and spoke:
    "Telemachus, it wasn't
Without God's will that this bird flew by on the right,

A truly ominous bird if I ever saw one.
Surely there is no line in Ithaca so kingly
As yours, and yours is the ruling house here for all time!"
       And thoughtful Telemachus replied: "May it be as
          you say, sir,
And if it is, you'll soon be aware of my kindness,
For so many will be my gifts to you that everyone
You meet will call you blessed."
       Then he turned
To his loyal friend Peiraeus, and said: "Peiraeus,
Son of Clytius, of all the men who went with me
To Pylos, you have been the most helpful, so now,
If you will, please make this guest of mine at home
In your halls, and until I arrive, see that he's honored
In every way."
       And spear-famous Peiraeus replied:
"No matter how long you stay out here, Telemachus,
I'll entertain him and make sure that nothing is lacking
In our hospitable welcome."
       So saying, he went
On board, bidding the rest of the crew to follow
And cast off from the stern. Soon they were all aboard
And in their places. Then, when Telemachus had bound on
His beautiful sandals and taken from the deck of the ship
His strong bronze-pointed spear, the men released
The ship-to-shore moorings, and shoving off sailed on
To the city, as they had been told to do by sacred
Odysseus' dear son Telemachus, who now walked on
With a rapid stride until he came to the farmyard
And his numerous swine, among whom the loyal swineherd
Was accustomed to sleep, with no ill will toward his masters.

BOOK

XVI

ODYSSEUS AND
TELEMACHUS

That morning at dawn, Odysseus and the worthy swineherd
Had kindled a fire and got the herdsmen off
With the droves of swine, and now they were fixing their breakfast.
As Telemachus approached, the loud-voiced hounds, instead
Of barking, began to wag their tails and fawn,
And alert Odysseus, hearing the sound of footsteps,
Noticed the fawning dogs and immediately spoke
To Eumaeus these winged words:
    "Eumaeus, surely
Some friend of yours is coming, or at least someone
Who's known here, for instead of barking, the dogs are wagging
Their tails, and I can hear footsteps."
    He had not finished speaking
When his own dear son stood in the doorway. The herdsman
Sprang up in amazement, dropping the bowls in which
He was mixing the sparkling wine. Then he went to greet
His master. His eyes brimming over with tears, he kissed
The young man's head, both beautiful eyes, and both hands.
As a loving father welcomes his own dear son

Who comes in the tenth long year from far abroad,
An only son, for whom he has suffered much,
Even so the worthy swineherd hugged Telemachus
And covered him with kisses, as though he had just escaped death.
Then he spoke, in a trembling voice, these winged words:
      "Telemachus, sweet light, you're back at last! When you left
In that ship for Pylos, I never expected to see you
Again. But come in, come in, dear child, just back
From so far away, so that I can look at you
To my heart's content right here in this house. You
Leave town so seldom to visit the farm and the herdsmen,
It's as though you enjoyed watching that pestilent mob
Of wooers."
      And thoughtful Telemachus answered him thus:
"So be it, good father. It's because of you that I've come,
That I might see you myself and find out from you
Whether my mother is still at home, or whether
She's already married some other man and left
The unmade bed of Odysseus for filthy cobwebs
To cover."
      And the master swineherd replied: "She's still
At home, all right, and patient as ever, though she
Still weeps away the miserable nights and days."
      Then Telemachus handed his spear to the herdsman
          and entered
Across the stone threshold. As he neared his father, Odysseus
Got up to give him a seat, but Telemachus stopped him
And said:
      "Keep your seat, sir. We'll find another
Somewhere in our farmhouse. In fact, here's just the man
To fix us one."
      He spoke, and Odysseus went back
And sat down, and when the swineherd had piled up
         green brushwood

And covered it with a fleece, the dear son of Odysseus
Sat down. Then before them Eumaeus set platters of pork
Left over from yesterday's meal, quickly heaped bread
In the baskets, mixed an ivy bowl of honey-sweet wine,
And sat down himself across from sacred Odysseus.
They all fell to and enjoyed the good things before them.
But when they had eaten and drunk as much as they wanted,
Telemachus said to the worthy swineherd:
          "Good father,
Where's your guest from? How did sailors get him
To Ithaca, and who did they say they were? I'm quite sure,
You know, that he didn't walk."
          Then, Eumaeus,
This was your answer: "To you, my child, I'll certainly
Tell the whole truth. He says he was born in broad Crete
And that he has wandered through countless cities all over
The world. Such is the life some god has spun
For him. Now, though, he's managed to slip away
From a Thesprotian ship and come to my lodge. I
Turn him over to you, to do with as you wish. He considers
Himself a suppliant of yours."
          And thoughtful Telemachus:
"Eumaeus, what you say hurts me deeply, for how can I welcome
This stranger at my house when I'm not at all sure that I am
Either old or strong enough to protect myself
Against a man's wanton and wrathful attack? And the heart
Of my mother is still undecided, whether to stay
And keep house for me, respecting the bed of her husband
And public opinion, or whether to go on and marry
The best and most generous of those Achaeans who woo her
In the palace. But since this stranger has come to your house,
I'll give him a good cloak and tunic to wear, a pair
Of sandals, and a two-edged sword, and I'll see that he gets
Wherever his heart and soul tell him to go. Or,

If you'd rather, you can take care of him here at the farm,
And I'll send clothes for him and all of his food,
So that he won't exhaust the supplies of you and your men.
But I won't allow him to go and mix with the wooers.
They have more than their share of stupid arrogance, and if
They should taunt and make fun of him, it would grieve me
       greatly.
It's hard for one man to do much against so many,
No matter how strong he may be. To say the least,
Their advantage is great."
      Then noble, long-suffering Odysseus
Spoke to him thus: "My friend, I'm sure you won't mind
If I put in a word at this point. The way you say
The wooers carry on in your palace, and you such a fine man,
Has greatly upset me. But say, don't you care?
Or have all the people followed the voice of a god
And come to hate you? Or is it the fault of your brothers,
Whose fighting support you should have no matter how rough
Things get? I only wish that I were as young
As I feel and either the son of matchless Odysseus,
Or Odysseus himself—for whose return there's still hope.
Then any man could cut my head from my shoulders
If I didn't go to the halls of Laertes' son
Odysseus and make much trouble for all those men!
And if they did overwhelm me, with their many against
My one, why I'd much rather die, slain
In my own palace, than go on watching these constantly
Horrible things, strangers roughly mistreated,
Slave women shamefully dragged through the lovely halls,
Wine drawn off and wasted, bread devoured—
And the whole wretched mess without point, purpose, or end!"
      Then thoughtful Telemachus: "I'll certainly set you
       straight, sir,
And that quite frankly. No, all the people

265

Don't hate me, nor do I blame brothers, whose fighting support
One should have no matter how rough things get. Zeus has kept
Our house alive through a line of only sons.
Arceisius had but one son, Laertes, who had
But one, Odysseus, who also had only one—
Me, in whom he had little joy before leaving
Our halls for the war. So now you know why our house
Is swarming with blackguards. All the island princes,
From Dulichium, Samos, and wooded Zacynthus, as well as
The powerful lords in craggy Ithaca—all
Are wooing my mother and wasting my wealth. So far
She neither refuses their loathsome offers completely,
Nor can she make up her mind and end them. Meanwhile,
They're devouring my house and soon will utterly ruin me.
These things, though, all lie in the lap of the gods.
But now, Eumaeus, I want you to go with speed
To gifted Penelope and tell her she has me back safe
From Pylos. I'll stay here, and when you have told her—
And her alone—come back. See to it that none
Of the other Achaeans hears it, for many of them
Would welcome the chance to harm me."

      Then, Eumaeus,
This was your answer: "I know what you mean. You're talking
To a man of some sense. But tell me frankly what you think
About my taking the news to poor old Laertes,
Who greatly grieved for Odysseus but still looked over
The crops from time to time and ate and drank
With the slaves on the place when he had a mind to. But since
The day you left in that ship for Pylos, they say
He will no longer eat and drink as he did, or look over
The crops occasionally. Now he just sits around
All the time, moaning and groaning and weeping the flesh
From his bones."

      And prudent Telemachus answered him thus:

"I'm sorry indeed to hear that, but in spite of our grief
We'd better let him alone. If it were at all possible
For mortals to have whatever they wished for, our first wish
Would be for the day of my father's return. No,
When you've told Penelope, come back here to the lodge,
And don't go wandering the fields in search of Laertes.
But tell my mother to send her servant the housekeeper
Secretly out to tell the old one."

      These words
Got the herdsman going. He bound on his sandals and left
For the city. Nor was it unknown to Athena that swineherd
Eumaeus was no longer at home. She now approached
The lodge in the form of a lovely woman, tall
And wonderfully skillful, and stood out beyond the door
Where Odysseus could see her. Telemachus neither saw nor felt
Anything unusual, since the gods by no means appear
To all in such visible form. But Odysseus and the dogs,
They saw her, and the dogs, too frightened to bark, slunk
        whimpering
Away to the far side of the yard. Then Odysseus saw her
Nod, and leaving the lodge he went out beyond
The high wall of the yard till he stood in her presence, and Athena
Spoke to him thus:

      "Zeus-sprung son of Laertes,
Resourceful Odysseus, now is the time to reveal
Yourself to your son in all frankness, so that you two
May plot death and doom for the wooers before you enter
The famous city. I'll join you soon myself,
For that's a battle I'm really most eager for!"

      Then, with a touch of her golden wand, Athena
Changed his rags to a fresh clean cloak and tunic
And renewed his physique and youthful vigor. Once again
His face filled out, his color returned, and the beard
On his chin grew dark. This done, she departed, and Odysseus

267

Re-entered the lodge. There his dear son was astounded,
And fearing that a god was before him he looked away
And spoke:
    "You seem quite different, stranger, than you did
Just now. Your clothes are all changed and your color is not
What it was. Surely you're one of the sky-ruling gods.
Be merciful then, that we may give golden gifts,
Richly wrought, and fittingly sacrifice to you. But spare us,
Please."
    And patient, noble Odysseus replied:
"I'm no god. Why compare me with the immortals?
But I am your father, for whom you've groaned and suffered
Much, the victim of violent men!"
    So saying,
He kissed his son, and the tears he'd completely held back
Until now rolled down his cheeks to the ground. But Telemachus,
Who couldn't as yet believe that this was his father,
Spoke to him thus:
    "But you're not my father Odysseus.
Some demon *is* trying to trick me, so that I can grieve
And groan even more. No mere mortal could do
What you've done without help from some god, one who
        could easily
Make him young or old as he pleased. Just now
You were old and dressed in rags, but now you really
Do resemble the gods who rule the wide sky."
    Then Odysseus, always resourceful, spoke to his son:
"Telemachus, you have no real reason for so much amazement
And wonder that I, your father, am here in the house.
You can be very sure that no other Odysseus will ever
Come here. But I am home at last, after all that
Wandering and pain, back in the twentieth year
In my own country. These changes, of course, are the work
Of conquering Athena, who makes me look as she pleases—

Now like a tramp, then again like a well-dressed young man.
It's no trouble at all for the sky-ruling gods to ennoble
A man or degrade him."
    With this, he sat down, and Telemachus
Threw his arms around his father and wept,
And they both gave in to a longing for sobbing and wailing
With cries more constant than those of birds, sea-hawks
Or taloned eagles, when farm folk take their fledglings
From the nest—nor were the tears of those two
Any less pitiful. And now they would surely have wept
The sun away, if Telemachus had not come up soon
With these questions:
    "But tell me, dear father, what kind of ship
Did you come in? Who did the sailors that brought you say
They were? For of course nobody gets here on foot."
    Then patient Odysseus replied: "Son, I'll tell you
Exactly. Phaeacians brought me, ship-famous men
Who help on their way all who come to them.
While I was asleep, they brought me over the sea
In a fast ship of theirs and landed me in Ithaca.
And they gave me wonderful presents, lots of bronze,
Garments, and gold, which, by grace of the gods,
Lie hidden in caves. Now I've come here, as Athena
Thinks best, to plan with you the death of our enemies.
So come now, tell me about the wooers, who
They are and how many, that I may honestly face
The facts and decide whether we'll be a match for them
By ourselves, or whether we'd better look around for others
To help us."
    Then Telemachus, prudent as ever, replied:
"Father, all my life I've heard what a wise,
Spear-wielding warrior you are, but now you're going
Too far, even for you. What you say astounds me.
Against men so many and strong, we two would not

Have a chance! For there aren't just ten of those men, or twice
That number, but more, many more. How many I'll tell you
Right here and now. There are fifty-two able young men
From Dulichium, and with them six servants, twenty-four more
From Samos, twenty young Achaeans from Zacynthus, and a dozen
From Ithaca itself, all of them princes, and Medon
The herald is with them, and a sacred bard, and two squires,
Skillful in the carving of meat. If we battle all these
In the palace, I'm afraid our taking their violence to task
Will indeed be bitter and baleful, but for us, not them!
So please try to think of someone to help us, preferably
One who'd be not only willing but eager."

    And long-suffering Odysseus replied: "All right, I have
A question I'd like you to hear and consider. Will Athena
And Father Zeus be enough on our side, or should I
Try to think of some other helper?"

    Then Telemachus,
That tactful young man, replied: "These helpers you mention
Are certainly good ones, even though they rule all mankind
And the immortal gods from way up there in the clouds."

    And again the staunch Odysseus: "Don't worry, those two
Will soon be present, once we begin in my halls
The screaming struggle to see whom Ares favors,
Us or the wooers. But tomorrow at dawn I want you
To go to the palace and mix with the wooers. Later on
The swineherd will lead me to town disguised as a beggar,
Old and miserable. And no matter how badly they treat me,
You must not interfere. Even if they haul me by the feet
Through the house and out of the door, or hit me with things
They throw, you just stand by and watch. Of course
You can tell them to stop their senseless behavior and gently
Try to dissuade them with words. But they won't pay any
Attention to you at all: for truly the day
Of their doom has all but arrived! And here's something else

I want you to keep in mind. When wise Athena
Tells me it's time, I'll give you a nod. At this signal
Take all the weapons of war that lie in the hall
And put them away in the inmost recess of the lofty
Storeroom. Then, when the wooers miss them and begin
Asking questions, put them off with as soft an answer
As possible, saying:

      " 'I've taken them out of the smoke,
Since wherever the fire's breath has touched them, they're all
          smutched up,
And they don't look at all as they did when Odysseus left
For Troy. Then too, Cronos' son has put this greater
Concern in my heart, that you may be in your cups
And get to fighting among yourselves, thus wounding
One another and bringing disgrace on your feast and yourselves
As wooers. For iron just naturally draws a man to it.'

    "For us, though, leave a sword and spear apiece
And two leather shields where we can make a break
For them and arm ourselves, while Pallas Athena
And all-knowing Zeus cast a spell on the wooers. And here's
Something else I want you to keep in mind. If you're really
My son and one of our blood, don't tell a soul
That Odysseus is back in the palace. Don't let Laertes
Know, or the swineherd, or anyone there in the household,
Including Penelope herself. The two of us
Will find out whose side the women are on, and together
We'll check on the farmhands to see who still cares for us,
Who reveres us, and who has no regard for me
And nothing but scorn for a Prince so young as yourself."

    And his gifted son replied: "Father, when you know
Me better, you'll see that I'm neither a fool nor a coward.
But I don't think what you suggest will do either of us
Any good, and so I ask you to please reconsider.
While you go wandering around all that time from farm

To farm testing the men, those gluttons in the palace
Are perfectly free to go on devouring your home,
Nor will their overreaching spare anything you have.
I do think you ought to check on the women, though,
As to which have dishonored you and which are innocent.
But as for the men on the farms, I would much rather
See to them later, if you've really had a sign
From aegis-bearing Zeus."
    While they were talking, the ship
So sturdy that brought Telemachus and all his friends
From Pylos put into port. Having crossed the deep harbor,
They drew the black ship well up on the shore, and squires
Gladly unloaded the gear and carried the handsome
Gifts straight to the house of Clytius. And for fear
Wise Penelope might be alarmed and let the tears flow,
They sent a herald to tell the good Queen that Telemachus
Was at the farm and had told them to sail the ship
Around to the city. So the herald and worthy swineherd
Met, both bound for the Queen with similar news.
But when they got to the palace of the sacred King,
The herald no sooner found himself mid the handmaids
Than he called out, and said: "Even now, O Queen,
Your son is back from Pylos!"
    But the swineherd walked up
To Penelope and told her all that her son had asked him
To tell her. This done, he went out through the hall and the yard
And returned to the swine.
    The surprised and unhappy wooers
Left the hall and walked out behind the high wall
Of the yard. There, in front of the gates, they sat down,
And Eurymachus, son of Polybus, began:
    "My friends,
Brash Telemachus has done a great deed, completed
The journey we said he'd never complete. But come,

Let's launch a black ship, our best one, and round up some sailors
To row out and tell the others to get back here
Immediately."
  These words were scarcely out of his mouth
When Amphinomus happened to turn in his place and see
A ship already in the deep harbor, with men
Aboard her furling the sail and manning the oars.
Laughing lightly, he spoke to the comrades around him:
  "No need for a message now! They're already back.
Either they heard the news from some god, or spotted
The ship going by and then were unable to catch her."
  They all got up and went down to the shore, where quickly
They beached the black ship. Then, while proud squires unloaded
The armor, the wooers went in a body to the place
Of assembly, nor would they let anyone else, whether young
Or old, sit with them there. Eupeithes' son
Antinous now addressed them:
  "Confound it all!
Just look how the gods have saved this man from destruction.
Day after day and watch after watch, our look-outs
Sat on the windy crags, and not one night
Did we spend ashore, but always from sundown to dawn
We scoured the sea in our swift ships that we
Might ambush Telemachus and put him to death. Meanwhile,
A god brings him home. But right here and now let us plan
Woeful destruction for Telemachus, some certain death
He cannot escape, for I don't think we can finish
This business of ours while he's alive. His mind
Is a good one and he knows how to use it, and the people no longer
Bear us any good will at all. So come,
Before he gets the Achaeans together in a meeting,
Nor will he be slow to do so. He's an angry man now,
And when he gets up among them and tells how we plotted
His death and then couldn't catch him—when they hear, I say,

273

Our evil deeds, nobody there will have
A good word for us. In fact, we'll be lucky to find
Ourselves uninjured and not in exile somewhere
Among strangers. So come now, let us act first and get him
In a field well out from town, or on the road.
We could then divide his estate in all fairness among us
And give the house to his mother and the man she marries.
But if you don't like this plan and would rather he lived
And kept what belonged to his fathers, then let us stop gathering
Here and eating these splendid dinners. Let us all
Go home and try to win his mother with gifts
Of our own, until she marries the man who offers
The most and is destined to be her husband."

      He spoke,
But for a while nobody else said a word.
Then Amphinomus addressed the assembly. He
Was the brilliant son of King Nisus, son of Aretias,
And led the wooers from the fertile grain and grass lands
Of Dulichium. Penelope's favorite and a man of excellent
Sense, he now, in an effort to help, addressed them:

      "My friends, if I were you, I surely would not
Kill Telemachus. King-killing is a terrible thing!
In any event, let us try first of all to discover
The will of the gods. If the oracles of almighty Zeus
Are for it, I'll not only urge all of you on—I'll kill him
Myself! But if the gods withhold their approval,
I advise you all to lay off."

      Thus Amphinomus,
And the wooers liked what he said. They got up and re-entered
The house of Odysseus, where again they all sat down
In the gleaming chairs.

      Now prudent Penelope changed
Her mind and decided to visit her horribly proud
And insolent suitors. For Medon the herald overheard

Their scheming, and he had told the Queen all about
The murderous plot in the palace against her son.
So down to the hall she went, and her women with her.
There, by one of the pillars of the massive roof,
The lovely lady stood before the wooers,
Her face partly concealed by a shining veil,
And called Antinous by name, rebuking him thus:
     "Antinous, you trouble-maker! you insolent
          overreacher! it's hard
To believe that you're the one folks call the smartest
And most eloquent young man in Ithaca, slave of greed
That you are! How could you weave that fatal plot
Against Telemachus, and show no regard at all
For those in need of help and sacred to Zeus?
Such weaving of evil plots is gross impiety.
Don't you know that your own father once came
To this house as a suppliant, scared half to death of the people?
He had joined with Taphian pirates in raiding our friends
The Thesprotians, and the people were furious at him and ready
To tear out his heart and completely devour his estate,
Which was large and delightful. But Odysseus restrained them
          and kept
That bloodthirsty mob from violence—the same Odysseus
Whose home you're now so meanly consuming, whose wife
You're wooing, and whose son you are trying to kill! You've already
Caused me worry enough, believe me. So I'm telling
You now—let this be all, and you tell the others!"
     Then Polybus' son Eurymachus answered the Queen:
"Wise Penelope, daughter of Icarius, cheer up,
And don't let these things disturb you so deeply. As long as
I live and see light on this earth, no man alive
Or yet to be born shall lay a hand on your son
Telemachus. For I give you my word here and now that such
A man's black blood would soon be flowing about

275

My spear. Many's the time that city-sacking Odysseus
Took me on his lap, put roasted meat in my hands,
And held red wine to my lips. Telemachus, then,
Is the dearest friend I have, and I assure you
He certainly need not fear death, at least from the wooers.
From the gods, no man can avoid it."

      Thus he spoke
These words of comfort, though he himself was plotting
Death for her son. So she went back upstairs
To her bright chamber, where she wept for her dear husband
Odysseus, till blue-eyed Athena shed sweet sleep
On her lids.

      That evening the worthy swineherd got back
To Odysseus and his son, who had slaughtered a yearling pig
And were busy preparing supper. But before the herdsman
Could arrive and recognize Odysseus, Athena came up
And with a touch of her wand made him old again and clothed
In filthy rags. For she was afraid the secret
Might be too much for Eumaeus, who might go off
With the news to constant Penelope.

      Telemachus was first
To greet him: "My good Eumaeus, you're back. What
Is the news in town? Have the wooers, those manly fellows,
Returned from their ambush, or are they still waiting out there
To take me on my way home?"

      Then, Eumaeus,
This was your answer: "I had no desire to go
Through town asking questions. When I had delivered
      my message,
I wanted only to come back here at once.
I did fall in with a herald on the way, whom your crew
Had sent to run the news to your mother, and he
Was the first to tell her. And above the city, on the hill
Of Hermes, I saw something else—a swift ship, loaded

With men and shields and two-pointed spears, putting into
Our harbor. I thought at the time it must be the wooers,
But I really can't say for sure."

    At these words, the strong
And sacred young Prince glanced at his father and smiled,
But only when the swineherd was not looking.

    When the work was done and supper ready, they all
Sat down and found the meal quite equal to
Their excellent appetites. But when they were no longer hungry
Or thirsty, they began to think of their beds, and soon
Each one of them received the gift of sleep.

BOOK

XVII

FROM LODGE
TO PALACE

At the first red streaks of dawn, Odysseus' dear son
Telemachus, eager to be off for the city, fastened
His beautiful sandals, picked up the mighty spear
That fitted his hand so well, and spoke to his herdsman:
    "Good father, I'm going into town, so that my mother
Can see me. For I don't think she'll stop her woeful weeping
And wailing until she does. Now here's what I want
You to do. Lead this unfortunate stranger to the city,
Where he can beg his bread and water from anyone
Willing to give it. As for me, I can't be responsible
For everybody. I've troubles enough of my own. And if
This greatly angers the stranger, so much the worse
For him. At any rate, I like very much to speak frankly."
    Then resourceful Odysseus replied: "I assure you, friend,
I have no wish to stay here. Handouts in town
Are far more frequent than in the country, and I am
No longer young enough to live on a farm
And do all the chores some overseer tells me to do.
So go, and this man will do as you say and lead me,

But not till I've warmed myself at the fire and it's warmer
Outside. For these clothes of mine are so wretchedly ragged,
I'm afraid the morning frost might be too much
For me. And you say it's a long way into town."
   He spoke, and Telemachus strode rapidly out through
    the farm,
Brooding an evil end for the wooers. When he reached
The fair-lying palace, he leaned his spear against
A tall pillar and went inside across the threshold
Of stone.
   Eurycleia the nurse, spreading fleeces on the chairs
So curiously carved was far the first to see him.
Weeping, she hurried to meet him, and the other maids
Of stalwart Odysseus crowded around, tenderly
Welcoming him and kissing his head and shoulders.
   Then from her room came wise Penelope, like Artemis
Or golden Aphrodite, and with a burst of tears
She threw her arms about her darling boy,
Kissing his head and beautiful eyes, and sobbing
These winged words:
   "You're back, Telemachus! Sweet light,
You're back! I never expected to see you again
When you left in that ship for Pylos, so secretly and against
My will, to seek some word of your dear father.
But tell me what you've seen or heard of him."
   Then gravely came his reply: "Mother, please don't
Get me all upset when I've just escaped looming
Destruction. Instead, go bathe yourself and put on
Fresh clothes, then go upstairs with your ladies and promise
In prayer to all the gods that you will offer
Unblemished hecatombs, if ever Zeus fulfills
Our hopes of retribution. I'm going to the place of assembly
To invite a man home, one who came from Pylos
With me. I sent him on with my godlike companions

279

And told Peiraeus to entertain him at his house with honor
And every kindness until I arrived."

    He spoke,
But no winged words came back from his mother. She bathed
Herself, put on fresh clothes, then promised in prayer
To all the gods unblemished hecatombs, if ever
Zeus fulfilled their hopes of retribution.

    But Telemachus,
With spear in hand and two flashing-swift hounds at his heels,
Went out through the hall. And such was the heavenly grace
Athena shed on him that all the people
Gazed in wonder as he approached. The proud suitors
Crowded around him with praise on their lips and murder
Deep in their hearts. But he shouldered his way through the mob
And sat down with Mentor, Antiphus, and Halitherses,
His father's old friends, who asked him many questions
About the trip. Then spear-famous Peiraeus arrived
With the stranger, having walked with him through town
        to the place
Of assembly, and Telemachus got up at once to meet
His guest. But Peiraeus was the first to speak.

    "Telemachus,
As soon as you can, send some women to my house
And by them I'll send the gifts Menelaus gave you."

    But thoughtful Telemachus replied: "Peiraeus, none of us
Knows what's going to happen. Should the proud wooers
Secretly murder me in the palace and divide
What is rightfully mine, I would rather for you to keep
And enjoy those things than for one of them to get them.
But if I succeed in sowing fatal seeds of death
For them, then I'm sure that you'll be as glad to bring
Those gifts to my house as I will be happy to have them."

    With this, he led his weary fugitive guest
To the stately palace, where they threw their cloaks on the chairs,

Both reclining and straight, and entered the polished baths.
When the maids had bathed them and rubbed on the oil,
        they gave them
Tunics and fleecy warm mantles to wear. Then they left
The gleaming baths and sat down in the chairs, and a maid
Brought water in a golden pitcher and poured it out
Above a silver basin, that they might wash their hands,
And she drew up before them a polished table, whereon
The respected housekeeper put generous helpings of bread
And other good things to eat.
        Across from Telemachus,
By one of the hall's great pillars, his mother leaned back
In a chair, spinning fine thread on her distaff. And when
They had both enjoyed the good things lying before them
And were no longer hungry or thirsty, brooding Penelope
Was the first to speak:
        "Telemachus, I'm going upstairs
To my room and lie down on my bed—a bed of sorrow
And tears ever since the day Odysseus left
For Troy with the sons of Atreus. But still you have not
Seen fit to tell me—before my noble suitors
Come thronging in—what you may have heard concerning
Your father's return."
        And her thoughtful son replied:
"Mother, I'll tell you everything. We went to King Nestor,
The people's shepherd at Pylos, and he welcomed me
In his palace with every kindness. Even as a father
Might welcome his son just back from a long stay abroad,
So he and his splendid sons took care of me.
But concerning much-suffering Odysseus, living or dead,
He said he'd heard nothing from any part of the world.
So he sent me on with horses and car to the son
Of Atreus, spear-famous Menelaus. There I saw Helen
Of Argos, for whom, by will of the gods, the Argives

And Trojans labored so long. Then battle-roaring Menelaus
Asked me why I had come to lovely Lacedaemon,
And when I had told him quite frankly, he answered me thus:
    " 'What folly! for those cowards want to lie in the bed
Of a man truly valiant. It's as if a deer were to leave
Her suckling twin fawns asleep in the thicket-lair
Of a mighty lion and go out to graze on the hills
And in the green valleys, while the lion returns to his bed
And ferociously slaughters them both. Even so will Odysseus
Bring down a doom most wretched upon those men!
And now, O Father Zeus, Athena, and Apollo,
I pray that he may come among them with strength
Such as that he possessed when once in populous Lesbos
He wrestled a bout with Philomeleides and threw him
Crashing to the ground, with applause from all the Achaeans—
If only he might come among them with strength such as that,
Then would their wooing be bitter, and swift their destruction!
But concerning the matter of which you so earnestly ask,
I will not swerve from the truth or try to deceive you.
Of all the unerring old man of the sea told me,
Not a word will I conceal or keep from you.
He said he had seen Odysseus, most unhappy,
On the island and in the home of the nymph Calypso.
She keeps him by force, and he has no ship, no oars,
No comrades to help him get home over the sea's broad back.'
    "So spoke the son of Atreus, spear-famous Menelaus.
When I had done all this, I set sail for home,
With an excellent wind sent to me by the immortals,
Who quickly brought me back to my own dear country."
    These words deeply moved his mother's heart.
And now Theoclymenus the seer addressed her thus:
"O honored wife of Laertes' son Odysseus,
Menelaus has no clear vision of things such as these.
But listen to me, for I prophesy to you with knowledge

Unerring, concealing nothing. And I swear by Zeus,
The first among gods, and by this hospitable board
And hearth of Odysseus, that at this very moment
Odysseus is in his own dear country, at rest
Or afoot, learning of these evil deeds and planning
A day of reckoning for all the wooers—so signified
The bird of omen I saw from the well-decked ship,
And so I proclaimed it to Telemachus."

   And wise Penelope
Replied: "Ah sir, may it be as you describe it,
And if it is, you'll soon be aware of my kindness,
For so many will be my gifts to you that everyone
You meet will call you blessed."

   While they were talking,
The wooers were enjoying themselves with their usual arrogance
In front of the palace of Odysseus, there where the ground
Had been leveled, throwing the discus and javelin. But when
It was time for dinner, and the shepherds came in with their flocks
From all directions, Medon, the favorite herald
Of the wooers, who was frequently present at dinner-time,
Spoke to them thus:

   "Fellows, now that you've all
Had enough recreation, let us go to the house and fix dinner.
It's not unpleasant to have one's dinner on time."

   He spoke, and the wooers got up and did as he said.
Once in the stately palace, they threw their cloaks
On the chairs and couches and prepared the meal, slaughtering
Huge sheep, fat goats and pigs, and a heifer from the herd.

   Meanwhile, Odysseus and the worthy herdsman were about
To set out for town, when thus the master swineherd:
"Sir, since you're really anxious to go to the city
Today, as my master ordered, we'd better get started—
Though I'd rather leave you here to look after the farm,
If it weren't that I fear and respect my master so much

And know how unpleasant rebukes from masters can be.
So come, the day is already old, and the closer
To evening it gets, the colder you'll find it outside."

    Then resourceful Odysseus answered: "I know, I know.
You're talking to a sensible man. Let's go, and you
Be my guide all the way. But give me a staff to lean on,
If you have one somewhere that's already cut, for you said
The road is rugged and slippery in places."

    So saying,
About his shoulders he slung his grimy old pouch,
All torn and ragged and hanging by an old piece of rope,
And Eumaeus gave him a staff that suited him well.
Thus they set out for the city, leaving the dogs
And herdsmen to care for the farm, the swineherd leading
His King in the form of a wretched and ancient beggar,
Woefully dressed and hobbling along with a staff.

    As they walked down the stony path and drew near
The city, they came to a clear-flowing fountain,
       where the townsfolk
Got their water—a fountain fashioned in rock
By Ithacus, Neritus, and Polyctor and surrounded by a grove
Of poplars, thriving in the well-watered ground. The cold water
Poured from the rock above, and on top of that
An altar was built to the nymphs, where all who came by
Made offerings. There they met Dolius' son Melanthius,
Who, with the help of two herdsmen, was driving in
The choicest goats from all the herds to furnish
A feast for the wooers. And with words so violent and vile
That they quickly aroused the wrath of Odysseus, he began
To insult them:

    "Well now, sure as can be, if it isn't
The lousy leading the lousy! As always God
Brings two of a kind together. You loathsome hog-herder,
Where are you taking this filthy pig of a beggar,

This spoiler of dinners? He's just the man to scratch
His back on doorposts and beg for garbage, but hardly
One who will ever be given a sword or cauldron.
If you'd give him to me to work on the farm, he could clean out
The pens and tote fodder for goats, and perhaps he might drink
Enough whey to build up those miserable legs of his.
But he's too far gone in worthless ways to ever
Do anything useful. He'd rather go cringing and begging
His way through the country in the futile hope of filling
His bottomless belly! But I'll tell you this right now,
And you can believe me. If he ever shows his face at the palace
Of sacred Odysseus, those men there will throw
At his head and massage his ribs with many a footstool
And whatever else they can find as he goes through the house!"

     He spoke, and in passing the fool gave Odysseus a kick
On the hip, which wasn't enough, however, to knock him
From the path, so firm he stood. Then, for a moment,
Odysseus was undecided whether to lash out
And kill the man with his staff or pick him up
By the waist and bash his head on the ground. But he held himself
Back and stood it. The swineherd, though, looked the blackguard
Straight in the face and denounced him, then lifted his arms
And prayed this earnest prayer:
     "O nymphs of the fountain,
Daughters of Zeus, if ever Odysseus made
Burnt-offerings to you of lean thigh-pieces of lambs
And kids wrapped in the glistening fat, answer
My prayer that God will guide my master home
Again. Then, sir, he would surely scatter those hot
And arrogant airs you flaunt, always hanging
Around in town while worthless shepherds are out there
Ruining the flocks!"
     Then Melanthius, goader of goats:
"Well, well, how the cur snarls! malicious and vicious

Indeed. Someday I'll take him far away from here
In a well-benched black ship and sell him for plenty. I only
Wish I were as sure that silver-bowed Apollo
Would strike Telemachus down in the palace today,
Or that the wooers would finish him off, as I
Am certain that distant Odysseus will never return!"

    With this, he strode off and left them plodding along,
And soon he came to the royal palace, went in
At once and sat down across from his favorite, Eurymachus.
The waiters supplied him with meat, and the staid housekeeper
Put bread before him.

    Outside, Odysseus and the worthy
Swineherd drew near the palace in time to hear Phemius
The bard strike up a few chords on the curving lyre
In prelude to his song for the wooers, at which Odysseus
Took the swineherd's arm and said:

    "Eumaeus,
This must be the splendid house of Odysseus. Anybody
Could tell it at once from all the others. Here building
Sprawls on building, the courtyard wall is crowned
With excellent battlements, and the double gates seem amply
Thick and strong. No man would be likely to take
This palace by storm. And it's obvious that inside a big feast
Is on, for I smell the aroma of roasting meat
And hear the resounding voice of the lyre, which the gods
Have made the banquet's companion."

    Then, Eumaeus,
You answered him thus: "You're right, but then you're not
Unperceptive in other things as well. And now
Let's make up our minds as to what we're going to do.
Either you can go first into that fair-lying palace
Where the wooers are and leave me out here, or if
You'd rather you can stay here and let me be the first
To go in. I warn you, though, don't linger too long

Out here, since someone may see and throw something at you
Or strike you. Now think which way you want it to be."
　　　And noble, long-suffering Odysseus answered him thus:
"I see what you mean, for I do have some understanding.
And I think I'll stay here while you go in first, since I
Am not unaccustomed to blows and flying objects.
Mine is a tough old heart from many trials
In wave and war. What's one more misery to me?
But a gnawing belly is an evil no man can hide
And the cause of many horrors. On its account
Even ships of many benches are fitted out
To cross the barren and unresting sea in raids
On hostile men."
　　　As they were talking, a hound
Lying there lifted his head and pricked up his ears—
Argus, the very dog that stalwart Odysseus
Had raised from a pup but had never got to hunt,
Since before there was time he had to leave for Troy.
Time was when Argus was the constant companion of young men
In the field, hunting the wild deer, goat, and hare.
But now, with his master gone, he lay neglected
On one of the many large piles of mule and cattle
Manure which lay in front of the doors till the slaves
Of Odysseus could take it away to fertilize great fields.
There lay Argus the hound, crawling with fleas
And dog-wrecking lice. Even so, when he knew Odysseus
Was near, he wagged his tail and dropped his ears,
But hadn't the strength to move any nearer his master.
Looking away, Odysseus wiped a tear,
Easily hiding his grief from Eumaeus, whom quickly
He questioned thus:
　　　"Eumaeus, isn't it odd
That so noble a hound should be lying out here in the dung?
Handsome he is, though I really can't be sure

287

Whether he was equally gifted with speed, or merely
One of those table-dogs men keep for their proud appearance."
    Then, Eumaeus, this was your reply:
"Surely the man died far from home who owned
This dog. If he were in brawn and performance what he was
When Odysseus left him for Troy, believe me you
Would marvel at his splendid speed and endurance. No beast
Whose trail he followed through the depths of the forest ever
Escaped him, so keen was he on the scent. But he is
In bad shape now. His master died far from home,
And the slovenly women pay him no mind at all.
Servants who lose their masters are no longer inclined
To do a very good job, for Zeus, who sees all,
Takes half a man's worth away on the day he becomes
A slave."
    Then Eumaeus entered the stately palace
And went straight to the hall where the lordly wooers
        were feasting.
But Argus now, after nineteen long years, no sooner
Saw Odysseus again, than he gave in to fate
And lay still in the grip of black death.
    The first to greet
The swineherd as he came through the hall was godlike
        Telemachus,
Who nodded and called him over. Looking around,
Eumaeus picked up a nearby stool, the one
Whereon the carver sat when slicing much meat
For the feasting wooers. This he took over and placed
At the Prince's table directly across from him
And sat down. And a herald put a helping of meat before him
And bread from a basket.
    Soon after him, Odysseus
Entered the palace in the guise of a wretched old beggar,
Woefully dressed in rags and hobbling along

With a staff. He sat down in the doorway on the ashen threshold,
Leaning on a pillar of cypress, which long ago
Some builder had skillfully hewn out true to the line.
Then Telemachus beckoned the swineherd over beside him,
And taking a whole loaf of bread from the beautiful basket
And a double handful of meat, he said:

    "Take this
To the stranger there and tell him to make the rounds
And beg from all the wooers. Shame and need
In the same old man make a mighty poor combination."

    With this saying in mind, the swineherd went over and spoke
These winged words to Odysseus: "Stranger, Telemachus
Sends you this food and says for you to make
The rounds and beg from all the wooers. Shame,
He says, is no good at all in a poor old man."

    To which resourceful Odysseus replied with a prayer:
"Lord Zeus, grant that Telemachus may always be one
Of the blessed and have whatever his heart desires."

    With this he took the food in both hands and set it
In front of his feet on his worn and ragged old pouch,
And he ate so long as the bard continued his song
In the hall. When he had eaten and the sacred bard's song
Was done, the wooers raised a great din in the palace.
But Athena stood close to Odysseus, son of Laertes,
And urged him to go and gather up scraps from the wooers
In an effort to tell the good men there from the bad,
Not that she was inclined to save any of them
From destruction. So he made the rounds from left to right,
Stretching out his hand to each of them, like one
Who had never been anything else but a beggar. They pitied
Him and gave, astonished at his appearance
And asking who he was and where he came from.

    Then up spoke goatherd Melanthius: "Listen to me,
O wooers of the famous Queen, for without a doubt

I've seen this man before. I'm sure the swineherd
Brought him here, but I don't really know where he claims
To be from."

At this Antinous railed at Eumaeus:
"Now, hog-herder, isn't that just like you!
But why did you bring this fellow to town? Haven't
We already got enough tramps and bothersome beggars?
Don't you think plenty such plate-lickers congregate here
To consume the goods of your master without your inviting
This wretch?"

Then, Eumaeus, you answered him thus:
"Your birth, Antinous, is nobler by far than your words.
Who would deliberately go out and ask a perfectly
Foreign stranger in, unless he were
Some gifted man—a prophet or priest, a builder,
Or sacred bard of delightful song? Such men
Are always welcome throughout the boundless earth,
While no man wants to burden himself with a beggar.
But of all the wooers, you're always the meanest to those
Who serve Odysseus, and especially hard on me—
Not that I care, so long as constant Penelope
And godlike Telemachus continue to live in the palace."

At which point wise Telemachus interfered: "Enough!
Don't argue with that one. Antinous is full of evil
And always trying to stir up strife with insults,
Or make another do so."

He spoke, then turned
To Antinous with these winged words: "Thanks a lot,
Antinous, for your fatherly advice, that I should order
This stranger from the hall. God forbid! But give him
Something yourself. I don't begrudge it. In fact,
I'm telling you to. Nor, when it comes to such giving,
Do you need my mother's permission, or any servant's
Here in the house of Odysseus. But you, Antinous—

You'd much rather eat all that yourself than give any
Of it to another."
      And Antinous replied: "Telemachus,
What a big bold speech that was! If all the wooers
Would give him what I'd like to give him, he wouldn't show up
In this house again for a good three months, believe me!"
      As he spoke, he reached under the table and brought out
          the stool
On which he rested his shining feet when he dined.
But all the others gave till the pouch was full
Of leftover bread and meat. And now Odysseus
Was about to go back to the threshold without having to pay
For testing the Achaeans, but pausing before Antinous
He spoke to him thus:
      "Give, my friend. You
Don't look like the meanest man here, but more like the noblest,
More like a king. So you ought to give even more bread
To me than the others, for which I'd always speak well
Of you wherever I went on the boundless earth.
I too once lived in a splendid house of my own
As a man of means, and many's the time I've given
To a homeless wanderer, no matter who he was
Or what he needed. I had innumerable slaves
And everything else one needs to live in luxury
And be considered rich. But Zeus, the son of Cronos,
Drained all of it away—because, I guess,
That's what he wanted to do—and me he sent
To my ruin on an almost endless voyage to Egypt
With a band of scavenging pirates, and at last we anchored
Our graceful ships in the great Egyptian river.
Then I gave the strictest of orders to my trusty companions
To stay by the ships and guard them, and I sent some scouts
To high vantage points to get the lay of the land.
But the crews gave in to their own wanton violence, and carried

Away by their strength, they began to pillage and plunder
The fine Egyptian farms. They abducted the women
And children and murdered the men. But their cries were heard
In the city, and at dawn the whole plain was full of foot soldiers
And chariots and the flashing of bronze. Then Zeus, the hurler
Of lightning, filled my men with ignoble panic,
And such were the dangers that pressed from all sides, that not
One man had the courage to stay where he was and fight.
Thus, with keen bronze, the Egyptians cut us down by the dozen,
And others they led up to their city as slaves. But me
They gave to a guest, Iasus' son Dmetor,
Who took me to Cyprus, where he was the mighty ruler.
And from there I've come to this place through sorrow and pain."

     Then Antinous replied: "What demon has brought
        this nuisance
To spoil our dinner? Stand out there in the middle,
Well away from this table, or very shortly you'll come
To a really bitter Egypt and Cyprus! presumptuous
And shameless tramp that you are, to go around begging
From men such as these, who are of course more than generous,
Since what they give belongs to somebody else
And each has plenty before him."

     Then resourceful Odysseus
Stepped back and said: "Ah me, you have, I see,
More good looks than good sense. From wealth of your own
You wouldn't give a pauper so much as a grain of salt—
You who sit here now at another's table
With plenty before you and haven't the heart to give me
A bit of bread."

     At this Antinous got angrier
Yet, and scowling he spoke these winged words:
"Well now, it seems you won't get out of here
In such good shape as you thought, not after an insult

Like that!"
      Then seizing the footstool he hurled it and struck
Odysseus on the right shoulder blade, but boulder firm
He stood, unstaggered by the blow. Quietly, but shaking
His head and brooding revenge in the depths of his heart,
He returned to the threshold, put his bulging pouch on the floor,
And sat down. Then he addressed the wooers:
      "Listen,
O wooers of the wonderful Queen, that I may speak
As the heart in my breast commands. A man who is struck
While defending his own, his cattle or silvery white sheep,
Need have no grief or regret. But Antinous has dealt me
This blow solely on account of my miserable belly,
A terrible curse and the cause of untold human horrors.
So if there are gods and avenging Furies for beggars,
May dateless death, not marriage, soon come to Antinous!"
      Then Antinous, son of Eupeithes, replied: "Just sit there,
Stranger, take it easy and eat, or some of these fellows
Might take offense at your words, drag you out through the house
By the hand or foot, and tear off all your skin."
      But all the others were full of blame for Antinous,
And one of the brash young men would speak to him thus:
"Antinous, you may regret hitting that poor old tramp.
Too bad for you if he should be some god
Come here from heaven, as indeed the gods do haunt
These mortal cities, variously disguised as foreigners
While taking in the hubris and lawfulness of men."
      So said the wooers, but Antinous paid no attention.
Meanwhile, grief in the heart of Telemachus, on account of
The blow, was great and growing, though no tears at all
Fell from his lids to the ground. Without a word
He shook his head, brooding revenge in the depths
Of his heart.
      When wise Penelope heard what had happened

293

Below, she spoke out thus among her women:
"So too may the archer Apollo strike you, Antinous!"
    At which the housekeeper Eurynome said: "If only
Our prayers might be answered, not one of those men would see
Fair Dawn of the beautiful throne."
    Then thoughtful Penelope:
"Nurse, they're all hateful and evil-minded men,
But Antinous especially is like the dark spirit of ruin.
Some poor tramp wanders about the palace,
Forced by need to beg from the men, and all
The others gave him more than enough to fill
His pouch, but Antinous threw a footstool and struck him
On the right shoulder blade."
    So she, among the women
Sitting with her in the chamber, while noble Odysseus
Was eating. Then she summoned the worthy swineherd, and said:
"My good Eumaeus, bid the stranger come here
To me. I want to welcome him and ask
If he's heard of brave Odysseus, or seen him, perhaps,
With his very own eyes. He's apparently traveled a lot."
    And this, Eumaeus, is what you said in reply:
"If only, my Queen, the Achaean lords would be quiet,
For the stranger's words would charm your very soul.
I had him with me in my lodge for three days and three nights,
Since I was the first he came to after running away
From a ship, but still he had not finished the story
Of his woeful life. And as a man looks spellbound
At a gifted bard who sings the songs the gods
Have taught him and that mortals could go on listening to
Forever, even so he charmed and delighted me
As he sat in my lodge. He says he's a friend of the house
Of Odysseus and claims to live in Crete, where the kindred
Of Minos are kings. From there he's been rolling on
Through many torments, till now he turns up here.

294

He swears he's heard of Odysseus, close by in fertile
Thesprotia, alive, loaded with treasure, and headed
For home!"
     Then prudent Penelope answered him thus:
"Go bring him here, so that he can tell me this
Himself. As for the others, let them go on
Enjoying themselves as they sit at the gates or here
In the house, for such is their merry mood. All
They own lies safe in their homes, where no one consumes
Their bread and sweet wine but the servants. But day after day
Our house is full of these men, killing our cattle,
Our sheep and our goats, reveling and riotously feasting,
And drinking reckless drafts of the flaming wine,
Completely wasting whatever they touch! For there's no one
To stop them, no man like Odysseus to keep our house
From ruin. But if Odysseus does come to his country
Again, he and his son will soon exact
Full payment for the violent and lawless deeds of these men."
     Then all of a sudden Telemachus gave out a sneeze
So remarkably loud it resounded throughout the house.
Penelope laughed and spoke these winged words
To Eumaeus: "Do go and bring the stranger to me.
Don't you see that my son has sneezed a most ominous sneeze
To all I have said. Now no uncertain death
Shall come for all the wooers. Not one shall escape
From death and the fates! And here's something else to remember.
If I am convinced that all he says is true,
I'll give him an excellent cloak and tunic to wear."
     The swineherd took it all in, then went to Odysseus
With these winged words: "Good father, gracious Penelope,
The mother of Telemachus, in spite of the misery she suffers,
Wants you to come where she can follow her heart
And inquire concerning her husband. And if she's convinced
That all you say is true, she will give you a cloak

And tunic, which is what you need most. Then you can beg
Your way through the country and get bread for your belly
      from anyone
Willing to give it."
      And patient, noble Odysseus:
"Eumaeus, soon now I'll tell the whole truth to the daughter
Of Icarius, gracious Penelope. For Odysseus and I
Have gone through a lot of misery together, and my knowledge
Of him is valid. But frankly I am afraid
Of this crude mob of suitors, whose arrogance and violence
Reach the iron sky. Just now, as I went through the hall,
Harming no one, this man threw and struck me a painful
Blow, which neither Telemachus nor anyone else
Did anything to ward off. So tell Penelope to wait
In the palace till sundown, anxious though she is.
Then she can question me concerning the day
Of her husband's return, and give me a seat somewhat nearer
The fire, for my clothes are in very sad shape, as you
Well know, since you are the first to whom I made
My plea."
      The swineherd listened and left, but had scarcely
Got through the door when Penelope said: "But Eumaeus,
You didn't bring him. What can he be thinking of?
Can he be terrified of someone in the palace, or just bashful
About being here in the house? A bashful beggar
Is a mighty poor fellow indeed."
      Then, Eumaeus,
This was your reply: "He sends a sensible
Answer, as any man would judge, and is only trying
To avoid the violence of arrogant men. He wants you
To wait till sundown, and surely, O Queen, it will be
Far better for you to talk with the stranger alone."
      Then thoughtful Penelope: "The stranger is not unwise.
What he fears might very well happen, considering what foolish

And surpassingly wicked men these are."
    When he
Had told her all, the worthy herdsman went
Through the mob of wooers, held his head close to Telemachus
To keep the others from hearing, and spoke to him thus:
"My friend, I'm going out to look after the swine and the farm,
Your living and mine, and leave you to take care of things here.
Look out for yourself first of all and stay on the alert,
For many Achaeans are plotting evil against you.
May Zeus demolish them all before anything like that
Happens to us!"
    And thoughtful Telemachus answered:
"So be it, father. Go when you've had your supper,
But come on back in the morning and bring fat boars
For sacrifice. The gods and I will take care of things here."
    So the swineherd sat down again in his place at the table
And ate and drank to his heart's content. Then he
Returned to the swine, leaving the hall and the courts
Crowded with feasting men, dancing and singing
And enjoying themselves, now that evening had come.

BOOK

XVIII

THE FIGHT WITH IRUS

Now who should arrive but a most notorious beggar,
A man who was constantly eating and drinking and was known
Throughout the city for his ravenous gut. He had neither
Strength nor endurance, though in bulk he was huge. His name
Was Arnaeus, for so his good mother had called him from birth.
But all the young men called him Irus, since he would run errands
Whenever anyone bade. Now he came up
To Odysseus and began to insult him, trying to drive him
Out of the house—his own house—with these winged words:
    "Get out of the door, old man, before somebody drags you
Out by the foot! Don't you know that all those men
Are winking at me and saying for me to start dragging?
I don't have the heart. But get up now, or in this quarrel
Of ours you're likely to feel my fist in a hurry!"
    Then resourceful Odysseus scowled up at him, and said:
"My friend, I'm not bothering you in any way,
Nor do I begrudge what any man gives you, no matter
How much it is. This threshold is plenty big
For both of us, and surely you needn't begrudge
What other folks have. You seem to be a wanderer
Like myself, but then, if the gods are willing,

We might be lucky yet. I advise you, though,
Not to say too much about fists and fighting, or I,
Old as I am, just might get mad and splatter
Blood from your mouth all over your chest! Then maybe
Tomorrow I'd have a little more peace, since I don't think
You would be likely to show up again in the hall
Of Odysseus, son of Laertes."

    Then the vagabond Irus
Really got mad, and said: "Damnation! how
The filthy glutton runs on, just like an old slut
In the kitchen. But wait till I give him a left and a right
To the jaws and scatter his teeth on the ground like those
Of a crop-eating boar! Gird up your rags, so that everybody
Will know we're going to fight, if you really want
To fight with a younger man."

    As they were bickering
There on the threshold before the high doors and getting
Each other more and more on edge, the powerful Prince
Antinous heard the ruckus and bursting with laughter
Spoke thus among the wooers: "Never before,
My friends, has a god brought such delightful sport
To this house. That stranger and Irus are picking a fight
With each other. But quick! let's help them get together."

    At this they leaped up, and laughing all crowded around
The ragged beggars. And Eupeithes' son Antinous
Shouted: "Listen, you manly wooers. I have
A suggestion. Here are goat paunches that we stuffed with rich
Blood pudding and set on the fire for supper. Let the winner,
Who proves himself the stronger man in the match,
Go take his pick of these, and let him always
Feast with us, with no competition at all
From other beggars."

    This speech pleased them all.
Then resourceful Odysseus, trying to trick them, spoke thus:

"Friends, a poor old fellow like me, already
Beaten by pain and misfortune, can't really fight
With a younger man. Even so, this baneful belly
Of mine is driving me on to get a good licking.
First though, I want you all to swear a great oath
That none of you will do Irus the favor of laying me
Out at his feet with a foul and treacherous blow
From a heavy fist."

    He spoke, and every man there
Did as he said and swore not to strike him. When
They had ended the oath, the strong and sacred Telemachus
Had this to say: "Stranger, if your own manly spirit
Bids you stand up to this fellow, you have nothing to fear
From any Achaean, for whoever strikes you will have
A much larger fight on his hands. I am your host,
And the very prudent lords, Antinous and Eurymachus,
Will back me up."

    Then everyone there had praise
For these words of the Prince. So Odysseus tucked his rags
In his belt and girded his loins, revealing his handsome
Huge thighs, wide shoulders, and powerful arms—all
The work of Athena, who drawing near had thus
Transformed the people's shepherd. All the wooers
Were utterly astonished, and one would glance at the man
Beside him and say:

    "It won't be long now before Irus,
Un-Irused, will get what he asked for and no longer be fit
For errands at all, judging from the looks of that thigh
The old man shows from beneath his rags!"

    As for Irus,
He nearly collapsed, but the servants tucked in his rags
By force and dragged him forward, fat and shaking
All over with fear. Then Antinous chided him thus:
"You clumsy bully! you'd surely be better off dead,

Or not born at all, if you're gutless enough to shake
And be so deathly afraid of this poor old man!
But let me tell you this, and you can believe it.
If this fellow is stronger and wins, so help me I'll throw you
Aboard a black ship and pack you off to the mainland
To mortal-maiming King Echetus, who will slice off
Your nose and ears with the ruthless bronze and rip out
Your privates to provide raw meat for the dogs to divide."

    At this he began to shake all the more, but they led him
Into the ring and both men put up their hands.
And now the noble, long-suffering Odysseus could not
Make up his mind whether to strike him down dead,
Or stretch him out on the ground with an easier blow.
Thinking, he decided in favor of hitting him lightly,
So as not to attract too much notice from those looking on.
Then Irus drew back and drove at the King's right shoulder,
But Odysseus struck him square on the neck just under
The ear and crushed in the bones. At once, the red blood
Ran out of his mouth and he fell in the dust with a groan,
Grinding his teeth and beating the ground with his feet.
But the lordly wooers threw up their hands and nearly
Died laughing. Then Odysseus took the man's foot and
               dragged him
Out through the door and courtyard to the gates of the portico,
Where he propped him up by the wall, shoved his staff in his hand,
And spoke these winged words:
               "Sit there and scare off
The hogs and the dogs, and miserable wretch that you are
Don't ever try to lord it over strangers and beggars,
Or you may get something a good deal worse than this!"

    So saying, about his shoulders he slung his grimy
Old pouch, all torn and ragged and hanging by an old piece
Of rope. Then he went back and sat down on the threshold,
And the merry wooers came crowding in, laughing

And greeting him thus:
    "Stranger, may Zeus and the other
Immortals grant you your heart's desire, whatever
You want most in the world, since you have ended
The Ithacan career of this insatiable beggar.
Very soon now we'll ship him off to the mainland
To mortal-maiming King Echetus."
      At these ominous words
Odysseus rejoiced. Meanwhile, Antinous set
Before him a huge paunch stuffed with the rich blood pudding,
And Amphinomus served him two loaves from the basket,
      then raised
A golden cup to him, and said:
    "Your health,
Good father. Here's hoping you have better luck from now on,
Despite the very bad way you're in at the moment."
      And resourceful Odysseus replied: "Amphinomus,
      you strike me
As a truly sensible man, and so was your father—
Judging from what I've heard of Nisus of Dulichium,
A man both wealthy and brave. His son they say
You are, and you speak with great humanity. Therefore,
I say this to you, and I hope you'll pay some attention.
Of all the creatures that breathe and move on earth,
She nourishes none more utterly helpless than man.
So long as the gods keep him well and supply him with prowess
He assumes he'll never have any evil to suffer.
But when from the blessed gods the evil does come—
Well his heart though unwilling must endure it
      steadfastly. For the way
Men think and feel on earth depends on what kind
Of day the Father of gods and men brings to them.
I too was once a happy and prosperous man,
But carried away by my own exuberant strength

And counting on my father and brothers, I did not a few
Quite thoughtless and wicked things. Therefore, let no man
Anywhere ever be lawless, but let him quietly
Enjoy whatever the gods may give. But now,
I see the wooers foolishly plotting evil,
Wasting the wealth and insulting the wife of a man
Who will not, I say, be away from his friends and his country
Much longer. In fact, he's very near home right now!
So I hope some god will see you safely home
And that you won't be here to meet him when he comes.
For once he gets home and under these roof-beams, the parting
Between him and the wooers will certainly not be bloodless."
　　　He spoke, and poured a libation, then drank a draft
Of the honeyed wine and handed the cup back to Amphinomus,
Marshaller of hosts, who now went through the hall
Dejectedly shaking his head, for his spirit foreboded
The evil to come. Still, he did not escape
That fate, since Athena detained him too, as one
Now bound to fall at the hands of Telemachus, violently
Slain by the spear. And again he sat down in the chair
That he had left empty.
　　　Now, the bright-eyed Athena
Put it into the heart of prudent Penelope, the daughter
Of Icarius, to make a personal appearance before
The wooers, that she might increase their desire and enhance
Herself in the eyes of her husband and son. So forcing
A laugh, she called the housekeeper by name, and said:
　　　"Eurynome, my heart desires as never before
To show myself to the wooers. Also I want
A few words with my son, to tell him for his own good
Not to mix with the insolent wooers, who pretend to be friendly
But are really plotting against him."
　　　And the housekeeper Eurynome
Answered: "Surely, child, all this is well spoken,

But first have a bath and fix your face. Don't go
With tear stains on both cheeks. But go, by all means, for grieving
All the time is no good. Remember what
You've always prayed hardest to the immortals for is to see
Your son a grown and bearded man, and so
He now is."

    Then thoughtful Penelope replied: "Eurynome,
Out of your care and concern for me, don't try
To persuade me to primp and prepare myself with water
And oil. The glow I once had departed, by will
Of the sky-ruling gods, on the day my husband sailed off
With the fleet. But go tell Autonoe and Hippodameia
To come here to me, that they may stand beside me
In the hall. I won't go among men by myself. I'd be
Too embarrassed."

    She spoke, and the old one went out through the chamber
To find the women and tell them to come. Meanwhile,
The bright-eyed goddess Athena had another idea.
She shed sweet sleep on the daughter of Icarius, who now
Leaned back on her couch and slept, as all of her limbs
Relaxed. Then the radiant goddess gave immortal gifts
To her, so that the Achaeans might marvel at sight
Of such beauty. She began by renewing her lovely face
With ambrosial balm, of the sort fair-crowned Aphrodite
Uses when she joins the Graces in their beautiful dance.
And she made her taller and more voluptuous, and her skin
More creamy white than new-sawn ivory. When these things
Were done, the goddess departed, and the white-armed maids
Came up from another chamber. At the sound of their chatter
Sweet sleep let Penelope go, and she rubbed her cheeks
With her hands, and said:

    "Ah me, in the midst of all
That pain, soft sleep enfolded me. If only
Holy Artemis would send me this moment so soft

A death! so that I wouldn't have to go on with a heart
Full of misery, wasting my life away with yearning
For the versatile prowess of my beloved husband,
The most remarkable man among the Achaeans."
       Then she went down from the bright upper room, attended
By the two handmaids. When they reached the hall she stood,
Lovely by one of the pillars of the massive roof,
Her face partly hid by a shining veil, and confronted
The wooers, with a trusted maid on either side.
One look was enough to stagger the men and charm
Their hearts with desire. Each of them prayed that he
Might lie with the lady. But she spoke to Telemachus, her own
Dear son:
       "Telemachus, your thinking is no longer so fine
And firm as it used to be. You were indeed smarter
When only a child. But now that you're a grown young man,
So handsome and tall any stranger would know you at once
For the son of a wealthy man—now you no longer
Show such good judgment. What a miserable thing has happened
Here in these halls in your allowing this stranger
To be so badly mistreated! Suppose some guest
Of ours, while sitting here in the house, should be
Thus roughly handled and seriously injured? Then everyone
Would put the blame and disgrace on you!"
       And Telemachus
Gravely replied: "Mother, I don't blame you one bit
For being so angry about what happened. But I
Am no longer a child, and I understand quite well
What's right and what's wrong. Even so, I'm not always able
To plan things wisely, for these men distract me with malice
At every turn, and I have no one to help me.
Believe me, though, this bout between the stranger and Irus
Didn't turn out at all as the wooers wanted,
For the stranger was too much for him. Ah Father Zeus,

305

Athena, and Apollo, if only this very moment
The wooers were likewise defeated within our house
And scattered about the hall and yard with their heads
Slumped down in a daze, like Irus, who even now
Is sitting out there by the courtyard gate with his head
Hung down like a drunkard, unable to pull himself
Together enough to get on his feet and go home
Wherever he usually goes."

      Such was their talk,
But Eurymachus interrupted thus to compliment the Queen:
"Daughter of Icarius, wise Penelope, if all
The Achaeans in Iasian Argos got one look at you,
By tomorrow morning you'd have more wooers than ever
To feast in your halls, since surely in face and figure
And good sense to match you excel all other women."

      And prudent Penelope said: "Eurymachus, what beauty
Of face and form, what excellence I had, the immortals
Destroyed on the day the Argives sailed for Ilium,
And my husband Odysseus with them. If he might only
Return and take care of my life again, my fame
Might amount to something. But now I just suffer, so many
Are the woes some god has sent against me. When he left
His country that day, he took my right arm by the wrist,
And said:

      " 'My wife, not all the well-greaved Achaeans
Will come back from Troy unharmed, for they say the Trojans
Are warlike men, spear-hurlers, bow-shooters, and drivers
Of swiftly-drawn chariots, that decide a pitched battle
      more quickly
Than anything else. So I don't know whether God
Will bring me back, or whether I'll fall at Troy.
Therefore, I leave you in charge of everything here.
In the palace look after my father and mother, as now,
Or even more, with me so far away.

But when you see our son a bearded young man,
Marry the man of your choice, and leave your home.'

"He said it, and now it's all happening just that way,
And a hateful wedding night will surely be forced
Upon me, accursed as I am and deprived of joy
By Zeus. Meanwhile, my heart and soul are bitterly
Afflicted, for never before did wooers behave
As you do. Men who want to compete for the hand
Of any real lady bring splendid cattle and sheep
Of their own, as a feast for friends of the bride, and to her
They give wonderful presents. They don't just devour the living
Of somebody else completely without repayment!"

She spoke, and noble, much-suffering Odysseus was delighted
To see her charming their hearts with soft talk and extracting
Their presents when her true heart and mind were elsewhere.
Then Antinous, son of Eupeithes, spoke to her thus:

"Daughter of Icarius, prudent Penelope, if any
Of us decide to bring gifts, be sure that you
Accept them. Refusing a gift is a serious matter.
Meanwhile, we will not go back to our lands or anywhere
Else, till you marry the best Achaean among us."

Thus Antinous, and the wooers liked what he said.
They each sent out a herald to fetch a gift.
Antinous' man returned with an ample robe,
Finely embroidered and fitted with twelve golden buckles,
Each with a curving tongue. Quickly another
Came back to Eurymachus with a golden chain, curiously
Wrought, and strung with sun-bright beads of amber.
The squires of Eurydamas brought a beautiful pair of earrings,
Glowing and graceful three-drop clusters. From the home
Of Prince Peisander, son of Polyctor, came a precious
And lovely necklace. And all the Achaean lords
Gave one fine gift or another. Then the fair lady
Went back upstairs to her room, and the handmaids carried

For her the exquisite presents.

    Now the wooers began
To enjoy themselves with dancing and merry songs,
As they waited for evening to come. When darkness fell on
Their fun, they stood in the hall three braziers to give them
Some light, and in them they piled up newly split wood,
Dry and well-seasoned. Then in the midst of each
They thrust a blazing torch, and the servant girls
Of patient Odysseus took turns at tending the fires,
Till God-sprung Odysseus himself spoke to them thus:

    "Masterless maids of long-absent Odysseus, go
To the rooms of the Queen you revere and give her what comfort
You can, as you sit with her there and twist the yarn
Or card the wool with your hands. I'll furnish light
For all of these men, even though they wish to stay up
For Dawn of the beautiful throne. I can take it, believe me."

    At this the girls giggled and glanced at each other.

      But Melantho,
The fair-cheeked daughter of Dolius, began to insult him
Most hatefully. She had been raised by Penelope herself,
Who had cherished the child like one of her own and given her
The toys her heart desired. Even so, her heart
Held no grief at all for Penelope. But Eurymachus she loved
And slept with him regularly. Now she reviled Odysseus
With harsh and shameless words:

    "You wretched old fool!
You won't go sleep in a smithy or some public place.
You'd rather stay here and go on running your mouth,
Totally unafraid in the midst of all these lords.
Surely you must be drunk, or else you always
Rattle your brains and babble this way. Can it be
That your head is swollen at beating that hobo Irus?
You'd better be careful, or someone a lot more man
Than Irus will club your head with his big beefy fists

And send you out of the house all streaming with blood!"
        Fiercely scowling, resourceful Odysseus replied:
"I'll go in a hurry, you bitch, and tell Telemachus
How you talk. He'll cut you up right here
In little pieces!"
        At this the girls scurried away
Through the hall, their knees trembling with fear,
                for they believed
What he said. But Odysseus stayed by the blazing braziers,
Watching them all and tending the fires, though other things
Really possessed his pondering heart—events
That would not fail to occur.
        But Athena was not
About to allow the haughty wooers to check
Their outrageous behavior, for it was her will that the heart
Of Odysseus, son of Laertes, should be even more full
Of misery and pain. So now Eurymachus, son
Of Polybus, started to taunt Odysseus and so
Amuse his companions.
        "Hear this, you wooers of royalty.
I can't hold it back any longer. This man is surely
God-sent to the palace of King Odysseus. For it seems
That the light of those torches is coming from the top of his head,
On which there isn't a hair in the way, not one!"
        Then he called out to Odysseus, sacker of cities:
"You there, how would you like to hire out to me
And be sure of good pay for building stone walls and planting
Tall trees on a new piece of land out here in the country?
I'd furnish you food throughout the year, as well as
Clothes and sandals. But I guess you're too far gone
In worthless ways to ever do anything useful.
You'd rather go cringing and begging your way
                through the country

In the futile hope of filling your bottomless belly!"
  And resourceful Odysseus: "Eurymachus, I only wish
The two of us might have a match at mowing
When the long days of springtime come, both of us
With a curving scythe in our hands and more than enough
Tall grass to test our laboring and last us all day,
Nor would we eat a bite until it was dark.
Or I wish we had oxen to plow, the best there are,
Great glossy beasts that have had their fill of grass,
Both the same age and tireless under the yoke,
And that we had a fine four-acre field
Of arable land—then you'd see whether or not
I could cut a long straight furrow clear across that field.
Or I wish that Cronos' son would send us war
From somewhere or other and that I had a shield, two spears,
And an all-bronze helmet that fitted me well—then you
Would see me in the midst of the foremost fighters, and perhaps
You would stop making jokes about this belly of mine.
But you're a cruel and arrogant bully, and it's obvious
You think of yourself as a big, important man
Because the men you associate with are few and worthless.
If Odysseus might only come back to his own native land,
I'll tell you those doors over there, wide as they are,
Would be much too narrow for you when you made your dash
For the great outdoors!"
  This made Eurymachus furious,
And scowling fiercely he spoke these winged words:
"You tramp! I'll teach you to run your mouth so fearlessly
In the midst of all these lords. Surely you must be
Drunk, or else you always rattle your brains
And babble this way. Can it be that your head is swollen
At beating that hobo Irus?"
  Then he grabbed a footstool,
But the startled Odysseus sat down at the knees of Amphinomus

Of Dulichium, so that Eurymachus struck the right hand
Of a wine-pourer, who fell back in the dust with a groan,
                    as his pitcher
Clanged on the ground. Throughout the shadowy hall
The wooers broke into an uproar, and thus would one of them
Say to the man beside him:
            "If only that stranger
Had died in his wanderings elsewhere before he got here,
Then he wouldn't have caused such chaos among us. Now
We brawl about beggars and have surely spoiled our fine feast
When such things prevail!"
            Then the strong and sacred Telemachus
Spoke to them thus: "Gentlemen, you're raving mad,
And the effects of your eating and drinking are all too obvious!
Some god is urging you on. But now that you've had
A good dinner, go home and to bed—when you want to, that is.
I'm not throwing anybody out."
            At this bold speech
From Telemachus, they bit their lips in amazement. But
            Amphinomus
Spoke to them thus, he the son of King Nisus
And grandson of Aretias: "My friends, nobody can argue
With that, or take offense at words so justly
Spoken. Enough of mistreating the stranger and servants
Here in the house of godly Odysseus. But come,
Let the bearer pour the first drops in the cups, so that we
Can make our libations and go home to bed. We'll leave
This troublesome stranger in the halls of Odysseus for Telemachus
To care for. After all, this is the house he came to."
            These words pleased them all. So the warrior Mulius,
A herald from Dulichium and squire to Amphinomus, mixed them
A bowl and poured for each man there, and they made
Their libations to the blissful gods and drank all they wanted
Of the honey-sweet wine. Then they all went home and to bed.

311

BOOK

XIX

THE SCAR OF
ODYSSEUS

Royal Odysseus, left behind in the hall,
Pondering with Athena death for the wooers, soon spoke
To Telemachus these winged words: "Telemachus, now
We must take all the weapons of war from the hall and put them
Away. Then, when the wooers miss them and begin
Asking questions, put them off with as soft an answer
As possible, saying:
    " 'I've taken them out of the smoke,
Since wherever the fire's breath has touched them, they're all
            smutched up,
And they don't look at all as they did when Odysseus left
For Troy. Then too, Cronos' son has put this greater
Concern in my heart, that you may be in your cups
And get to fighting among yourselves, thus wounding
One another and bringing disgrace on your feast and yourselves
As wooers. For iron just naturally draws a man to it.' "
    He spoke, and Telemachus obeyed his dear father. Calling
The old Eurycleia, he spoke to her thus: "Good nurse,

I want you to keep the women in their rooms, while I
Put all my father's fine weapons away in the storeroom.
They have lain here uncared for and smutched by the smoke
      ever since
My father left home when I was a child. Now I
Am going to put them away where the fire's breath
      won't touch them."
      And his dear nurse Eurycleia: "Very well, my child.
I hope you'll always want to take care of this house
And guard all its treasures. But come, who'll get a light
And carry it before you, since you don't want the maids to do it?"
      Then thoughtful Telemachus answered: "This stranger here,
For I won't let anyone be idle who eats my bread,
No matter how far he comes from."
      No winged words
Came back from the nurse. She went to the stately chamber
And bolted the women's doors. Then Odysseus and his son
Leaped up and began to carry in the helmets,
The sharp-pointed spears, and the bossed and studded shields.
And before them went Pallas Athena with a golden lamp,
Suffusing a glorious light throughout the hall.
Then all at once Telemachus turned to his father,
And said:
      "Father, surely I see a great wonder
Here, for the walls and fair panels, the beams of fir
And the lofty columns are glowing as with the light
Of a blazing fire. Surely some god is here
In the house, some sky-ruling god!"
      And resourceful Odysseus
Replied: "Hush! You must restrain yourself
And ask no questions. This is the way of the gods
That rule Olympus. But go on to bed, while I
Stay here to stir up still more the maids and your mother,

313

Who, I am sure, will weep and question me closely."
      He spoke, and Telemachus went out through the hall
         by the light
Of the flaring torches to lie down in his room, just
As he usually did when delicious sleep was approaching.
There he lay down and waited for bright morning to come,
While again Odysseus the King was left in the hall,
Pondering with Athena death for the wooers.
      Then Penelope
Came down from her room, like Artemis or golden Aphrodite,
And they set a chair for her at her place by the fire,
An antique chair inlaid with whorls of ivory
And silver and made, with a foot-rest attached, by the craftsman
Icmalius. On this they flung a great fleece, and Penelope
Sat down. The white-armed maids came out of their chamber
And cleared away much leftover food, as well as
The tables and cups which the haughty young lords had used
In their recent carousing. And they emptied the braziers, casting
The embers to earth, and piled them high with more wood
For light and for warmth. But now Melantho began
A second time to revile Odysseus:
      "You nuisance!
Are you going to be here all night, roaming the house
And spying on the women? Get out, you tramp! and make
The most of that supper you got, or pretty soon
You'll get the works with a torch. Then I bet
You'll get out!"
      This time quick-witted Odysseus frowned
At her, and said: "Woman, you're surely possessed!
Why do you come at me with such ill will?
Is it because I'm a beggar, so dirty and poorly
Dressed? That's how beggars are, and I
Am such by necessity, not choice. I too once lived
In a splendid house of my own as a man of means,

And many's the time I've given to a homeless wanderer,
No matter who he was or what he needed.
I had innumerable slaves and everything else
One needs to live in luxury and be considered rich.
But Zeus, the son of Cronos, drained all of it
Away—because, I guess, that's what he wanted
To do. Therefore, my good woman, look to it, or you're liable
To lose that favored place of glory you hold
Among the handmaids. Watch out, for your mistress may
Get angry at you and rebuke you severely, or Odysseus
Might come home, as there is indeed still reason
To hope that he will. And even if such as you
Are right in believing him dead, his son is now,
By grace of Apollo, as good a man as his father—
Yes, Telemachus. He doesn't miss one wanton thing
You women do in the palace! He's no longer a child,
You know."

     He spoke, but brooding Penelope had heard
It all, and now she rebuked the handmaid thus:
"Be very sure, you brazen bitch, that I
Did not miss a bit of the horrible thing you did,
And believe me you'll pay for what happened with all you've got!
For you knew perfectly well, since you heard me say so,
That out of my deep distress and here in my home
I wanted to question this stranger concerning my husband."

     Then she spoke thus to Eurynome the housekeeper:
          "Eurynome,
Go get a chair and fleece for our guest, so that he
Can sit down and tell me his story and hear all the questions
I want to ask him."

     She spoke, and Eurynome quickly
Fetched a polished chair and spread a fleece
Upon it. Then patient Odysseus sat down, and Penelope
Began her questioning: "Sir, first of all, tell me this.

Who are you and where are you from? Your city, your parents,
Where are they?"
    And resourceful Odysseus replied: "My lady,
No mortal man on the boundless earth could really
Object to anything from you, for word of your worth
Extends to the wide sky itself, like the fame of a blameless
And god-fearing king, who rules, upholding the right,
Over many strong men, and the black earth teems with wheat
And barley, the trees bow down with fruit, the flocks
Are unfailingly fruitful, and the sea supplies fish—and all
Because of good guidance from him. His people thrive.
So question me here in your home of anything else,
But not of my family and country, if you don't want memories
To fill my heart even fuller of pain, for I
Am a sigh-worn, weary man. Even so, it's not right
For me to sit here weeping and wailing in somebody
Else's home. Constant grief is no good.
Nor would I like to be blamed by you or your maids
And have you say that the wine has gone to my head
And turned into tears."
    And Penelope: "Sir, what beauty
Of face and form, what excellence I had, the immortals
Destroyed on the day the Argives sailed for Ilium,
And my husband Odysseus with them. If he might only
Return and take care of my life again, my fame
Might amount to something. But now I just suffer, so many
Are the woes some god has sent against me. For all
The island princes, from Dulichium, Samos, and wooded
Zacynthus, as well as the lords in sunny Ithaca—
All are forcing their wooing upon me and ruining
My house. That's why I neglect my guests and those
Who come begging, to say nothing of public heralds. I go on
Melting my heart away with longing for Odysseus.
These men try to hasten my marriage, and I

Weave tricks to prevent it. The first was inspired by a god.
I had a great loom set up and began to weave yards
Of fine cloth, explaining myself this way to the men:
    " 'My ardent young suitors, gallant Odysseus is dead,
And you can't wait for me to marry again,
But you, my wooers must try to be patient until
I finish this shroud for lord Laertes, for him
When the painful fate of leveling and grievous death
Arrives. Naturally, I would not have my labor
Go to waste, nor any Achaean woman
Speak ill of me for not providing a shroud
For one who has amassed so great a fortune.'
    "To this their proud hearts agreed, and daily I wove
At that great web. But at night I unraveled my work
By the light of torches. Thus for three wily years
I beguiled the Achaeans, but when the fourth arrived
And winter gave way to spring, as the months went by
And the countless days, the wooers by means of my women—
Those irresponsible bitches—came in and caught me,
Shouted reproaches at me, then forced me to finish
The work against my will. Now I don't know
How I'll avoid this marriage. My parents are urging
It on me and my son is impatient, for now he's grown
And fully aware that these men are wasting his wealth
And ruining an estate that he is quite able to manage
With honor and glory from Zeus. But tell me who
You are, for surely you weren't the child of an oak
Or stone, like him in the ancient fable."
    And Odysseus,
Able as ever, replied: "O honored wife
Of Odysseus, son of Laertes, won't you ever
Stop asking about my family? Very well, I'll tell you,
But now you're increasing my misery, for so it must be
When a man has been far from his country as long as I have,

Roaming through so many cities and suffering so much.
Even so, I'll answer your questions. Out there in the midst
Of the wine-blue sea is the wonderful country of Crete,
A fair and fertile island of countless men
And ninety cities. Nor do they all speak the same language,
For besides Achaeans and the spirited natives of Crete,
There also live Cydonians, three Dorian clans,
And noble Pelasgians. One of their cities is Knossos
The huge, where Minos was King from his ninth year on,
Minos who lived in close communion with Zeus
And fathered high-hearted Deucalion, who fathered me
And royal Idomeneus. Idomeneus departed for Ilium
With the curving ships and the sons of Atreus. My famous
Name is Aethon, but Idomeneus was older than I
And a better man. There in that island I saw
And befriended Odysseus. For a storm had driven him off
His course for Troy and out past Malea to Crete,
Where he just did manage to get out of the gale and into
The difficult harbor at Amnisus, where he anchored his ships
Not far from the cave of Eileithyia. Then at once he went up
To the city and asked for Idomeneus, who, he said,
Was his dear and greatly respected friend. But the tenth
Or eleventh dawn had come and gone since Idomeneus
Sailed with the curving ships for Ilium. So I brought
Him home and welcomed him warmly with many good things
In the house. And for the men who followed him
I got from the people enough barley and sparkling wine
And bulls for sacrifice to fully content their hearts.
There for twelve days that mighty blow from the North
Held the noble Achaeans, a wind stirred up by some
Hostile god and such a blast that even on land
They couldn't stay on their feet. But finally it fell
On the thirteenth day, and quickly they put out to sea."
     All these stories he told as though they were true,

And as Penelope listened her tears ran down
And her fair cheeks seemed to melt like snow on the lofty
Mountains when the East Wind thaws what the West Wind
       drifted
There and the water flows down to the flooding rivers.
So now her lovely cheeks, as she mourned and wept
For the man who at that very moment was sitting beside her.
And Odysseus deeply pitied his weeping wife,
But his eyes stood artfully fixed between his lids
Like horn or iron, so no tear fell. When she
Had cried enough, she spoke to him thus:
    "Now sir,
I feel I must try to find out if that was indeed
My husband and those godlike comrades of his that you
Entertained in your home. Tell me what kind of clothes
He had on and something about the man himself
And the men who were with him."
    And subtle Odysseus replied:
"My lady, it's hard for a man who has been away
For so long to tell of a man who left his country
Now more than nineteen years ago. But I
Will describe the image that's still in my heart. He wore
A fine purple cloak, fleecy and double thick,
And on it a clasp with two tongues, a real work of art.
For there a hound was portrayed with both front feet
On a spotted fawn, pinning it down as it writhed
And slashing away with his teeth. The men all marveled
At this, how there on the golden clasp the hound
Was slashing away and throttling the fawn, while the fawn
Was lashing out with its feet and struggling to flee.
And I noticed the tunic he wore, how soft it was.
It shone on his body like the skin of a well-dried onion,
Or the sun itself. Truly, a great many women
Looked at him in wonder. But let me add,

And mark this well, that I don't know whether Odysseus
Wore those clothes at home, or whether some comrade
Of his gave him those things when he went aboard
The swift ship, or maybe even some stranger. Many men
Were fond of Odysseus, since few among the Achaeans
Were equal to him. I myself gave him a sword
Of bronze, a fine purple cloak of double thickness,
And a tasseled tunic, and sent him away with honor
In his well-decked ship. Then too, a herald was with him,
A man somewhat older than he, and I can also
Tell you of him. Curly-haired, round-shouldered, and swarthy,
His name was Eurybates, and Odysseus preferred him to all
Of his other comrades, since, with regard to mind,
He had more in common with him."

　　　　When she heard him tell
So surely of these familiar tokens, Penelope
Felt in her heart more like crying than ever.
But when she had taken her fill of tearful lamenting,
She spoke to him thus: "I pitied you, sir, before,
But now you shall be a cherished and honored guest
In my home. For I gave him those clothes you describe myself,
Took them out of the storeroom, folded them all,
And put on that gleaming clasp for him to enjoy.
But never again will I welcome my husband back
To the country he loved so dearly. Surely his lot
Was sorry indeed when he left in that hollow ship
To lay his eyes on evil, unspeakable Troy!"

　　　　Then resourceful Odysseus replied: "O honored wife
Of Laertes' son Odysseus. Now don't keep spoiling
Your lovely complexion and wearing your life away
With tearful grief for your husband. Not that I blame you,
For any woman weeps when she loses the husband
With whom she's made love and had children, even though he was
No Odysseus, who, they say, resembles the gods.

But dry your tears and listen to what I tell you,
The whole truth, of how not long ago I heard
That Odysseus was near and on his way home, close by
In the fertile Thesprotian country, very much alive
And loaded with valuable treasure, as he visits his way
Through the land. But his faithful companions and hollow ship
He lost in the wine-dark sea as they went from the island
Thrinacia. For Zeus and Helios, whose cattle his comrades
Killed, were angry at him. Thus they all sank
In the foaming sea, but he on the keel of his ship
Was washed ashore by the waves in the land of the Phaeacians,
A people close kin to the gods. They heartily honored
Him quite as though he were a god, and insisted
On seeing him safely home. And surely Odysseus
Would have been here long ago, if he had not thought it
More profitable to travel throughout the world and gather
Wealth, and without a doubt no man alive
Can touch him when it comes to a knowledge of how to get rich
All this I had from Pheidon, the Thesprotian King,
And in my presence he swore, as he poured libations
There in his house, that a ship was launched and a crew
Standing by for the sole purpose of taking Odysseus
Home. But I left before he returned, since a ship
Of theirs chanced to be leaving for wheat-rich Dulichium.
And he showed me all the treasure Odysseus had amassed.
Truly it would have sufficed to keep both him
And his heirs to the tenth generation, so great was the wealth
Stored for him in the halls of the King. But Odysseus,
He said, had gone to learn the will of Zeus
From his lofty-leaved oak in Dodona, hoping to learn
Just how to go back, after being so long away,
To his own dear country, whether incognito or not.
He is, then, safe and close to home, and not much
Longer will he be away from his friends and his country.

And I give you this oath. First by Zeus, the highest
And best among gods, and by the hearth of noble
Odysseus to which I have come, I swear that all
I have said shall happen. In this very month, in the dark
Of the moon, Odysseus shall be here in the palace!"
   And thoughtful Penelope answered: "May it be
     as you say, sir,
And if it is, you'll soon be aware of my kindness,
For so many will be my gifts to you that everyone
You meet will call you blessed. But in my heart
I know how it will be. Odysseus will never
Come home, and you will never get a ship out of here.
For now we have no men in this house who are leaders
Of men as Odysseus was—if there ever was
An Odysseus—nobody to welcome sacred strangers
And send them on their way. But maids, wash the feet
Of our guest and make up a bed for him with plenty
Of robes and bright blankets to keep him warm till Dawn
Of the golden throne arrives. Then, the first thing
In the morning, bathe him and rub him with oil, so that he
Will feel like taking his place by Telemachus at breakfast
In the hall. And woe unto any man there who is worthless
Enough to taunt him! That man will never get anywhere
Here, no matter how fierce his anger. For how,
Good sir, would you know whether I am indeed any wiser
Or more considerate than other women, if I let you
Sit here and eat in my house all ragged, unkempt,
And uncared for? Our lives are soon over. If one is unfeeling,
And cruel in his thoughts, all men call down curses
Upon him while he is alive, and after he's dead
They mock and scorn him. But if one is kind-hearted and generous,
Strangers carry his fame throughout the world
And many are they who call that mortal good."
   Then resourceful Odysseus answered: "O honored wife

Of Laertes' son Odysseus, I haven't had
Any use at all for cloaks and bright blankets since the day
I rode away from the snow-crowned mountains of Crete
In my long-oared ship. So I'll go lie down as usual,
For many a sleepless night on some foul pallet
I've lain and waited for Dawn of the beautiful throne.
And I have no great affection for foot-baths either,
Nor shall any of these maid-servants here in the palace
So much as touch a foot of mine, unless
There is some really ancient and sober old woman who has borne
In her heart as many sorrows as I have. Only such
Would I allow to touch my feet."
     And Penelope,
Thoughtful as ever, replied: "Dear sir, never
Has one so wise, of those we've had from abroad,
Been a more welcome guest in my home, so keen and prudent
Is all that you say, and I do have just such an old woman,
A very understanding old woman, who lovingly nursed
And reared my unfortunate husband from the time she took him
Into her arms on the day his mother bore him.
She shall wash your feet, feeble though she is.
So come, discreet Eurycleia, get up and wash
The feet of a man the same age as your master.
By now the hands and feet of Odysseus must look like
These of our guest, for men in trouble grow old
In a hurry."
     Then the old one covered her face with her hands
And lamented, recalling Odysseus, as the hot tears fell:
"Ah, my child, what misery is mine at not
Being able to help you! Surely Zeus hated you most
Of all men, despite your god-fearing heart. For no
Mortal man ever burnt to Zeus, the lover of lightning,
So many rich thigh-pieces and select hecatombs as you
So prayerfully did, in hopes of reaching old age

323

In comfort and rearing your royal son. But now
To you alone God gives no day of returning—
And surely, sir, in some far foreign place
When he came to somebody's marvelous mansion, the women
Mocked and made fun of him too, as these bitches here
Have all done to you. It is so you won't have to endure
Their vulgar, insulting remarks that you won't have them
Washing your feet, but I will gladly wash them,
As Icarius' daughter Penelope has asked me to do.
Deep sorrow moves my heart, and so for her sake
And yours I'll wash your feet. But let me say this.
Many are the weary strangers we've had in the palace,
But never before have I seen any man who so
Resembled another as you resemble Odysseus
In build, and voice, and feet."
      Then shrewdly he answered:
"Old one, all who have seen us both do say
That we look very much like each other, just as you also
Have noticed and said."
      After these words, the old woman
Took the gleaming cauldron she used for foot-baths and poured in
Enough cold water, to which she added the warm.
And Odysseus sat down at the hearth, but quickly he turned
His back on the fire, for all of a sudden it struck him
That as she took hold of his feet she might notice a scar
He had, and so the truth would be out. Sure enough,
She had scarcely begun to wash the feet of her lord
When she discovered the scar of a wound Odysseus
Had suffered from a boar's white tusk when long ago
He had gone to Parnassus to visit Autolycus, his mother's
Accomplished father, and all of his sons—Autolycus,
With whom no man could compete as liar and thief.
This talent of his was a gift from a god, Hermes,
Whom he continued to please with legs of lamb

And kid burnt on the altar. So Hermes was always
Glad to help him. Now once Autolycus had come
To the wealthy island of Ithaca and found that his daughter
Had just given birth to a son, and as he finished
His supper, Eurycleia laid the child in his lap, and said:
     "Autolycus, now you find a name for your daughter's
         dear child,
For whom we have long been praying—yes indeed we have."
     And Autolycus answered: "My son-in-law and daughter, give
The boy whatever name I say. Now since
I come here as one who is *odious* to many, both men
And women, all over the bountiful earth, let his name
Be *Odysseus,* child of wrath! And when he becomes
A man and visits the great palace of his mother's people
At Parnassus, where all my treasures are, then
I will give him of them and send him home rejoicing."
     So Odysseus had gone to receive the splendid presents
Of Autolycus, and he and his sons welcomed him warmly,
Shaking his hands and saying how glad they were
To have him. And Amphithea, his grandmother, hugged Odysseus
And kissed his head and both of his beautiful eyes.
Then Autolycus asked his noble sons to prepare
The feast, and they were quick to get started. They led in
A five-year-old bull, and when they had flayed and carved
The carcass, they skillfully chopped up the meat in small pieces,
Put it on spits, roasted it well, and served out
The helpings. Thus they feasted all day until sundown
And found the meal quite equal to their excellent appetites.
But when the sun set and darkness arrived, they all
Went to bed, where each of them received the gift
Of sleep.
     But early next day, at the first red streaks
Of morning, the sons of Autolycus and noble Odysseus
Set out with the hounds on a hunt. Up the steep side

Of forest-clad Parnassus they climbed till they came, before long,
To the windy ravines. The Sun was just striking the fields,
As he rose from the gliding deep stream of Oceanus,
          when the beaters
Came into a glade. Before them the hounds were hot
On the scent, and behind came the sons of Autolycus and valiant
Odysseus, he, with the others, pressing hard on the hounds
And swinging his spear that cast the long shadow. There
In a thicket-lair a huge wild boar was lying,
A thicket so dense that no raw wind or rain
Or blazing hot sun could pierce it, and the littered leaves
Lay deep on the ground beneath. Then about the boar
Came the beat of the feet of the men and the dogs, pressing in
On him close, and the boar charged out of his lair and stood,
With bristling back and eyes aflame, at bay
Before them. Odysseus rushed in, his long spear held high
In his powerful hand, eager to strike the first blow.
But the boar was faster, and charging from the side he slashed
Above his knee a long deep gash in the flesh, though not
To the bone. And the point of Odysseus' bright spear went in
At the boar's right shoulder and clean through his body,
          sending him
Down in the dust with a squeal, where his life flew from him.
Then the dear sons of Autolycus took care of the carcass
And skillfully dressed the wound of godlike Odysseus,
Staunching dark blood with an incantation. Quickly
They reached their dear father's house, and when, with their care,
The wound was well and they had given Odysseus
Wonderful presents, they sent him swiftly and happily
Home to his own dear Ithaca. His father and mother
Were more than glad to see him and asked all about
The visit, and especially about the scar. And he told them
Exactly what happened, how the white tusk of a boar
Had gashed him there when he and the sons of Autolycus

Had gone on a hunt to Parnassus.
    As she handled his limbs
The old nurse felt the scar and knew what it was.
She let his foot fall, and his leg, as it fell and tilted
The basin, made the bronze ring and the water run out
On the ground. Then joy and grief together seized on
Her soul. Her eyes were brimming with tears and her voice
Cracked as she touched the chin of Odysseus, and said:
    "Indeed you are Odysseus, dear child! Until
I had handled the limbs of my lord, I didn't know you."
    With this she looked at Penelope, as much as to say
Her darling husband was home, but Penelope could not
Meet the glance and get the message, for Athena
Turned her attention elsewhere. Quickly, Odysseus
Felt for the nurse's throat and tightened his right hand
Upon it, while with his left he drew her closer,
And said:
    "Good mother, why do you want to destroy me?
You nursed me yourself at this your breast, and now
In the twentieth year I've come to my country again,
Having toiled through many hardships. So since, with the help
Of a god, you've found out and know in your heart who I am,
Be utterly quiet about it! so that no one else
In the palace will know. Or else—and believe me, I'll do
What I say—if a god defeats the lordly wooers
Through me, I'll execute you, nurse or no nurse,
Right here in these halls along with the other women!"
    Then wise Eurycleia: "My child, what words are these
That you let pass the barrier of your teeth!
You know how firm and steadfast my spirit is.
I'll be as close as solid stone or iron.
And here's another thing for you to remember.
If a god does defeat the lordly wooers through you,
I'll speak of all the women in this palace

And tell which ones disgrace you and which do not."
    And resourceful Odysseus said: "Good mother, why talk
About them? You surely don't have to. I'll watch them all
And find out about them myself. So hold your tongue,
And leave all this to the gods."
    He spoke, and the old one
Went off through the hall to fetch more water, since the first
Was all spilled. When she had washed his feet and rubbed them
Richly with oil, Odysseus again drew his chair up
Nearer the fire, warming himself, and covered
The scar with his rags. Then brooding Penelope continued
Their talk:
    "Sir, I'll ask you one more little thing,
And that's all, for now it will soon be time for sweet sleep,
At least for him who can sleep in spite of his troubles.
But to me some god has given immeasurable misery,
For though by day I get some relief from my sorrow
And mourning by seeing to the household chores and supervising
The maids, when night arrives and sleep that comes
To all, I lie on my bed, grieving and restless,
With a throbbing heart hard pressed with cutting cares.
As when Pandareus' daughter, the leaf-green nightingale,
Perches in early spring amid the deep foliage
Of trees and pours out her voice of great range with numerous.
Sweet variations, wailing for her own dear Itylus,
Son of King Zethus, the child she blindly killed
With a sword, even so my heart, like her sorrowful song,
Varies from doubt to doubt, whether to stay
With my son and look after all that I own, the servants
And this my huge high-vaulted home, respecting
The bed of my husband and public opinion, or whether
To go on and marry the best of these Achaeans,
The one who woos me here in the palace and offers
Gifts without limit. Then too, so long as my son

Was an irresponsible child, he wouldn't allow me
To marry and leave my husband's house, but now
That he's grown he begs me to go, since he is so worried
About his estate that the wooers are daily devouring.
But come, I want you to hear this dream of mine
And say what it means. I have twenty geese that come up
From the water to eat wheat in the house, and it does
      my heart good
To watch them. But a bent-beaked great eagle swooped down
      from the mountain
And broke all their necks, and leaving them dead and tumbled
In a heap in the hall, he flew off in the shining sky.
Then I began weeping and wailing right there in my dream,
And the fine Achaean ladies crowded around me
As pitifully I grieved for my geese the eagle had killed.
But then he returned, and perching outside on one
Of the jutting roof-beams, he spoke with the voice of a man
And stopped my lamenting thus:
      " 'Take heart, O daughter
Of far-famed Icarius. This is no dream, but a vision
Of truth that shall be fulfilled. The geese are the wooers,
And I, an eagle before, have come back now
As your husband, bringing a terrible doom on all
Of them.'
      "He spoke, and honey-sweet sleep let me go.
I looked around and there in the hall by the trough
I saw all the geese eating the wheat, just as
They always did."
      And resourceful Odysseus replied:
"My lady, no matter how much you twist it, this dream
Of yours can have no other meaning, for Odysseus
Himself has shown you how it will be. It's very
Clear that the wooers will all be destroyed. Not one

Will avoid this death and the fates!"
        Then wise Penelope
Answered: "Dreams, sir, are jumbled, inscrutable things,
And are by no means always a source of truth.
Through two separate gates our insubstantial dreams
Come to us. One is made of horn, the other
Of ivory. Those that pass through the gate of sawn ivory
Are deceptive dreams, and the words they bring are false.
But those that come through the gate of polished horn
Tell truly to the mortals that see them of things that really
Happen. But such, I fear, was not the gate
Through which my weird dream came, much to the sorrow
Of my son and myself.
        "And here's something else for you
To consider. That ominous day is almost here
That will take me away forever from the house of Odysseus.
For I'm about to propose a contest of strength
And skill, using the identical ax-heads, twelve
In all, that Odysseus would set up on props like those
Beneath a new keel, and align the handle-holes
Just so. Then he would stand at a distance and shoot
An arrow through all of them. Now this is the trial
I intend to set for the wooers. Whoever most easily
Strings the bow with his hands and shoots an arrow
Through all twelve axes, with him I will go, and leave
This house to which I came as a bride, this
Most lovely house, full of so many good things,
Which I shall remember, I'm sure, even in dreams."
        And the quick Odysseus replied: "O honored wife
Of Laertes' son Odysseus, put it off no longer,
This contest in the hall. For believe me, resourceful Odysseus
Will be here long before these men, fumbling
His polished bow, will ever string it and shoot
An arrow through iron!"

Then thoughtful Penelope answered:
"If it were really your wish, sir, to go on sitting
Here in the palace with me, pleasing me so,
No sleep should ever fall on these lids of mine.
But it cannot be that men should go without sleep
Forever, for the gods have set a just portion of time
For all that mortals do on the bountiful earth.
So now I'm going upstairs to my room and lie down
On my bed—a bed of sorrow and tears ever since
The day Odysseus left to lay his eyes
On evil, unspeakable Troy. There I'll lie down,
And you sleep here in the house. Either spread a pallet
For yourself on the ground, or let the maids make up
A bed for you."
                    So saying, she went back upstairs
To her bright chamber, but not alone, for her women
Accompanied her. When they reached the upper room,
She wept aloud for her dear husband Odysseus
Till blue-eyed Athena shed sweet sleep on her lids.

BOOK

XX

OMENS OF DEATH
FOR THE WOOERS

Out in the portico noble Odysseus lay down
For the night. On the ground he spread the undressed hide
Of an ox and on it a number of fleeces from some
Of the sheep the wooers were constantly killing. Then
He lay down, and Eurynome covered him up with a blanket.
While he was lying there, unable to sleep
And pondering within his heart an evil end
For the wooers, the women who made a practice of sleeping
With them came out of the hall, giggling and joking
Among themselves. At this the heart of Odysseus
Leaped with rage, and for a time he couldn't decide
Whether he should overtake them and kill them all on the spot,
Or let them sleep this last and final night
With the arrogant lords. And the heart in his breast growled
Like a bitch that senses a stranger and stands, snarling
And full of fight, over her helpless puppies.
Even so his heart growled, indignant at such depravity.
But striking his breast, he argued thus with himself:
    "Endure it, heart! You bore a thing more beastly

Than this that time the lawless Cyclops devoured
Those noble comrades of mine. Then you endured
Until that cunning Nobody got you out of the cave
You thought you were going to die in."

      Thus he restrained
The heart in his breast, that now obeyed his command,
Doggedly enduring. But he himself lay tossing
From side to side like a paunch of rich blood pudding
That a man who is eager to roast it turns quickly this way
And that above a large and blazing hot fire. Even so
Odysseus tossed and turned, pondering how
He might come to grips with the shameless wooers, he being
But one and they so many. At last Athena
Came down from the sky, and coming up close to him
In the form of a woman, she stood at his head, and said:

      "Why again are you lying awake, most wretched of men?
This is your house, and in it lie your wife
And your child, and he such a man as anyone would like
To have for a son."

      And resourceful Odysseus replied:
"What you say, O goddess, is nothing but the truth. Still
There's something that keeps coming up in my mind—namely,
How I may lay my hands on the shameless wooers,
Since I am only one man and there's always a crowd
Of them in the palace. And I worry about something else
More difficult yet. For suppose, by the will of Zeus
And yourself, I should manage to slay them all, where
Could I go and be safe? Give this some thought, if you will."

      And the blue-eyed goddess Athena replied: "Poor wretch,
Many's the man who puts his faith in a friend
Much weaker than I, in a mortal with nowhere near
My resources. For I am a goddess, your guardian goddess
Through all your trials. But let me make myself clear.
If we were surrounded by fifty bands of alert

333

And bloodthirsty men, even so, you would be able
To drive off their cattle and splendid fat sheep! Now then,
Give in and get some sleep. These all-night vigils
Are wearing indeed, and soon you'll be out of this trouble."
    When the beautiful goddess had let sleep fall on his lids,
She returned to Olympus. But care-loosening sleep had no sooner
Relaxed his limbs than his faithful wife awoke
And sat up weeping in her soft bed. Having found
Some relief in her tears, that lovely lady thought first
Of Artemis, and prayed:
    "O Artemis, powerful goddess,
If only right now you would strike my breast with one
Of your arrows and thus deliver my soul, or if only
The whirling winds would snatch me up and carry me
Down the dim ways and cast me out where the sea
Runs into the stream of circling Oceanus, just as
They did Pandareus' daughters! The gods had slain
Their parents and left the girls bereft in the halls,
Where fair Aphrodite took care of them with cheese,
Choice honey, and delicate wine. Hera endowed them
With looks and discretion beyond all other women,
Chaste Artemis made them grow tall, and Athena saw to it
That they were expert in the glorious handwork of women.
But as glamorous Aphrodite was ascending to lofty Olympus
To ask for them the gift of thriving marriage—
While she was on her way to ask this of Zeus,
The lover of lightning, him who has full knowledge
Of everything, including the luck and haplessness of mortals—
The harpy winds snatched the maidens away
And gave them in bondage to the hateful Furies. O that
The gods who live on Olympus would cause me to vanish
As they did, or that fair-haired Artemis would strike me down,
So that I might go beneath the hateful earth
With Odysseus bright in my mind and never give joy

Of any kind to a lesser man!
  "So long as
One weeps by day with a heart full of sorrow, but is able
To sleep at night, misery may be endured,
For when sleep envelops the lids all is forgotten,
The good along with the bad. But a god has so wrought
That even my dreams are wretched. Again tonight
There lay beside me here a man like him,
Just as he was when he left with the army, and my heart
Rejoiced, since I didn't know I was dreaming, but thought
It was finally true."
  Soon after her prayer came Dawn
With a sky full of gold. But Odysseus heard her crying,
And dreamily musing it seemed to his heart that she stood
At his head and knew who he was. Then, having picked up
The blanket and fleeces on which he had slept and put them
Inside on a chair and carried the oxhide outdoors,
He lifted his hands to Zeus and prayed to him thus:
  "O Father Zeus, if you gods meant well in bringing me
Home over sea and land, after tormenting
Me so, let one of those inside who are now
Waking up utter some ominous word for me,
And reveal, O Father, some god-sent omen out here."
  Thus he prayed, and wise-counseling Zeus heard his prayer,
And at once from above the mist, from the dazzling peak
Of Olympus, he thundered. Godly Odysseus rejoiced,
And just inside the house where the people's shepherd
Kept his mills, a woman grinding spoke
The ominous word. Twelve women in all were accustomed
To work at these mills, grinding out barley-groats and fine
Wheat flour, the marrow of mortals. Now all the others
Had ground their grain and fallen asleep, but she,
The feeblest of all, was still at work. But now
She stopped her mill and spoke this sign for her master:

"O Father Zeus, ruler of gods and men,
Most mightily then you thundered from the starry sky,
But since there isn't a cloud in sight you must be
Showing somebody a sign. Please grant now
Even for miserable me just this one thing.
May the wooers today feast in the halls of Odysseus
For the last and final time. Those men who have made me
Grow feeble, painfully laboring to furnish them groats
Of barley, may they this day partake of their very
Last meal!"
    She spoke, and noble Odysseus rejoiced
At this word of good omen and the ominous thunder of Zeus.
Now he felt sure that vengeance on the guilty was his.

    Meanwhile, the other women servants in the beautiful house
Of Odysseus had met at the hearth and were busy rebuilding
The blaze of the undying fire. And Telemachus got up
From his bed and dressed. He slung his keen blade
        from his shoulder
And on his shining feet bound beautiful sandals.
Then, like a god in appearance, he took his strong spear,
Sharp-pointed with bronze, and walked out to the door of the hall,
Where he stood and spoke thus to the good Eurycleia:
    "Dear nurse,
Have you shown, with bed and food, all due respect
To the guest in our house, or is he lying somewhere
Completely disregarded? That's Mother, you know. Wise
Though she is, she'll take a notion to honor some wretched
Mortal, but completely ignore a much better man
And send him away."
    Then discreet Eurycleia replied:
"Now, my child, I wish you wouldn't accuse
Your blameless mother. The man sat here and drank wine
As long as he wished, but when she asked him to eat
He said he was no longer hungry. And when he began

To think of going to bed, she told the maids
To make one for him. But he, like a man altogether
Unlucky and wretched, refused both bed and blankets,
And slept in the portico on the undressed hide of an ox
And the fleeces of sheep, though we did cover him up
With a blanket."

      She spoke, and Telemachus, with spear in hand
And two flashing-swift hounds at his heels, went out
          through the hall
To join the well-greaved Achaeans at the place of assembly.
But lady-like good Eurycleia, the daughter of Ops,
Peisenor's son, called thus to the maids:
      "Come now!
Some of you get busy and sweep out and sprinkle the hall
And cover the shapely chairs with purple tapestries,
While others thoroughly sponge off all the tables
And wash out the wine-bowls and well-wrought two-handled cups.
Let others go to the spring and quickly fetch water,
For the wooers will not be away from the hall much longer.
They'll be back very early this morning, since today is a feast-day
For all."

      The women all listened to her and were quick
To obey. Twenty sped off to the spring of dark water,
While the others performed with skill the household chores
And the strong men servants came in and deftly split
Some wood. Then the women returned from the spring,
          and behind them
The swineherd, driving the best and fattest three hogs
In the herd. Leaving these to root around for food
In the ample yard, he gently spoke to Odysseus:
      "Well, friend, do the lordly Achaeans show any more respect
For you, or do they still make sport of you there
In the hall?"

      And able Odysseus answered: "Ah,

Eumaeus, if only the gods would make those men pay
For the wanton and wicked outrages that they contrive
With no shame at all in somebody else's home!"

While they were talking, the goatherd Melanthius arrived
Along with two herdsmen leading the choicest goats
From all the herds to furnish a feast for the wooers.
They tethered the goats beneath the echoing portico,
And Melanthius taunted Odysseus with these cutting words:

"Stranger, can it be that instead of making tracks
You're going to keep on begging in the palace and making
An utter nuisance of yourself? I'm afraid that we
Won't say good-by until we've had a taste
Of each other's fists! For the way you beg is disgraceful,
And, you know, this isn't the only place
Where Achaeans are feasting."

To this the prudent Odysseus
Said not a word, but he shook his head and brooded
Revenge in the depths of his heart.

And now a third man
Approached, Philoetius, the master cowherd, driving in
For the wooers a young heifer and sleek fat goats that the boatmen
Who run the public ferry had carried over
From the mainland. He carefully tethered them under the echoing
Portico and came up close to question the swineherd:

"Who's the stranger, swineherd, just recently come
To our house? What people does he claim to be of? Where
Are his folks and fatherland? Poor beggar! He has the build
And bearing of a ruling king, but the gods can spin plenty
Of trouble for a world-wandering man, king or no king."

With this he went up to Odysseus, stretched out a friendly
Right hand, and spoke these winged words: "Welcome,
Good father. May you have better luck from now on,
Despite the very bad way you're in at the moment.
O Father Zeus, no other god is more ruthless

Than you! It argues a lack of compassion when you
Bring men, whom you yourself give life, into
All manner of misery and pain. Just now, good sir,
When I first saw you, I broke out with sweat, and my eyes
Are brimming with tears, for you remind me so much
Of Odysseus, who, I suppose, is a ragged wanderer
Very much like yourself—that is, if he's still alive
And in sight of the sunlight. If gallant Odysseus is dead
And already in the halls of Hades, I am
Indeed woebegone! When I was just a boy
Among the Cephallenians, he put me in charge of his cattle,
And now they've increased like ears of ripening grain,
Nor could the race of broad-browed cattle be more fruitful
For any mere mortal. But now I take orders from strangers
And supply them with meat, men who neither respect
The Prince's presence at home, nor tremble before the vengeance
And wrath of the gods. All they can think about now
Is dividing the goods of our long-absent lord. As for me,
I keep revolving over and over again
What I should do. For it certainly wouldn't be right,
With my master's son still alive, for me to take
The cattle and go into some foreign country. But
To stay here and suffer this misery, keeping cattle for strangers,
Is an even more wretched existence! I would have fled
Long ago and sought the protection of some other great king—
For I can no longer bear up beneath these woes—
But I keep on recalling my unlucky master, and hoping
That he may yet come back from somewhere and scatter
These suitor-men throughout the palace."
      Then able Odysseus
Answered: "Herdsman, since you are neither a bad
Nor stupid man and I can see for myself
That discretion is one of your traits, I'm going to tell you
Something and swear a great oath that it's true. By Zeus,

339

The first among gods, by this hospitable board
And the hearth of noble Odysseus to which I have come,
I swear that even while you are here, Odysseus
Shall come home, and you, if such is your wish,
Shall witness the slaying of these overbearing suitors
With your very own eyes!"

And the cowman: "Ah, my friend,
If only the son of Cronos would bring all that you say
To pass! Then you'd find out how strong I am
And what these hands can do."

Eumaeus likewise
Prayed to all the gods that sage Odysseus
Might return to his own home again.

While they were talking, the wooers were plotting as usual
Death and doom for Telemachus. But when a bird
Of omen, a high-flying eagle, came by on their left
With a trembling dove in his talons, Amphinomus spoke up
In the meeting, and said:

"My friends, our plan will not
Turn out as we wish, regarding the death of Telemachus.
But now we'd better start thinking of dinner."

Then they all
Agreed with Amphinomus, and entering the house of godly
Odysseus they threw their cloaks on the chairs and couches
And prepared the meal, slaughtering huge sheep, fat goats
And pigs, and a heifer from the herd. They roasted the vitals,
Heart, liver, and lungs, and gave out the helpings, and mixed bowls
Of wine, while the swineherd handed out cups. Philoetius
Served bread in beautiful baskets, and Melanthius poured
The wine. Then all reached out for the good things before them.

Craftily planning, Telemachus told Odysseus
To sit within the firm-founded hall beside
The stone threshold, and he placed for him there a battered old seat

And a low little table. Then he helped him to some of the vitals,
Poured wine in a golden goblet, and said:

   "Now sit
Right here with these men and drink your wine. I myself
Will see to it that you receive no taunts or blows
From them. This isn't at all a public place,
But the home of Odysseus, and it was for me that he built it.
Therefore, you wooers, let's have none of your fisticuffs
And wise remarks, so no fighting or fussing will start."

   At this bold speech from Telemachus, they all bit their lips
In amazement. But Antinous, son of Eupeithes, spoke thus:
"I know it's not easy, Achaeans, for us to respect
The word of Telemachus, but in spite of his threatening tone
Let us accept it. For if Zeus, the son of Cronos,
Had not objected, we would already have silenced
Him in the palace, shrill though his voice is!"

   So spoke Antinous, but Telemachus ignored what he said.
The heralds, meanwhile, were leading through town the holy
Hecatomb of the gods, and the long-haired Achaeans of Ithaca
Gathered in a shady grove of far-darting Apollo.
Those in the hall, having roasted the rest of the meat
And drawn it from the spits, carved up the helpings and fell
To the glorious feast. And the waiters, obeying the word
Of Telemachus, beloved son of a godlike father,
Gave Odysseus a portion as large as their own.

   But Athena was not about to allow the haughty
Wooers to check their outrageous behavior, for it
Was her will that the heart of Odysseus, son of Laertes,
Should be even more full of misery and pain. Now among
The wooers was a man uncouth and lawless, Ctesippus
By name, from a mansion somewhere in Samos. Bolstered
By trust in his boundless possessions, he wooed the wife
Of long-absent Odysseus, and now it was he who spoke
To the insolent wooers:

"Quiet, you manly lovers,
So I can talk! The stranger there has already
Had an equal helping, as indeed he should,
For it would be neither right nor mannerly to neglect
Any guest of Telemachus, no matter who he may be.
But say, I want to give him a friendly gift
Of my own, something extra, so he will be able
To give the bath-woman a present, or one to some other
Slave in the palace of royal Odysseus."
        So saying,
He took a cow's foot from the basket and let it fly
With all the strength of his beefy arm. But Odysseus
Bobbed his head, and to himself he smiled
One grim, sardonic smile, as the cow's foot struck
The solid wall. And now Telemachus spoke,
Harshly rebuking Ctesippus:
        "It's a very good thing
For you, Ctesippus, that the stranger ducked in time
And caused you to miss, or I would surely have hurled
My sharp spear clean through you! Then instead of a wedding
To celebrate here, your father would have found himself
With a funeral feast on his hands. So let there be
No barbarous behavior in my house. For now I see
And understand all that goes on here, both good and bad.
Before, I was only a child. Even so, we still
Put up with this brawling, this slaughtering of sheep
                and consuming
Of wine and bread, since it is hard indeed
For one man to hold so many men back. So please,
Out of your malice do me no further damage.
But if you're really determined to shed my blood
With the bronze, then so I wish it to be. For it's better,
Much better, to die than to go on watching these constantly
Horrible things, strangers roughly mistreated

And slave women shamefully dragged through the lovely halls!"
      For some time after these words, they all remained silent,
Till at last Agelaus, son of Damastor, spoke:
"My friends, nobody can argue with that, or take
Offense at words so justly spoken. Enough
Of mistreating the stranger and servants here in the house
Of godly Odysseus. But I would like to make
A gentle suggestion to Telemachus and his mother,
Which I hope will make sense to them. So long as your hearts,
Telemachus, were full of hope that wise Odysseus
Would return to his home, no one could blame you for waiting
And discouraging the wooers here, for had Odysseus
Really returned, that would surely have been
The better way. But now this much is clear—
That he will never return. So go sit down
By your mother and tell her she must marry the best
And most generous man here, so that she may keep house for him,
While you, eating and drinking, enjoy in peace
All that your fathers have left you."
      Then thoughtful Telemachus:
"No, Agelaus, by Zeus and the woes of my father,
Who has either died far from home or is wandering still,
I swear that I do nothing at all to delay
My mother's marriage. In fact, I actually tell her
To marry the man of her choice and I promise innumerable
Wedding presents. But I just can't bring myself
To order her from the palace. God forbid!"
      Telemachus spoke, and Pallas Athena befuddled
The wits of the wooers and stirred up hysterical laughter
Among them: They laughed with jaws so loose they did not
Seem to be theirs, and the meat they were eating was all
Bedabbled with blood. Their eyes brimmed up with tears
And their hearts with maudlin emotion. Then godlike
            Theoclymenus

Spoke to them thus:
>   "Ah, miserable ones, what horror
Is this you suffer? You are shrouded in night from head
To foot, a blaze of screams is kindled, your cheeks
Are streaming with tears, and the walls and beautiful beams
Are spattered with blood. The door and the court are crowded
With ghosts trooping down to enter the gloom of Erebus.
The sun is blotted completely from the sky
And a dark and evil mist hangs over all!"

>   Nothing but merry laughter answered the seer,
Till Eurymachus, son of Polybus, spoke up among them:
"Quick, boys! this newly come foreigner here is out of
His mind. Show him outdoors so he can go
To the market-place, since it seems too dark for him here."

>   But godlike Theoclymenus answered: "Believe me,
>   Eurymachus,
I need no help from you or your ushers. I've eyes
And ears of my own, two feet, and a mind within
Not at all malformed. These will see me out,
And so I go, for I see the evil that's coming
On all of you here—disaster which none of you wooers,
Who outrage those in the house of godly Odysseus
And plot all manner of wicked folly, can possibly
Flee or shun."

>   He spoke, and left those stately
Halls for the house of Peiraeus, who welcomed him gladly.
But the wooers all exchanged glances and tried to stir up
Telemachus by making fun of his guests. Thus one
Of the haughty young lords would say:

>   "Telemachus, when it comes
To company, surely you must be the most unfortunate
Man in the world. Just look at this filthy tramp,
Always in need of bread and wine, worthless
In all the skills of work and war, and nothing,

344

In short, but so much useless weight to burden
The earth. And here just now this other fellow
Gets up to prophesy. But say, if you'll listen to me
You'll be glad you did. Let us throw these strangers on board
A big ship and pack them off to Sicily, where you
Would be sure to get a very good price for them!"

     So the wooers, but Telemachus ignored what they said.
He just kept watching his father in silence, still waiting
For him to make the first move against that mob
Of graceless men.

     Meanwhile, thoughtful Penelope,
The daughter of Icarius, had placed her exquisite chair
Where she could hear every word that was said in the hall.

     Now the feast they had made with so much laughing
          and joking
Was a rich and tempting one indeed, for the wooers
Had slaughtered a great many victims. But surely no feast
Could ever have been less pleasant than that which a goddess
And powerful man were soon to serve them! For they
Were the ones who started the whole miserable business.

BOOK

XXI

THE STRINGING
OF THE BOW

Now the bright-eyed goddess Athena put it into the heart
Of Penelope, daughter of Icarius, to set before the wooers
In the home of Odysseus the bow and gray iron axes,
To begin their death with a contest. She climbed the high stairs
To her room, took in her strong hand the bent key
Of handsome bronze with handle of ivory, and with
Her women proceeded on into the far regions
Of the palace to the chamber where her lord's treasures were lying,
The bronze and gold and richly wrought iron. There too
Were kept the curving bow and excellent quiver
Bristling full of groan-fraught arrows—gifts
From a friend of Odysseus whom he once met in Lacedaemon,
Eurytus' son Iphitus, a man who closely resembled
The immortals themselves. The two had met in Messene
At the house of fiery Ortilochus. Odysseus was there
To collect a public debt, for the men of Messene
Had come to Ithaca in their many-benched ships and lifted
Some three hundred sheep, along with their shepherds. For these
Odysseus had come a long way, though he was still

A young man, for his father and the other elders had entrusted
Him with the mission. As for Iphitus, he had come
In search of a dozen mares he had lost, brood mares
With the tireless little mules they had foaled. Later, these
Were the cause of death and doom for Iphitus, when he reached
The house of Zeus's hard-hearted son, stout Heracles,
The master of mighty labors. For Heracles killed him
In cold blood, his own guest in his own house, without regard
For the table he had already set before him there
Or the gods' dire wrath! He feasted, then murdered the man,
And kept the mares where they were—in his own stables.
It was in quest of these that Iphitus met
Odysseus and gave him the bow, which great Eurytus
Had carried in days gone by and, dying, had left
To his son in the lofty palace. And Odysseus gave
To Iphitus a keen-edged blade and sturdy spear.
So their warm friendship began, but they never feasted
Each other, since before there was time the son of Zeus
Had murdered Iphitus, Eurytus' son, him
Who resembled the immortals themselves and gave Odysseus
The bow. This weapon gallant Odysseus never
Took to war with him aboard the black ships. He always
Left it at home in loving memory of
A dear friend, but in his own land he bore it about.
        When the lovely Queen reached the storeroom, she stepped
                on the oaken
Threshold, which long ago a builder had hewn out
True to the line, then fitted the posts, and hung
The gleaming doors. She quickly undid the thong
From the handle, put in the key, and with one deft thrust
Shot the bolts back. Struck by the key, the gleaming doors
Groaned like a bull that roars in the pasture and flew open
Before her. Up she stepped on the raised floor-boarding
Where the chests of fragrant clothing stood, and stretching

Up high with her hand she lifted down from its peg
The fine bright case containing the bow. And there
She sat down, with the case across her knees, and wept
Aloud as she drew out her husband's bow.
But when her tears had brought her some relief,
She started for the hall and the lordly wooers there
With the curving bow in her hands and the quiver full
Of groan-fraught deadly arrows, and her women went with her,
Bearing the chest that contained the ample iron
And bronze gaming-gear of her lord. In the hall she stood,
Lovely by one of the pillars of the massive roof,
Her face partly hid by a shining veil, and confronted
The wooers, with a trusted maid on either side.
Then, without hesitation, she spoke to them thus:

      "Your attention, proud wooers! you that have so rudely
Descended, with your endless eating and drinking, on the house
Of a man who has been so long away, and with
No other excuse except your desire for me
To marry someone of your number. Well then, my wooers,
Since it seems that I am the prize, hear this. I confront you
Now with the mighty bow of sacred Odysseus!
Whoever most easily strings the bow with his hands
And shoots an arrow through all twelve axes, with him
I will go, and leave this house to which I came
As a bride, this most lovely house, full of
So many good things, which I shall remember, I'm sure,
Even in dreams."

      She spoke, and told Eumaeus,
The worthy swineherd, to set before the wooers
The bow and gray iron axes, which he did,
But couldn't hold back his tears. He wept, and when
The cowherd saw his master's bow, he too
Gave way to weeping. Whereat Antinous poured

Contempt on them:
  "You childish peasants, who think
Of nothing but the passing day! Pair of miserable
Boors that you are, why now are you blubbering this way
And depressing this lady so much, when her heart is already
Mired in the misery of losing her darling husband?
Either sit down and stuff yourselves in silence,
Or go outside and cry. But leave the bow here
As a final tough test for the wooers. For I don't think
This gleaming bow is going to be easily strung.
Nobody here is the man Odysseus was.
Though I was a child when I saw him, I still remember."

  Such were his words, but all the time he was secretly
Hoping that it would be he who strung the bow
And shot an arrow through iron. Instead, he was
To taste the first arrow from the hands of matchless Odysseus,
Whom he, at that very moment, was meanly dishonoring,
And encouraging similar evil in all of his comrades.

  And now the jubilant Prince, the strong and sacred
Telemachus, said: "Well, of all things! Zeus,
The son of Cronos, must have taken my wits
Away. For my dear mother, wise though she is,
Says she'll marry another and leave this house,
And here I am gleefully laughing, crazy as can be!
But come, you wooers, since she is the prize you seek—
A lady whose like cannot be found in the whole
Achaean country, neither in sacred Pylos,
Argos or Mycenae, nor in Ithaca itself
Or on the dark mainland. But this you know already.
What need is there for me to praise my mother?
So come, don't draw this business out with your
Excuses, or put off any longer the stringing
Of the bow. We want to know the outcome. In fact,
I'd like to have a try at it myself.

If I can string it and shoot an arrow through iron,
I won't take it so hard when my honored mother
Says good-by to this house and goes away
With another, since then she'll be leaving me here the proven
Master in the contests of my father."
  So saying,
He threw off his purple cloak and sprang to his feet.
Then, from around his shoulders, he took the sharp sword
And dug a long trench, in which he set up the axes
And stamped the earth down firm around them, having brought
The handle-holes into alignment. All looked on
In amazement to see him do so well what he
Had never seen done before. Then he took his stand
On the threshold and addressed himself to the bow. Three times
His eager attempts made the bow quiver, but each time
He relaxed his effort too soon, though still his heart
Was hopeful that he would be the one to string
The bow and shoot that arrow through the twelve iron axes.
And now at last he might very well have strung it,
As on his fourth and final time he strove
With all his strength, but Odysseus checked his zeal
With a nod of his head. Whereat the strong and sacred
Young Prince spoke among them again:
  "Oh well, I guess
I'll always be weak and good for nothing. Either that,
Or I'm still too young, not sure enough of my strength
To stand up for myself when another gets rough and quarrelsome.
But come, you men much stronger than I, take
Your turns at the bow, and let's have done with the contest."
  Against the smooth, well-jointed door, he leaned
The bow, and beside the fine tip on the threshold he leaned
The swift arrow, then sat down again in the chair he had left.
And Antinous, son of Eupeithes, spoke to them thus:
"Let each man here take his turn, going from left

To right, and starting back there where the wine is poured."
    This they all liked, and the first to arise was their teller
Of omens, Oenops' son Leiodes, who always
Sat by the lovely bowl at the far end
Of the hall. He alone despised blind violent deeds
And was full of indignant blame for all the wooers,
And now his turn at the bow and swift arrow came first.
Making his way to the threshold, he braced himself
And gave it a try. But stringing that bow was much
Too much for him, and as he tugged at the string
His soft and delicate hands grew very tired.
Then he spoke thus to the wooers:
                        "Friends, I'm not
The man. Let somebody else take a turn. For believe me,
This very bow will take the heart and life
From many princes, but surely it's better to die
Than to go on day after day living and waiting
But never attaining that for which we are here.
Now many a man still hopes to have his desire
And marry the wife of Odysseus. Well, when you've had
Your turn at the bow and seen what I mean, go court
Some other fair-gowned Achaean lady and try
To win her with your gifts. Then Penelope can marry the man
Who offers the most and is destined to be her husband."
    He spoke, and against the smooth, well-jointed door
He leaned the bow, and beside the fine tip he leaned
The swift arrow, then sat down again in the chair he had left.
But Antinous called him by name and chided him thus:
"Leiodes, what hard and terrible words are these
That just got by the barrier of your teeth!
I blame you much for speaking so, saying
That this same bow will take from princes the heart
And life, just because you can't string it. Blame that
On your honored mother, for you weren't born to draw

351

A bow and shoot. But others here in this princely
Band of wooers will string it, and that right quickly!"

He spoke, and called out to goat-goading Melanthius: "Come,
Get busy, Melanthius, and build up the fire on the hearth.
Then beside it put a large seat with a covering of fleece
And bring out from within a sizable cake of tallow,
So that when we young lords have warmed the bow and rubbed it
With fat, we can give it a try and end the contest."

Melanthius quickly rekindled the still-glowing fire,
Placed a large seat with a covering of fleece beside it,
And brought out from within a sizable cake of tallow.
With this the young lords tried to limber the bow, but when
They attempted to string it not one of them was nearly
Strong enough, though Antinous and handsome Eurymachus,
The wooers' chief men, by far the first in valor,
Were still holding back from the contest.

The cowman and swineherd
Of godly Odysseus had left the hall together,
And now Odysseus himself went out of the house
To join them. Outside the courtyard gate, he spoke to them
Quietly: "Cowman, and you there, swineherd, should I tell you
Something, or not? My heart says I should. But say,
How willing would you two be to fight for Odysseus,
If suddenly from somewhere a god should bring him back?
Whom would you help, the wooers or Odysseus?
Answer me as your heart and soul command."

And the cowman replied: "If only Father Zeus
Would grant this wish of mine, that our master would
Return, god-guided, home! Then you would see
How strong I am and what these hands can do."

And Eumaeus likewise prayed to all the gods
That sage Odysseus might come home again.

When he knew for sure exactly how they felt,
He spoke to them thus: "Well, truly, here I am!

Really me, home again in the twentieth
Year, after many hardships. I'm well aware
That you are the only two servants I have who are glad
To see me. Not one of the others have I heard praying
For my return. So I'll speak frankly to you,
And what I say you can depend on. If God
Gives me the victory over these blackguards, I'll find you
Each a wife and give you things of your own,
Including new houses near mine, and from that time on
I'll look on both of you as friends and brothers
Of Telemachus. But here, see this—an unmistakable sign
I want to show you, so you will feel in your hearts
That you know me and be convinced—right here, the scar
I got long ago from the white tusk of a boar
On a hunting trip to the wilds of Mount Parnassus
With the sons of Autolycus."
      So saying, he shuffled his rags
And showed the great scar. When the two men had seen it
      and examined it
Closely, they threw their arms about wise Odysseus,
Weeping in loving welcome and covering his head
And shoulders with kisses. So too Odysseus kissed
Their heads and hands. And now the light of the sun
Would have set on their weeping, if Odysseus hadn't
      restrained them,
Saying:
      "Stop this weeping and wailing before
Someone from the hall comes out and sees us and tells those
Inside. Let's go back in, but not together.
I'll go first, then you, and watch for this sign.
When the insolent wooers refuse me the bow and the quiver,
Then you, my good Eumaeus, carry the bow
Through the hall and hand it to me, and tell the women
To lock the tight-fitting doors of their chamber, and bid them

Stay there and go on working in silence. No matter
What unseemly noise of groaning and thud they hear
From within these walls, let none of them come rushing out!
And to you, my noble Philoetius, I give the task
Of barring the courtyard gate and tying it fast
With a rope."

So saying, he entered the fair-lying palace,
Where he took the same seat as before, and then the two servants
Of sacred Odysseus followed him in.

By now
The bow had come to Eurymachus, who was turning it over
And over to warm it in the firelight. But still he could not
String it, and loudly his proud heart groaned as he lost
His temper and blurted: "Confound it all! I really
Feel for myself and all the rest of you, too.
Not so much on account of the marriage, sorry
Though I am about that, for there's no lack of other
Women, some right here in sea-girt Ithaca,
Some in cities elsewhere. What bothers me
Is our apparent failure to equal the strength
Of godlike Odysseus, since none of us is able
To string his bow. What an utter disgrace!
One that will reach the ears of our children's children."

Then Eupeithes' son Antinous answered him thus:
"That, Eurymachus, will never happen, nor do you
Really believe it yourself. For today throughout
The land is a holy feast of the archer god
Apollo, and who would bend a bow on such
An occasion? Cheerfully put it aside, and what's to
Keep us from leaving the axes right where they are?
I think it unlikely that anyone will enter the hall
Of Laertes' son Odysseus and take them away.
So come, let the bearer of wine pour drops in all
Of the cups, that we may make our libations and give

The curved bow a rest. Then, in the morning, tell
Goat-goading Melanthius to drive in the very best goats
From all the herds, so that we can lay leg of goat
On the altar of Apollo, the glorious archer, and then
Have a try at the bow and put an end to the contest."
      With this they were glad to agree, and when the heralds
Had poured water over the hands of the suitors, their young
Attendants filled the bowls brimful of wine
And after first drops for libations poured liberally for all.
When each had poured to the gods and drunk in accord
With the wish of his heart, the resourceful, shrewd Odysseus
Called for their attention:
      "You wooers of the famous
And wonderful Queen, hear what my heart has to say.
I appeal especially to Eurymachus and godlike Antinous,
Since his advice was surely wise, to put
The bow down for the present, trusting the gods with the outcome,
And in the morning God's chosen man will win.
But say, let me have a try at that burnished horn bow,
That I, right here among you, may find out whether
My hands and limbs are still as supple and strong
As once they were, or whether the wear and tear
Of a wanderer's life has seriously weakened me."
      At this they all lost their tempers, for they were afraid
That he might really string that gleaming bow, and Antinous
Severely rebuked him, saying: "You miserable intruder,
Without one grain of sense to your name! Aren't you
Satisfied to feast your fill in this high company,
Getting your share of the food and hearing our talk
Which surely no other beggarly stranger hears?
You must be another wounded victim of wine—
Honey-sweet wine that does a staggering damage
To all who gulp it without moderation. It was wine,
You know, that got the best of the Centaur, famous

Eurytion, on his visit to the Lapithae, in the hall of Peirithous,
His great-hearted host. There he got silly drunk
And completely out of control, thus angering the heroes.
They sprang up and seized him, sheared off his ears and nose
With the ruthless bronze, and dragged him out of the house
And through the gate. Off he went, crazy
With pain and loaded down with the sin and blind folly
Of his own stupid heart. So started the feud between
Mankind and the Centaurs. But first he found pain for himself,
And too much wine was the cause of it all! Even so,
I say, if you string this bow, much the same treatment
Will be your lot in this land wherever you go.
In fact, we'll pack you off at once aboard
A black ship to mortal-maiming King Echetus, from whom
There is no escape. So take it easy and drink
Your wine, and don't ever struggle to compete with men
Who are younger than you."

      Then brooding Penelope said:
"Antinous, it is both ugly and wrong to deprive
The guests of Telemachus of anything rightfully theirs,
No matter who they may be. Do you really believe
That if this stranger has sufficient faith in his strength
To string the great bow of Odysseus he will then lead me off
To his home and make me his wife? I dare say he
Has no such hope in his heart. So don't let a thought
So foolish make anyone mope at his meat at this feast.
For believe me, nothing—but nothing!—could be more unlikely."

      And Polybus' son Eurymachus answered her thus:
"Daughter of Icarius, wise Penelope, it's not
That we think the beggar will lead you off with him—
That is indeed unlikely. What worries us
Is the slanderous gossip of men and women, this sort
Of thing from some low-down Achaean: 'Truly,
Those fellows wooing the wife of a matchless man

Are poor excuses for men! They can't put the string
On that burnished bow of his, but some beggar comes wandering
Along, strings it with the greatest of ease, and shoots
An arrow through iron.' So they will talk, and such
Would be our disgrace."

    Then brooding Penelope said:
"Eurymachus, there is no such thing as good reputation
For men who devour and dishonor the house of a prince.
So why take this matter to heart? Our guest is tall
And very well-built, and says he's the son of a noble
Father. But come, give him the bow and let us
See the result. I'll tell you this right now,
And I mean what I say. If he does string the bow and is glorified
By Apollo, I'll give him a good cloak and tunic to wear
And a fine sharp javelin to protect against dogs and men,
Along with a pair of sandals and a two-edged sword,
And I'll see that he gets wherever his heart and soul tell him
To go."

    Then thoughtful Telemachus answered her gravely:
"Mother, with regard to that bow—nobody who lords it
In rocky Ithaca or in any of the islands from here
To horse-pasturing Elis has a better right than I
To give it or not to whomever I please. Nor is there
Anyone here who is man enough to stop me,
Even if I should decide to make a present
Of it to this guest of mine to take on his way!
Go, then, upstairs to your room and keep yourself busy
With the loom and spindle, and see that your maids are busy.
Leave the bow to men—men in general,
But most of all to me, since I am now head
Of this house."

    Then back to her room she went, amazed,
And took to heart the spirited wise words of her son.
There with her maids she wept for her dear Odysseus

Until from blue-eyed Athena the sweet sleep came.
    By now the worthy swineherd was on his way
To Odysseus with the well-curved bow, but the hall full of wooers
Cried out at him, and thus a proud young lord
Would shout: "Hey! you wretched, meandering swineherd,
Where do you think you're going with that bent bow?
By grace of Apollo and the other immortal gods,
You'll soon be alone with your pigs, where the speedy hounds
You raised yourself can make a good meal of you!"
    This great uproar in the hall filled him with fear,
And he put the bow down where he was. But Telemachus,
       from the other
Side of the hall, loudly threatened him thus:
"Come on, old fellow! let's get on with the bow.
You'll soon find out it's not easy to do what all of us
Tell you. Take heed, or I'm liable to drive you back
To that farm with a pelting of rocks. I may be younger
Than you, but I guarantee I'm a good deal stronger.
I only wish I had the same muscular edge
On all these wooers here. I'd soon throw many
A clobbered villain out of this house of ours
And send him on his way a much sadder man!"
    This gave the young lords a good laugh at the Prince's
       expense
And relieved the bitter resentment they felt toward him.
The swineherd went on through the hall with the bow till
       he reached
The fiery Odysseus and handed it to him. Then
He called Eurycleia, the nurse, and spoke to her thus:
    "Wise Eurycleia, Telemachus says that you
Are to lock the tight-fitting doors of the women's chamber
And see that they stay there and go on working in silence.
No matter what unseemly noise of groaning and thud
They hear from within these walls, let none of them come

Rushing out!"
     No winged words came back from the nurse,
Who went to the stately chamber and bolted the doors.
     Quickly, quietly Philoetius went out of the house
And barred the gates of the high-walled yard. Under
The portico lay a curving ship's rope, made
From fiber of byblus, and with this he tied the gates tight
And went back inside. He took the same seat as before
And kept his eyes fixed on Odysseus, who now was handling
The bow, turning it round and round and trying
It out in various ways, making sure that worms
Had not eaten into the long horns while its owner was absent
Then a young suitor would glance at his neighbor and say:
     "Aha! no doubt an old hunter—and filcher—of bows.
Or perhaps he's got some just like it at home. Either that
Or he wants to make one himself, judging from the way
He turns it around and around in his hands, evil
Old tramp that he is!"
     And another of the proud young lords
Would say: "I wish the fellow just as much luck
As he ever has success in stringing that bow!"
     So they mocked him, but resourceful Odysseus weighed
The bow in his hands and examined it all with care.
Then, with as little effort as a skillful bard
Employs when about a new peg on his lyre he strings
The gut of a sheep and makes it fast at both ends,
Odysseus now, with equal ease, strung
The great bow. And holding it in his right hand he tested
The string, which gave back a musical twang as sweet
As the voice of a swallow.
     At this the wooers grew ill
And their faces turned pale. Zeus, by way of a sign,
Gave out a loud clap of thunder, and long-suffering, noble
Odysseus rejoiced at this omen from the son of Cronos,

Crooked in counsel. All but one of the arrows
Were still in the hollow quiver—arrows soon
To be tried upon the Achaeans. But now Odysseus
Picked up the quick shaft that lay there bare on the table
Beside him, laid it on the bridge of the bow, and drew back
The string and notched arrow. Then he shot with sure aim
   straight ahead
Without even leaving his seat, and not one ax
Did he miss. In at the first handle-hole, clean through,
And out at the last it flew, burdened with bronze.
To Telemachus, then, he spoke thus:
  "Telemachus, the stranger
That sits in your palace does not disgrace you. I neither
Missed the mark nor worked very long in stringing
The bow. The scornful wooers are wrong in their taunts—
I have my old strength still! But now the hour
Has come, while light remains, to prepare a feast
For the wooers, and thereafter continue the fun with the lyre
And singing and dancing, fine things at a feast."
  He spoke,
And signaled with his brows. Then the dear son
Of sacred Odysseus slung his sharp sword about him,
Got a firm grip on his spear, and stood by a chair
Not far from his father, armed with the flashing bronze.

BOOK
XXII

THE SLAYING OF
THE WOOERS

Now able Odysseus stripped his limbs of their rags
And sprang to the ample threshold, bearing the bow
And quiver full of swift arrows, which he poured out there
At his feet, and spoke these words to the wooers:
                                                "At last
This final tough test is ended, and now I'll shoot
At a mark which no man ever has hit, to see
If Apollo will grant me that glory."
                                     With this he sent
At Antinous a sharp and bitter shaft. Now that
Young lord had a lovely two-handled cup in his hands
And was just on the point of raising it up to drink
Of the wine. He had in his heart no thought of death,
For who at a feast would ever suppose that one man
There among many, even though he were very strong,
Could bring on him dark doom and evil death?
But Odysseus' well-aimed arrow went in at the throat,
Clean through his soft neck, and the point stuck out behind.

He dropped the cup and slumped to one side, as a thick rush
Of blood came up through his nostrils, and he, with a quick
Convulsive kick of his foot shoved the table away
And spilled all the food on the ground, where bread and roast meat
Were bedabbled with blood. At this the clamoring wooers
Broke into a panic, leaped from the chairs, and ran
Through the hall, scanning the solid walls for weapons,
But not one shield or doughty spear was there
To lay hold of. So they screamed at Odysseus these furious words:
    "You'll have to pay dearly, stranger, for making a man
Your target! No more contests for you—your death
Is now certain! To say the least, for you have killed
The best young man by far in all Ithaca.
The vultures will pick your bones right here in this island!"
    Thus the bewildered wooers, who thought he had killed
The man by mistake. The poor fools did not know that they all
Had reached the end and were now bound fast in the bonds
Of utter destruction. Then scowling at them, resourceful
Odysseus replied:
    "You dogs! you must not have thought
I'd ever come home from Troy, judging from the way
You've been ruining my home and forcing the women to sleep
In your beds and lawlessly wooing my wife with me
Still alive—all without fear of the sky-ruling gods
Or the sure retribution of men. Now, at the end
Of your folly, you're all bound fast in the bonds of destruction!"
    At these words they all turned a ghastly pale olive with fear
And each looked frantically round him for some escape
From that dire death. Only Eurymachus answered:
"If you really are Odysseus, home again
In Ithaca, these charges you make against the Achaeans
Are accurate enough—there have been many blind acts
Of wickedness and folly, both here in these halls of yours
And out in the fields. But he who was to blame

For it all is already dead—namely, Antinous.
He was the man behind every one of those evils,
Not that he really desired or needed the marriage.
He had another idea, which Cronos' son
Did not see fit to fulfill: to fatally ambush
Your son and make himself king in the well-settled realm
Of Ithaca. But he got what was coming to him and now
He is dead. So spare your own people, and we will go
Through the land and gather full payment for all of the food
And drink consumed in your palace, and each of us
Will personally bring, by way of payment, wealth
Worth twenty oxen, thus making good your loss
With bronze and gold till your heart is warmed and relents.
But until we do, nobody could blame you for being
So angry."
        Then, still scowling, resourceful Odysseus
Replied: "Eurymachus, not if you gave me all
Your ancestral estate, plus all that you have now
Or could get from anywhere else, would I hold back
These hands of mine from slaughter until you wooers
Have paid in full for all of your crimes. And now
It's before you to choose, either to face me and fight,
Or to flee and try to escape death and the fates,
Though I have a notion that a number of you won't make it!"
        At this their knees shook and they went to pieces inside.
Then Eurymachus spoke up again: "Friends, there is
No mercy for us in those most ruthless hands.
Now that he has the burnished bow and the quiver,
He'll shoot from the polished threshold till all of us
Are dead. So come, make up your minds to fight!
Out with your swords and use the tables for shields
Against the quick-killing arrows, and all together
Let's rush him and try to knock him off of that threshold
And out of that doorway, and go out ourselves through town,

Where the cry would soon be raised, and soon this fellow
Will have shot his bolt for good!"
    So saying, he drew
His double-edged blade of sharp bronze and charged at Odysseus,
Fearfully yelling, but he had scarcely got started
When the King let fly an arrow, and the swift shaft
        struck him
In the chest by the nipple and lodged itself in his liver.
Eurymachus dropped his sword and doubled up over
The table, then sprawled out, writhing, and fell on the ground
Along with the food and two-handled cup. In torment
Of soul he beat the earth with his brow, as his feet
Lashed out in convulsion, overturning the chair, and darkness
Enveloped his eyes.
    Amphinomus next, sharp sword
In hand, made a headlong lunge for famous Odysseus,
Hoping he would yield him the doorway. Telemachus, though,
Was too fast for him, and throwing from behind he drove
The bronze point of his spear in between the man's shoulders
        and out
Through his chest, so that he fell with a thud and struck
His face hard on the ground. Telemachus sprang away
And left the long-shadowing spear in the fallen Amphinomus,
For he was greatly afraid that while he was trying
To draw out the spear, or stooped down over the corpse,
Someone would rush in with a sword and deal him a slash
Or a stab. So he ran to his dear father's side, and spoke
These winged words:
    "Father, I'll bring you a shield
And a couple of spears and a good bronze helmet to fit
Your temples, and when I get back I'll arm myself
And also give armor to the swineherd and cowman. For we
Had better be armed."
    To which his dauntless father:

364

"Run and get them, before I shoot all these arrows
And all alone as I am they force me out of
This doorway!"
    Telemachus did as his dear father wished.
He went to the room where the glorious arms were stored,
Took four shields, eight spears, and four bronze helmets
Thickly maned with horsehair, and carried them quickly
Back to his father. Then the Prince put on the bronze,
As did the two servants, who now took their stand, equipped
With the splendid armor, on either side of Odysseus,
The versatile and fiery.
    So long as he had the protection
Of arrows, he kept on shooting the wooers, picking
Them off one by one and piling them up in the hall.
But when the King's arrows gave out, he left the bow leaning
Between a doorpost of the firm-founded hall and the gleaming
Wall of the entrance. Then around his shoulders he hung
A hide shield of four layers, and on his noble head
He put the strong helmet with horsehair plume, defiantly
Waving above him, and he took up two bronze-pointed spears.
    At the rear of the hall in the well-built wall and raised
To the threshold level was a small back exit with tight
Folding doors leading into a passage emerging close by
The main entrance. Since the passage had only this one
        outside opening,
Odysseus bade the good swineherd to stand hard by it
And guard it. Agelaus, then, spoke thus to the wooers:
    "Friends, won't somebody mount through the door back there
And tell the people, that a cry may quickly go up
And the shooting days of this fellow be quickly ended?"
    And the goatherd Melanthius answered: "That can't be done,
Zeus-fed Agelaus. The fine double door from the hall
To the yard is too dangerously near where the passage comes out,
And the mouth of the passage is terribly narrow, so narrow

That one good man could hold it against us all!
But come, let me go to the storeroom and bring you armor
To wear, for I believe Odysseus and that brilliant
Son of his have laid the arms away
Nowhere else but here, right here in the house!"

    So saying, goatherd Melanthius went out at the rear
Of the hall to the storerooms of Odysseus, where he took
       twelve shields
And an equal number of spears and bronze helmets maned
With horsehair, and quickly carried them back to the wooers.
At sight of them arming themselves and brandishing spears,
Odysseus felt weak in the knees and his great heart sank.
The task ahead seemed hard indeed, but at once
He spoke winged words to his son:
    "Telemachus, surely
Some woman inside is raising the odds against us—
Either that, or Melanthius is!"

    Then gravely Telemachus
Answered: "Father, nobody's to blame for this
But me. I left the tight door of the storeroom open,
And their lookout was sharper than I. But go, good Eumaeus,
Close the storeroom door and find out whether
It's one of the women who helps them or, more likely,
Dolius' son Melanthius."

    While they were talking,
Goat-goading Melanthius started for the storeroom again
For another load of the excellent armor, but the swineherd
Saw him, and quickly spoke thus to his master nearby:
"Zeus-sprung son of Laertes, resourceful Odysseus,
There's that infernal fellow we all suspect
On his way to the storeroom again. But tell me what
You want done with him if it should so happen that I
Am the better man. Shall I kill him right there, or bring him
In here to you, so that he can pay for all

366

The outrageous things he's caused to be done in your house?"
    Then able Odysseus answered: "I, with the help
Of Telemachus, will hold the proud wooers in here, no matter
How fiercely they fight. You two go throw that wretch
In the storeroom, hog-tie his hands and feet, along with
A board, behind him, then attach a rope and haul him
Up a tall pillar till he almost reaches the roof-beams.
That way he'll live a long time and suffer hard pain."
    He spoke, and both were eager to do as he bade.
When they got to the storeroom, there was Melanthius rummaging
Around in a corner looking for armor, and so
He missed their arrival. Quietly they waited for him,
One on either side of the door, and as
The goatherd stepped over the threshold, in one hand
        a fine helmet,
In the other a broad, mildewy old shield—once
The shield of the young lord Laertes, but now out of use
For so long the stitching of its straps had rotted—right then
They jumped him and dragged him back in by the hair, threw
The terrified wretch to the ground, and forcing his hands
And feet together behind him tied him with cords
That cut, as the royal son of Laertes, long-suffering
Odysseus, had ordered, and they attached a rope
And hauled him up a tall pillar till he almost reached
The roof-beams. Then, Eumaeus, you mocked the man thus:
    "Now at last, Melanthius, you've got the soft bed you deserve!
Lie there and watch all night, nor is it likely
That you will be sleeping when early Dawn comes up
In gold from the streams of Oceanus, at that very time
You used to drive in the goats to furnish a feast
For the wooers here in the palace!"
    There they left him,
Bent back and bound with the cutting cords. They took up
Their arms, closed the bright door, and returned to Odysseus,

The fiery and fertile-minded. Then the four of them stood
On the threshold, breathing fury and confronting those
In the hall, the many and able. Now Pallas Athena,
Daughter of Zeus, drew near in the guise of Mentor,
And Odysseus rejoiced when he saw her, and said:
    "Mentor,
Dear fellow, keep us from ruin! Remember our friendship
And the good turns I've done you."
    He thought, as he spoke these words,
That Mentor was really Athena, the rouser of warriors.
But the wooers shouted together from out in the hall,
And the voice of Damastor's son Agelaus emerged,
Rebuking the goddess: "Mentor, don't let Odysseus
Trick you with words into fighting for him against us,
Unless you want to die for your misdeeds
Right after your comrades there, for we're surely going to
Kill them—both father and son! So remember, you'll pay
With your head, and when we have taken your life with the sword
We'll lump all you own, both indoors and out, with the things
Of Odysseus, nor will we allow your sons and daughters
To live in your house, and your excellent wife won't dare
To walk abroad in the streets of Ithaca!"
    This made
Athena so angry she took her rage out on Odysseus:
"You've no longer got it, Odysseus—that steady strength
And valor you certainly had when you fought without ceasing
For nine long years at Troy for high-born Helen
Of the lovely white arms! Many were the men you killed
In terrible combat, and your plan led to the taking
Of the wide-wayed city of Priam. So now, at home
Among your belongings, how is it you show such wailing
Reluctance to use against the wooers what valor
You have? Come on, old fellow, stand by my side
And watch me in action. I want you to see how Mentor,

Alcimus' son, repays a debt of kindness
In battle with blackguards."
    Even so, she did not increase
His prowess to the point of victory, but continued to test
The valor and might of father and son. She herself
Took the form of a swallow and darted up high in the hall
To perch on a smoky roof-beam.
    Now six of the suitors
Made an effort to rally the wooers—Agelaus, son
Of Damastor, Eurynomus, Amphimedon, and Demoptolemus,
Peisander, son of Polyctor, and fiery Polybus—
By far the most valiant of those who survived the thick hail
Of arrows and now still fought for their lives. Agelaus
Spoke thus:
    "Friends, the ruthless hands of that man
Are beginning to fail him. After those empty brags,
Mentor deserted him, and there they are
Alone at the door. So don't all throw your long spears
At once. Let the six of us throw first and see
If Zeus will grant us the glory of striking Odysseus!
Once he is down, the others won't be any trouble."
    They did as he said and savagely hurled their spears,
But Athena made all of them miss. One struck the door-post
Of the firm-founded hall, another the strong door itself,
While the ashen, bronze-heavy lance of a third crashed into
The wall. When they had dodged the volley, the gallant,
Enduring Odysseus spoke to them thus:
    "Now,
My friends, it's our turn! Hurl your spears right into
That mob of suitors, who would very much like to add
The slaughter and stripping of us to their other atrocities."
    He spoke, and they all let fly, hurling their spears
Straight and hard. Odysseus slew Demoptolemus, Telemachus
Euryades, the swineherd Elatus, and Peisander fell

369

To the keeper of cattle. All at one time they fell
And bit the huge dirt floor with their teeth, and the rest
Of the wooers retreated as far back as they could in the hall,
While the four on the threshold leaped out and recovered
       their spears
From the dead.
       Then again with all their might the wooers
Hurled their sharp spears, and Athena made most of them miss.
One struck the door-post of the firm-founded hall, another
The strong door itself, while the ashen, bronze-heavy lance
Of a third crashed into the wall. But Amphimedon did manage
To graze the wrist of Telemachus, the bronze just breaking
The skin, and Ctesippus' huge spear flew over the shield
Of Eumaeus and scratched his shoulder as it hurtled on down
To the floor. Then again the valiant foursome, led
By their versatile King, sent their sharp spears straight into
That mob of suitors. This time Eurydamus fell
To Odysseus, sacker of cities, while Telemachus killed
Amphimedon and the swineherd Polybus. Then the keeper
       of cattle
Landed his spear in the chest of Ctesippus, exulting:
     "Now, you mockery-loving son of a braggart,
Don't ever be foolish enough to talk big again!
Let gods do the judging, since they are so much more able.
That spear is your gift of welcome in return for the cow's foot
You recently gave to godlike Odyssus when he
Was a beggar here in the palace!"
       So spoke the keeper
Of the long-horned cattle. Then at close quarters Odysseus
Fatally wounded Damastor's son Agelaus
With a thrust of his spear, and Telemachus did the same
To Leiocritus, son of Euenor, driving the bronze
Clean through the small of his back, so that he pitched forward
And struck the floor with his face. Then Athena, high up

370

Near the roof, lifted the lethal, horrible aegis,
And the wooers went crazy with fear. They fled through the hall
Like a herd of stampeding cattle when the darting gad-fly
Attacks them and drives them along in the springtime, season
Of longer days. And as when eagles, with bent beaks
And talons, swoop down from the mountains and pounce
          on the smaller
Birds that cringe at the clouds and hug the plain
In their flight, unable to help themselves or escape
As the eagles dive down and destroy them while men enjoy
The sport, so now the valiant foursome smote
The wooers this way and that through the hall. Mid the bashing
Of heads a hideous groaning arose, and the whole floor
Ran with blood.
      Then Leiodes rushed in, and embracing
The knees of Odysseus spoke these words winged with pleading:
"Here at your knees, Odysseus, I beg you to have
Some regard and pity for me. I swear to you
That in these halls no woman has ever been wronged
By a wanton word or deed of mine. In fact,
I did my best to keep the others from doing
Such things. But they wouldn't listen to me and keep
Their hands to themselves. Blind folly brought on
         their harsh doom.
But I was only their priest, their teller of omens.
I've done nothing wrong, yet I shall be laid as low
As the others. Such is the thanks one gets for goodness!"
      With a look of grim disgust, resourceful Odysseus
Replied: "If, as you say, you were their priest,
Their teller of omens, then surely the times were many
When you must have prayed in this house that I would never
Attain my sweet return, and that my dear wife
Would go off with you and bear your children. So you

371

Shall not escape this bitter and painful death!"
    Then, with his powerful hand, he picked up the sword
Which the dying Agelaus had dropped and brought it down hard
On the neck of Leiodes, and right in the midst of a word
His head rolled down in the dust.
    Phemius the poet,
Terpes' son, he who was forced to sing
For the suitors, had so far managed to avoid dark doom,
And now he stood, still clutching the melodious lyre,
By the small back door and tried to decide what to do,
Whether to slip from the hall and sit in the yard
By the altar of almighty Zeus, god of the household,
The highly wrought altar whereon Laertes and Odysseus
Had burnt so many thighs of slaughtered oxen,
Or to rush right in and embrace the knees of Odysseus,
Pleading for mercy. He decided this would be better,
To embrace the knees of Laertes' son Odysseus.
So he laid the curving lyre on the ground between
The mixing-bowl and the chair all studded with silver
And rushed to the knees of Odysseus, pleading for mercy
In these winged words:
    "Here at your knees, Odysseus,
I beg you to have some regard and pity for me.
If you kill a poet, a singer for gods and men,
You'll surely be sorry. I've always been my own teacher,
And God has caused all kinds of songs to grow
In my heart, songs I can sing for you, as for
A god. So please leave my head where it is! Yes,
And your own dear son Telemachus will tell you this—
That I myself had no desire to come here
And sing for the feasting wooers. I didn't want to
At all, but they were many and strong and dragged me here
Whether or not."
    Close by, the strong and sacred

Telemachus heard what he said, and spoke to his father:
"Hold on! Don't put this innocent man to the sword.
And Medon the herald, who always cared for me
Here in the house when I was a child, is another
Man we must spare—that is, if he isn't dead
Already at the hands of Philoetius or the swineherd, or perhaps
He ran into you raging your way through the hall."

    The sensible Medon heard these words from where
He lay wrapped up in the newly flayed hide of an ox,
Cowering under a chair, hoping dark doom
Would miss him. Quickly he scrambled from under the chair,
Hastily ridding himself of the hide, and dashed in
To embrace the knees of Telemachus, pleading in these
Winged words:

    "Old friend, it's me! Hold on, and tell
Your father to, or he might just ruin me with
That sharp bronze blade, carried away by his strength
And furious at the wooers, who wasted his things in the palace
And foolishly showed no respect at all for you."

    Resourceful Odysseus smiled, and spoke to him thus:
"Calm down. My son has saved you from death, that you
May know and tell others how very much better it is
To do good than evil. Now go outside and sit
In the court away from the carnage, you and the songful
Bard, till I have finished my business here
In the house."

    So the two of them left the hall and sat
In the court by the altar of almighty Zeus, nervously
Looking about them, expecting death any moment.
Odysseus too looked about him, carefully searching
The house for survivors seeking to hide from dark doom.
But there they all lay in the blood and dust, piles of them
Heaped in the hall like so many fish that fishermen
Take in their nets from the hoary sea and heap

On the sand of the curving beach, where they all lie gasping
For waves of the brine till the bright sun takes their lives.
So lay the suitors heaped on one another.
Then resourceful Odysseus spoke to his son:
    "Telemachus,
Go call the nurse Eurycleia for me. I've something
To tell her."
    He spoke, and Telemachus obeyed his dear father.
Shaking the door of the women's chamber, he called
To the nurse: "Old one! get up and come on, you
That have charge of all our women servants here
In the palace. Let's go, my father has something to tell you
And wants you to come."
    No winged words came back
From the nurse. She opened the doors of the comfortable quarters
And followed Telemachus back to the hall. There,
Among the dead bodies, she found Odysseus, besmeared
With blood and gore like a lion that comes from feeding
On an ox in the pasture, a fearful sight with blood
All over his chest and on either side of his face.
Even so were the gory arms and legs of Odysseus.
When she saw the corpses and all that unspeakable blood,
She immediately started to raise her voice in rejoicing
At the great achievement before her. But Odysseus checked
Her glad ululation with these winged words:
    "Rejoice
Within your heart, old nurse. But restrain yourself
And raise no cry. To boast over fallen men
Is an unholy thing. The gods themselves determined
The fate of these men—the gods and their own cruel deeds.
For these men had no regard for any man
On earth, whether good or bad, no matter who
Came among them. Thus, by their own perverseness, they brought
Disgraceful death on themselves. But come, tell me

374

Which of the women have shamed me and which have not."

Then the dear nurse Eurycleia replied: "To you, my child,
I'll tell the whole truth as it happened. Here in the palace
There are fifty women servants in all, whom we
Have taught to do the chores, card the wool,
And bear up under the life of slaves. Twelve
Of these have gone their own shameless way, with no
Regard at all for me or Penelope herself!
Telemachus just now grew up, and his mother would not
Permit him to order the women around. But come,
Let me go up to the shining chamber above
And tell your wife. Some god has put her to sleep."

But thorough Odysseus replied: "Don't wake her just yet,
But tell those scheming and shameless women to come
To the hall."

When the old one had gone to summon the women
And tell them the news, Odysseus called Telemachus,
The swineherd, and cowman, and gave instructions to them
In these winged words: "Start taking the corpses outside
And order the women to help you. Then, when you've cleaned
The exquisite chairs and tables with water and sponges,
Lead the women from the firm-founded hall to a spot
Between the rotunda and excellent wall of the court.
There thrust your long blades home till there's no life left
In any of them and all have completely forgotten
Those Aphrodistic delights they had with the wooers
When they slept with them on the sly!"

Then the women came in
Together, wailing hysterically and shedding big tears.
They carried the corpses out and stacked them one
On another beneath the portico of the well-walled yard.
Odysseus himself gave the orders and sped up the bearing
Of bodies, forcing the women to do it. Then they cleaned
The exquisite chairs and tables with water and sponges.

Telemachus, the cowman, and swineherd scraped the floor
Of the well-built hall with hoes, and the women took up
The gore and threw it outdoors. When the hall throughout
Had been set in good order again, they led the women
From the firm-founded house to a spot between the rotunda
And the excellent wall of the court, where they hemmed them up
In a narrow place from which there was no escape.
Then gravely the brooding Telemachus spoke to the herdsmen:
    "I'll not give such as these a decent death,
Women who heaped disgrace on the heads of me
And my mother; and made a practice of sleeping with the wooers!"
    So saying, he tied the rope of a blue-bowed ship
To a massive portico pillar, then flung it around
The rotunda's dome, drawing it taut and high
So that none of the women could reach the ground with her feet.
Like long-winged thrushes or doves that come in to roost
In a thicket and find themselves in a net, a bed
Of misery and pain where they looked for nothing but sleep,
So the women held their heads in a row while nooses
Were laid on their necks, that they might die most wretchedly.
They twitched their feet for a while, but not very long.
    Then they led Melanthius out through the doorway
        and courtyard,
Sliced off his nose and ears with the ruthless bronze,
Ripped out his privates to furnish raw meat for the dogs,
And in their furious wrath hacked off his hands
And feet.
    When the work was done, they washed their own hands
And feet and went back in the house to Odysseus. Whereupon
He spoke to the cherished old nurse Eurycleia: "Fetch me
Sulphur for purging, old one, and fire. I want
To purify the hall. And tell Penelope to come here
With her women, and bid all the women servants in the palace

Come too."

      Then the dear nurse answered: "Yes, yes, my child,
All that you say is proper and fine. But first
Let me bring you a cloak and tunic to wear. What a shame
For you to stand like this in the hall with nothing
But rags across your broad shoulders!"

      But resourceful Odysseus
Replied: "Now the first thing I want is a fire in this hall."

      Eurycleia did not disobey. She brought the fire
And sulphur, and Odysseus purified hall, house, and courtyard.

      Then the old one went back through the beautiful
           house of Odysseus
To tell the women and bid them come, and they,
With torches in hand, came out of their quarters and flocked
Around Odysseus in loving welcome, hugging
His neck, clasping his hands, and tenderly kissing
His head and shoulders. And now a delicious desire
Took hold of him to give in to weeping and wailing,
As in his heart he knew them one and all.

BOOK

XXIII

ODYSSEUS AND PENELOPE

Chuckling out loud to herself, the old nurse hurried
Upstairs to tell her mistress her husband was home.
Stiffly hustling and bustling, her feet just trotted
Along till she stood above the Queen's head, and said:
   "Penelope, child, wake up! and see with your very own
Eyes what you've yearned to see for so long. Odysseus
Is home—late, but he's here, and he's killed those proud wooers
Who upset his household, ate up his wealth, and bullied
His son!"
   Then brooding Penelope answered: "Dear nurse,
The gods have addled your brains, they who are just as
Able to make the wise foolish as they are to give sense
To the simple. Now they have marred your mind, that used to
Be so well-balanced. What do you mean making fun
Of my misery this way, waking me up from the sleep
So sound and sweet that enveloped my lids and held me
To tell me this crazy stuff? Why I haven't slept
So well since Odysseus left for that horrible place

378

I can hardly bear to mention! But go on downstairs
And back to your quarters. If any other woman of mine
Had waked me up to hear this nonsense—believe me,
I would have sent her packing in much worse shape
Than she came! But in this at least you're lucky to be old."
      And the cherished old nurse replied: "I'm not making fun
Of you, dear child. What I tell you is so. Odysseus
Really is here in his home. That stranger—he
Whom everyone mocked and despised in the hall—that
Was Odysseus! And Telemachus knew he was here all the time,
But sensibly didn't reveal his father's plan
Before he exacted full payment for the violence done
By all those arrogant men."
      At this Penelope
Sprang out of bed and joyfully hugged the old woman.
Then, as the tears dropped from her lids, her words
Came winged with wonder: "But tell me, dear nurse—if he really
Has come as you say—tell me exactly how he,
All alone, was able to handle that shameless gang
Of wooers, who always stuck together here
In the palace."
      And the dear Eurycleia replied: "I didn't
See what happened myself, and I didn't inquire.
But I heard the horrible groans of dying men.
We women sat back in terror in the darkest corners
Of our strong quarters, shut in by the tight-fitting doors,
Until, at his father's request, your son Telemachus
Came and called me out of the chamber. Then
I found Odysseus standing among the dead bodies
Piled up all around him, lying one
On the other there on that foot-packed hard earthen floor.
What a thrill it would have been for you to have seen him
Standing there like a lion all besmeared
With blood and gore! Now all the bodies are stacked

Beneath the portico at the courtyard gates, and he
Has a great fire going and is purging the palace with sulphur.
He sent me up to get you, so come on now,
That both of your hearts may enter this joy together,
You who have suffered so much. But now your old
And great desire has been fulfilled: he
Has come home alive to his own hearth again and found
In his halls both you and his son, and from all the wooers,
Who damaged him so, he has exacted full payment
Here in his house!"
     Then thoughtful Penelope answered:
"Dear nurse, don't be too jubilant yet. You know
Very well how glad everyone of us would be
To see him again in these halls, most especially I
And the son we had together. But the story you tell
Is quite unconvincing. Apparently, some immortal
Has slain the lordly wooers in wrathful indignation
At their evil deeds and insolent, galling hubris.
For they had no regard for any man
On earth, whether good or bad, no matter who
Came among them. Thus, by their own perverseness, they suffered
This evil. But far-off Odysseus has lost every chance
Of reaching Achaea again, nor does he himself
Exist any longer."
     And the cherished old nurse replied:
"What kind of talk is that, my child, that you
Have just let by the barrier of your teeth,
Saying your husband will never come home again
When right at this moment he's here beside his own fire!
You've never had any real faith. But come, I'll remind you
Of an obvious mark of identity—namely the scar
He got long ago from the slashing white tusk of a boar.
I saw it while washing his feet and I wanted to tell you
Right then, but he in his wisdom and cunning held

My mouth and wouldn't let me. So come on with me.
I'll put my life at stake. If what I have said
Isn't so, kill me by any most wretched death
You can devise!"

Cautious Penelope answered:
"Dear nurse, it's difficult indeed to comprehend the ways
Of the eternal gods, no matter how wise you are.
But let's go down to my son and see the dead wooers
Along with the man who killed them."

With this she left
Her room and went downstairs, fiercely debating
Within her heart whether she should keep her distance
From her own dear husband and ask him some questions, or go
Right up and clasp him, kissing his head and hands.
But when she went in across the stone threshold, she sat down
In the firelight close by the wall across from Odysseus,
Who sat by a massive pillar with his eyes on the ground
Waiting to see if his noble wife would speak
When she saw him. Long and silently she sat there, utterly
Spellbound. At times she would look him straight in the face
And still not know who he was in those rags he had on.
Then Telemachus reproached her severely, saying:
"My mother—
What kind of mother are you to hold yourself
So far away from my father, instead of sitting
Beside him asking him questions? Surely no other
Wife would be so hard and unfeeling as to welcome
Coldly a husband who had just come back to her
And his home after nineteen long years of misery and toil.
But then your heart has always been harder than rock!"

And wise Penelope answered him thus: "My child,
The heart in my breast is so overcome with surprise
That I am unable to speak one word to him,
Unable to ask a question or even so much as

Look him in the face. But if he is really Odysseus
Come home again, the two of us will surely
Know each other, and that beyond doubt, since there
Are things known only to us, things hidden from everyone
Else."
        At this the patient, gallant Odysseus
Smiled, and spoke at once these winged words
To his son: "Telemachus, let your mother try me
Here at home. She'll change her mind for the better
Pretty soon. I'm dirty now and dressed
In rags, so she refuses to honor me
And can't bring herself to admit that I am Odysseus.
But come, let's try to decide what's best for us
To do. When a man kills one of his fellows, even one
Who has very few to avenge him, still the slayer
Leaves his country and kinsmen and goes into exile.
But those we destroyed were the very pillars of state,
The Ithacan best of their generation. Now there
Is something for you to think about!"
        But shrewdly
Telemachus answered: "That's one for you to solve,
My father. They say nobody alive can touch you
When it comes to thinking. We'll gladly back you up, though,
With all the strength we have, nor, I dare say,
Will there be any lack of courage in us."
        Then Odysseus
Of many devices replied: "Very well, I'll tell you
What I think is best. First of all, go bathe and put on
Your tunics, and tell the maids in the palace to dress
For a dance. Then let the sacred bard strike up
A jubilant tune on that melodious lyre
Of his, so anyone going by, some traveler
Or one of the neighbors, will say it's a wedding feast.
That way word of the wooers' demise will not

382

Get out all over town before we can get out
To our well-wooded farm. Once there, we'll see what advantage
The Olympian may choose to give us."
> All were glad
To do as he said. They bathed and put on their tunics
And the women adorned themselves. Then the sacred bard
Played on the curving lyre and got them all
In the mood for marvelous music and dancing. So the great hall
Re-echoed throughout with the dancing feet of men
And well-dressed women, and thus would one outside
Who heard the commotion say:
> "Aha! for sure now
Someone has married the much-courted Queen—the wretch!
She didn't have what it takes to keep the great house
Of her husband and hold out all the way until he
Got back."
> So they would say, who had no idea
What had really happened inside.
> Meanwhile, the housekeeper
Eurynome bathed great-hearted Odysseus, now
In his own home again, and when she had rubbed him with oil
She helped him into a beautiful tunic and mantle.
And Athena, daughter of Zeus, shed beauty abounding
Upon him. She made him seem taller and stronger and caused
His hair to curl like the hyacinth in bloom. As a craftsman
Who learned his art from Hephaestus and Pallas Athena
Overlays silver with gold and produces a work
Full of charm, so the goddess shed grace on the head and shoulders
Of Odysseus. And he came from the bath with the form and looks
Of an immortal god and sat down again in the chair
He had left across from his wife. Then he spoke to her thus:
> "Mysterious woman! apparently those who live
On Olympus gave you a heart more hard and unyielding
Than they did to any other truly feminine woman.

383

Surely no other wife would be so unfeeling
As to treat aloofly a husband who had just come back
To her and his own native land after nineteen long years
Of misery and toil. But enough! Nurse, go make up
A bed for me. I'll sleep alone, since surely
My wife has a heart of solid iron!"
    And Penelope
Shrewdly replied: "No less mysterious man!
Really I'm not at all haughty or coldly indifferent,
Nor am I scornful of you or amazed any more than
I should be. It's just that I have such a vivid memory
Of you as you were when you boarded that long-oared ship
And said good-by to Ithaca. But go, Eurycleia,
Make the big bed for him—outside the bedroom
He himself built. Put the strong bed out there
And make it with fleeces and blankets and lovely bright spreads."
    So she spoke, to see what her husband would say.
And Odysseus lost his composure and angrily spoke
To his clever and faithful wife: "Truly, woman,
Those words were bitter and painful! Who has moved
My bed? No easy job, I can tell you, no matter
How skilled a man were, though a god if he wished might come
And easily put it elsewhere. But no mere mortal
Alive, however young and lusty, would find it
Easy to pry that bed out of place—for I alone
Built it, and a greatly unusual feature went into
The careful construction of that elaborate bed.
A long-leafed olive tree grew in the court,
A fine and flourishing tree as thick as a pillar,
And I built up my bridal chamber around it with stone
On sturdy stone, thoroughly roofed it over,
And finished it up by hanging the jointed tight doors.
Then I cut off the long-leafed foliage, trimmed the trunk up
From the root, and expertly rounded it smooth and straight

With an adze. Thus I fashioned a post for the bed and bored it
All with an auger. From this beginning, I went on
With the work till I finished, richly inlaying the frame
With gold and silver and ivory and lacing it well
With thongs of crimson leather. This I describe
Was our secret, woman! But whether that bed is still solidly
There, or whether some man has cut through the stump
Of olive and moved the bed elsewhere, I wouldn't know."
     Struck by her husband's perfect description of the tokens
Between them, her heart beat fast and faster and her knees
Began to tremble. With a burst of tears, she ran straight
To Odysseus and threw her arms about his neck,
Kissing his head, and saying: "O don't be angry
With me any more, Odysseus. You were always more
Understanding than anyone else. Our misery came
From the gods, who begrudged us the joy of spending our youth
Together and coming to old age's threshold at last.
So don't be cross with me and resentful because
At first sight I didn't greet you this way. I've always
Shuddered to think that some man might come here
And take me in with his story, for those who would plot
Such evil to profit themselves are many. Surely
Helen of Argos would never have gone to bed
With that man from abroad if she had had any notion
That the fighting sons of Achaeans would fetch her back home
To her own dear country. But a goddess made even her,
Zeus's own daughter, succumb to that miserable business,
Nor had she ever so much as imagined that she
Would be subject to that horrible infatuation—the beginning
Of our troubles, too! But now that you have described
So well the secrets of our bed, known only to you
And me and just one other—the chambermaid Actoris,
Given to me by my father before I came here,
The one who kept the doors of our strong bridal chamber—

Now my heart is convinced, hard though it is."
     Her words made him feel even more like weeping than ever,
And weep he did, with his dear and loyal wife
In his arms. And to her he was as welcome as sight
Of land to swimmers whose sturdy ship Poseidon
Has battered and shattered at sea where wind and big wave
Beat hard upon it, and sweet indeed is the moment
When the few survivors, having swum inshore and struggled
Their way through the surf, set foot at last on dry land
And escape the treacherous sea with their bodies all crusted
With brine. Such was the gladness she felt to welcome
Her husband again, as she feasted her eyes upon him
And could not for a moment take her white arms from his neck.
     Now Dawn of the rosy fingers would have come up
On their tearful embracing, if the blue-eyed goddess Athena
Had not had other ideas. She held the long night
At the end of its course and refused to let Dawn, enthroned
In gold by the streams of Oceanus, yoke her youthful
Fleet-hoofed horses, Lampus and Phaëthon, who draw
Young Dawn in her course. Then Odysseus, thoughtful as ever,
Said to his wife:
     "My dear, our trials are by no means
Over. Labor unmeasured lies ahead of me still,
Long labor and hard which I must see through to the end.
For thus the soul of Tiresias foretold on the day
I descended to the house of Hades to seek out the truth
About the return of my comrades and myself.
But come, my dear, let's go to bed and enjoy
A night of sweet sleep together."
     And shrewd Penelope
Answered: "Your bed will be ready whenever you are,
For truly the gods have guided you home again
To your own native land and firm-founded house. But since
You thought of this trial and God put it into your heart,

Do tell me about it. I'm likely to learn of it later,
I think, so I might as well hear what it is right now."
　　　And Odysseus of many devices: "You really are
A strange one! How can you be so insistent? Well,
I'll tell you all about it, but believe me, you're not
Apt to like it any better than I do myself.
For Tiresias told me to go through many cities,
Taking a graceful oar along, and continuing
Inland until I meet men who know nothing at all
Of the sea, men who eat their food without salt
And are completely ignorant of red-cheeked ships
And wing-like, shapely oars. And he told me this sign
Which I will tell you. When I meet a man who asks
Why I carry a winnowing-fan on my shoulder, then,
He said, I'm to plant that oar in the earth and there
Most fitly sacrifice to mighty Poseidon a ram,
A bull, and a sow-mounting boar. Then I'm to go home
And sacrifice holy hecatombs to each of the immortal
Gods that rule the wide sky. And to me will come
An easy death from the sea, a peaceful death
In my comfortable calm old age with my people happy
And thriving around me. All this, he said, would happen."
　　　Then thoughtful Penelope replied: "Well, if the gods
Are really to give you a better old age, then we
Can hope that someday your troubles will be over and done with."
　　　While husband and wife were talking, Eurynome
　　　　　and the nurse
Put downy soft spreads on the bed by blazing torchlight.
But when they had stirred about and made the strong bed
The old nurse went back to lie down in her room, while Eurynome,
As maid of the chamber, led them along with a torch
In her hands and lit them to bed, then left them there
And went back. And they were happy indeed to be
In their old bridal chamber again.

But Telemachus, the cowman,
And swineherd stopped their dancing feet and those
Of the women and lay down for the night in the shadowy hall.
When the happy pair had known the deep delight
Of thrilling love, they enjoyed a long conversation.
The lovely lady told of all she had been through
In the palace watching that profligate gang of suitors
Wasting on her account whole herds of cattle
And excellent sheep and drawing off gallons of wine
From the large earthen jars. And Zeus-descended Odysseus
Described all the care and discomfort that he had inflicted
On others and all the sorrow and pain he himself
Had toiled his way through. She listened with keen delight,
And no sweet sleep fell on her lids till he
Had finished his story.
First he told how he
Overcame the Cicones and sailed on to the fertile land
Of the Lotus-eaters, and of all the Cyclops did
And how he made the pitiless monster pay
In full for devouring his gallant comrades. Then
He described how gladly Aeolus had taken him in
And tried to help him get home, though such was not
His lot at the time and a hurricane wind snatched him up
And swept him groaning across the fish-full deep,
And how he came to Telepylus of the Laestrygonians,
Who demolished all of his ships and well-greaved companions
Except those in the black ship with him, the only one
To escape. And he told of the wiles and treacherous tricks
Of Circe and the journey he made in his many-benched ship
To the dank and moldering house of Hades to consult
The soul of Theban Tiresias, and of seeing all
His dead comrades there and the mother who bore and nursed him.
And of hearing the dulcet song of the Sirens, and of sailing
By the Wandering Rocks, by dire Charybdis, and Scylla,

388

Whom none had ever gone by unharmed. Then
He told how his men had slaughtered the Sun's own cattle
And how high-roaring Zeus had shattered his ship
With a bolt of flaming thunder, killing all
Of his able companions, while he alone escaped
The baneful fates and reached the island Ogygia,
Where the nymph Calypso kept him in the yawning caves,
Yearning to make him her husband, pampering him
And offering to make him immortal and ageless forever,
To none of which the heart in his breast agreed.
And he told how he toiled his way through to the fine Phaeacians,
Who heartily honored him like a god and sent him
Home in a ship laden with presents of bronze,
Garments, and gold. So ended his story, and sweet
Limb-loosening sleep came on him, releasing the cares
Of his heart.
    Now the bright-eyed goddess Athena went on
With her plans. When she thought that Odysseus had
        made enough love
With his wife and had enough sleep, she quickly aroused
From the streams of Oceanus young Dawn of the golden throne,
That she might bring light to mankind. And Odysseus left
The soft bed and spoke these words to his wife:
    "My dear,
We've already had our share of trouble and trial,
You here at home, worried and weeping over
My painful return, while I, though eager to get here,
Was kept far from home bound in the bonds of suffering
By Zeus and the other gods. But now that we've had
The night together that both of us wanted so much,
I leave you to care for the house and all I possess.
As for the flocks that the arrogant wooers wasted,
I'll get a lot of them back by way of booty
And the Achaeans will contribute the rest till all of the folds

Are full. But now I must go to the well-wooded farm
To see my noble father, who is greatly distressed
About me, and to you, my dear, I want to say this,
Discreet and sharp though you are. The sun will no sooner
Be up than word will spread concerning the wooers
I slew in the hall. So take your women upstairs
To your chamber and stay right there. See no one else
At all and ask no questions."
     He spoke, and about
His shoulders he fastened his beautiful armor. Then
He awakened Telemachus, the cowman, and swineherd
       and told them
To get their weapons of war. They did as he said
And put on their armor of bronze, opened the doors,
And went out, with Odysseus leading the way. It
Was already broad daylight, but Athena hid them in darkness
And quickly guided their footsteps out of the city.

BOOK

XXIV

A COVENANT
OF PEACE

Meanwhile, Cyllenian Hermes had summoned the souls
Of the wooers. Wielding a wand of fair gold, with which
He puts to sleep or awakens whomever he wishes,
He aroused the spirits and got them started, and they
Came thronging behind him with many shrill gibbering cries.
As bats in the deepest depth of a marvelous cave
Flit squeaking and squealing about when one of their number
Falls from the rock where all had hung clustering together,
So these went gibbering along with the mighty deliverer
Hermes, who led them down the moldering ways,
Beyond the streams of Oceanus and the pallid Rock
Of Leucas, beyond the gates of the Sun and the country
Of dreams, till they came before long to the asphodel meadow,
Home of spirits, mere wraiths of men outworn.
Here they found the soul of Peleus' son
Achilles, and those of Patroclus, matchless Antilochus,
And Ajax, who next to the peerless son of Peleus
Had, of all the Danaans, the most manly bearing.
As these were milling and crowding about Achilles,

Up came the grieving ghost of Agamemnon, son
Of Atreus, and with him the spirits of those whose fate
Had been to die with him in the house of Aegisthus.
The spirit of Peleus' son spoke to him first:
    "Son of Atreus, because you were King of many
Powerful men in the land of the Trojans, where we
Achaeans suffered so much, we thought that you
Were always dearest of heroes to Zeus, the lover
Of lightning. But the doom of dreadful death, which no one
Born of mortals ever escapes, came on you
All too early, though how much better it would
Have been for you to have met your death and doom
At Troy in the glory of kingly honor and might
Accorded you in that land! Then all the Achaeans
Would have made you a tomb, and your story in days to come
Would have won great glory for you and your son as well.
But apparently you were fated to die a death
Surpassingly pitiful."
    Agamemnon's spirit replied:
"You were the fortunate one, O Peleus' son,
Godlike Achilles, to die on Trojan soil
Far from your home in Argos, and about you fell
In the fight for your body the noblest sons of Achaeans
And Trojans, as you, in all your greatness, forgetful
Of chariot-skill, lay in the swirling dust,
Mighty even in death. All day long
We fought, and would have continued to fight, if a storm
From Zeus had not ended the struggle. When we had borne you
Out of the battle and back to the ships, we laid you
On a bed and cleansed your beautiful body with warm water
And oil. Many indeed were the scalding tears
The Danaans shed about you, and many were the locks
Of hair they cut in their grief. When your mother got word
Of your death, she came from the sea with her deathless nymphs,

And a weird and wailing cry spread over the deep.
At this the Achaeans all trembled with fear and were just
On the verge of making a break for the ships, when one
Of our number, wise in ancient ways, stopped
Their stampeding. Nestor it was, he whose advice
Had won highest approval before. In an effort to help,
He raised his voice among them:
     " 'Hold on, Argives!
Young men of Achaea, don't panic! It's Achilles' mother,
Who comes from the sea with her deathless nymphs to look on
The face of her dear dead son.'
     "He spoke, and all
The great-hearted Achaeans checked their impulse to run.
Then about your body the pitifully wailing daughters
Of the ancient Sea-god stood, and they clothed your flesh
In immortal garments. And all nine Muses sang
In the dirge, sweetly echoing one another in lovely
Antiphonal song, till not one Argive there
Was tearless, so deeply stirred were they by that
Melodious chanting. So for seventeen days and nights
Immortal gods and mortal men together
Mourned your passing. Then on the eighteenth day
We gave you up to the flames, and about you we slew
Many fat sheep and splendid long-horned cattle.
And while your body was burning in the garments of gods
Along with many rich oils and much sweet honey,
A great and clamorous throng of armored men,
Foot soldiers and charioteers, moved in martial procession
Around your blazing pyre. At dawn, when the fire
Of Hephaestus had finally finished with you, we gathered
Your white bones, Achilles, and laid them away in oil
And unmixed wine. Your mother had given a golden
Two-handled urn, the work of renowned Hephaestus,
Which Dionysus, she said, had given to her. In this,

O noble Achilles, your white bones lie and mingled
Among them the bones of Menoetius' dead son Patroclus,
While the bones of Antilochus, one whom you thought the most of
Next to the dead Patroclus, lie in an urn
By themselves. Over those bones the formidable host
Of Argive spearmen built a great barrow, a matchless
And towering tomb raised on a jutting headland
Beside the broad Hellespont, that it might be seen far across
The wide water by men now alive and those yet to be born.
From the gods your mother requested exquisite prizes
Which she set in the midst of the lists for the noblest Achaeans
To win. Now you've found yourself present at the funeral games
Of many heroic chieftains, when young men gird
Themselves at the death of a king and prepare to compete,
But if you had seen those beautiful prizes set there
Only to glorify you by silver-footed Thetis,
Your goddess mother, surely your heart would have marveled
As never before, so great was the love of the gods
For you. Not even death obscured your name,
Achilles. All men will call you noble and glorify
You forever. But as for me, what possible
Pleasure can it be to me to have wound up the war
At last? For at my homecoming Zeus devised
A ghastly conclusion for me at the hands of Aegisthus
And those of my worthless wife."

    While they were talking,
The gods' bright bearer of news, the slayer of Argus,
Came down with the spirits of the wooers whom Odysseus
        had slain.
Amazement fell on the dead kings when they saw
        them approaching
And they both went straight to meet them. Agamemnon's soul
Recognized the dear son of Melaneus, illustrious Amphimedon,
At whose Ithacan home he had once been a guest.

So the spirit of Atreus' son spoke to him first:
    "Amphimedon, what happened to all of you picked
               young men
To send you down here all together beneath the black earth?
One who chose the very best men in a city
Could do no better! Did Poseidon stir up high winds
And waves and sink your ships, or were you slain
By enemies while rustling their cattle and fair flocks of sheep
Or fighting to win their city and women? Tell me
Your story, for I was once a guest in your house.
Don't you remember when I and godlike Menelaus
Came to your home on a mission to get Odysseus
To go with us to Ilium in the well-decked ships?
It took so long to persuade the sacker of cities
That a month went by before we arrived at Troy
Across all that wide water."
      Then Amphimedon's spirit replied:
"O most glorious son of Atreus, Agamemnon,
King of men, I do indeed remember
All you speak of, and to you, Zeus-fostered King,
I'll tell what happened to us and tell it straight,
How a miserable death was prepared for all of us.
Together we courted the wife of long-absent Odysseus,
And she would neither refuse our hateful offers
Completely, nor make up her mind and end them, plotting
All the while death and dark doom for us.
But talk of guile, hear what she did! At the palace
She had a great loom set up and began to weave yards
Of very fine cloth, explaining herself this way:
    " 'My ardent young suitors, gallant Odysseus is dead,
And you can't wait for me to marry again,
But you, my wooers, must try to be patient until
I finish this shroud for lord Laertes, for him
When the painful fate of leveling and grievous death

Arrives. Naturally, I would not have my labor
Go to waste, nor any Achaean woman
Speak ill of me for not providing a shroud
For one who has amassed so great a fortune.'

    "Such was her request, nor could our proud hearts
Deny it. There daily she wove at that great web,
But at night she unraveled her work by the light of torches.
Thus for three wily years she beguiled the Achaeans,
But when the fourth arrived and winter gave way
To spring, as the months went by and the countless days,
One of her women, who knew whereof she spoke,
Told us all, and we surprised her unraveling
That marvelous fabric. She finished it then, believe me!
Unwilling though she was.

    "It was when she had finished
Her weaving and had washed that ample robe till it gleamed
Like the sun or moon and had showed it to us, that some
Really fiendish demon brought Odysseus out of the blue
And landed him out in the country not far from the lodge
Of his swineherd. Then the black ship bearing his own dear son
Came back from sandy Pylos, and the Prince stopped off
At the very same lodge, where the two of them plotted dark death
For the wooers and entered the famous city—that is,
Telemachus came on ahead, and Odysseus later.
The swineherd brought him in, woefully dressed,
Hobbling along with a staff, and looking for all
The world like a wretched and ancient beggar. So sudden
And unlikely was his appearance that none of us,
Not even the older men, had any idea
Who he was. In fact, we talked quite ugly to him
And threw things at him. This pelting and taunting in halls
Of which he was the owner his heart steadfastly endured
For a while. But when the will of aegis-bearing Zeus
Sent him into action at last, he and Telemachus

Gathered up all the splendid arms, stored them
Away in a chamber, and shot home the bolts. Then
He was crafty enough to have his wife confront
The doomed wooers, by way of a contest, with a bow of his
And some gray iron axes, the beginning of the end for us.
Not one of us there came even close to stringing
That powerful bow, and when it came to Odysseus
We all shouted together that he shouldn't have
The bow, regardless of how much he talked. Only
Telemachus urged him on and told him to take it.
And the patient, noble Odysseus took that bow
In his hands, strung it with ease, and shot a shaft
Right through the iron axes. Then he took his stand
        on the threshold
And poured out the swift-flying arrows, fiercely scowling
From side to side. Prince Antinous was the first man
He shot, and he followed up, aiming and shooting
Those groan-fraught arrows till men lay around in heaps.
Soon it was clear that they had some god on their side,
For they tore through the hall in their rage, striking men down
Right and left. Mid the bashing of heads a hideous groaning
Arose, and the whole floor ran with blood. Such
Was our end, Agamemnon, and our bodies at this very moment
Still lie in the house of Odysseus just as we left them,
For as yet no word has gone out to our friends at home,
Friends who would tender to us the due of the dead
And wash the dark gore from our wounds and lay out our bodies
With grief and lamentation."
      Then the soul of Agamemnon cried:
"O fortunate son of Laertes, resourceful Odysseus,
How splendid in every way your wife has been,
So sensible and utterly loyal to you, the man
She married! Peerless Penelope, Icarius' daughter,
The good repute her excellence earned is undying.

397

The immortals themselves will make a delightful poem
For men on earth to sing in joyful praise
Of constant Penelope. How very different was Clytemnestra,
Tyndareus' daughter, who plotted and carried out
The murder of the man she married! Loathsome indeed
Her song will be among men, and even good women
Will suffer because of the shadow she threw on all
Of her sex."

So the two phantoms stood and spoke to each other
In the house of Hades in the hidden depths of the earth.

Now Odysseus and his companions had not been long
Out of town before they arrived at the well-worked farm
Of Laertes, an attractive place that he, long ago,
Had carved with much labor from out the surrounding country.
His house was there, and in the adjoining quarters
All about it the servants who did his bidding
Ate and sat and slept. Inside the house
Was an old Sicilian woman, who kindly cared for
The old man there on the farm well out from town.

Then Odysseus spoke to his son and the servants, saying:
"Go on inside the well-built house and kill
For our dinner the fattest pig on the place. I want
To try my father and see if he'll know me at sight
Or fail to recognize one who has been away
For so long."

He gave the servants his armor, and they,
Along with his son, went straight in the house. But Odysseus,
Intent on the trying, walked toward the fruitful vineyard.
As he went down through the great orchard approaching
        the vines,
He failed to find Dolius or his sons, or any
Of the other servants, for they had all gone to gather
Stones for the vineyard wall, with the aged Dolius
Heading the party. So he found his father alone

In the carefully tended vineyard, digging around
A plant. He had on a shabby old tunic, all patched
And dirty, and about his shins he had strapped a pair
Of sewn leather leggings to protect against scratches, while gloves
Kept the briars from his hands. A goatskin cap completed
The miserable garb of an even more miserable man.
When the much-enduring, noble Odysseus saw him,
So worn and heart-heavy with grief and old age, he stopped
By a tall pear tree and wept, uncertain in mind
And heart whether to hug and kiss his father
And tell him all about how he had come back at last
To his own fatherland, or whether to question him closely
And see how he felt about things. Pondering the problem,
He decided that it would be better to start by getting
The old one's reaction to a yarn he would tell him. So thinking,
Stalwart Odysseus went straight to where his father
Was still bent over digging around a plant.
Then his world-famous son stood by his side, and said:
        "Old man, when it comes to tending an orchard, you don't
Leave a thing undone. I've yet to see a plant
On this place, a fig tree, olive, or pear, a vine
Or vegetable plot, that wasn't perfectly tended.
But something else I must say—and please don't take
Offense—namely, that you yourself are not
At all well cared for. You're woefully old, badly
In need of a bath, and your clothes are a sight! I cannot
Believe your master neglects you because you are lazy,
Nor do you look, in form or feature, at all
Like a slave—more like a king, in fact, like one
Who lives as an old man should and sleeps on a fine
Soft bed after a good bath and dinner. But the truth, man!
Whose servant are you, and who owns the orchard you keep?
And another thing I'd like to be sure about:
Have I really landed in Ithaca? So said a fellow

399

Back there I met on the way, but I'm afraid
He wasn't too bright, for I couldn't get him to talk
Very much, and when I inquired concerning a friend
Of mine, whether he was still alive or dead
And already in the halls of Hades, he wouldn't listen
At all. But let me tell you about him, and do
Pay attention. Back in my own country I once had a guest
At the house—the most likable guest from abroad that I
Ever had—who said he was born in Ithaca, and that he
Was the son of Arceisius' son Laertes. I took him
Home, lavishly entertained him, and gave him fit gifts
Of friendship—seven talents of highly wrought gold,
A flowery mixing-bowl of solid silver,
Twelve cloaks of single fold, and an equal number
Of blankets, tunics, and beautiful mantles. In addition,
I let him choose for himself four women, experts
At weaving and working, shapely and good to look at."

    In tears his father replied: "Stranger, you've come
To the country you mention, but now it's in the control
Of wanton and wicked men. The numerous gifts
You so graciously gave were given in vain. Had you found him
In Ithaca still alive, he would have shown you
Warm hospitality and seen you off with gifts
Quite equal to those you gave. Such is but right
To one who starts a friendship. But tell me the truth
About this: how many years has it been since you
Entertained that guest, that unlucky guest, my son—
If there ever was such a man—my unfortunate son,
Who far from home and friends has more than likely
Been eaten by fish in the sea, or fallen prey
On land somewhere to beasts and carrion birds?
Nor did we whose son he is, his mother and father,
Have any chance to enshroud his lifeless body
And shed our tears above it, nor was his wife,

The gifted and constant Penelope, able to do
The right thing, to close his dead eyes and bewail her own
        husband
Laid out on his bier, as surely the dead deserve.
And further, I would like to hear you speak frankly of this:
Who are you and where are you from? Your city, your parents,
Where are they? And where did you leave the swift ship
        in which you
And your godlike companions arrived? Or were you a passenger
On the ship of somebody else, who set out again
As soon as they put you ashore?"
        And resourceful Odysseus
Replied: "I'll gladly tell you all about myself.
I'm from Alybas, where I live in a marvelous palace,
For I am the son of Apheidas the King, and the grandson
Of Polypemon. My own name is Eperitus. When I sailed
        from Sicania,
I had no idea of coming here, but a god
Drove me off course, and now my ship is moored
Well out from town not far from an open field.
But concerning Odysseus, it is going on five years now
Since that unfortunate man journeyed on from my country.
Yet, at the time, he had birds of good omen, birds
On the right, which made us both glad as we said good-by
In a spirit of hope that someday we'd meet again
In most hospitable surroundings and exchange fine presents."
        At this a black cloud of grief enveloped Laertes
And taking a dark double-handful of dust he poured it
Upon his gray head, while one groan followed another.
As he watched his dear father, the heart of Odysseus was moved
And at once his nostrils tingled with keen compassion.
Quickly he went and took the old King in his arms
And kissed him, saying:
        "I myself am the man, Father,

401

Right here with you, the same man you ask about!
I've reached my own country again in the twentieth year.
But stop the weeping and wailing, so that I can tell you
What's happened. Believe me, we've no time at all to waste.
Back in our palace I've killed the insolent wooers
And exacted full payment for all their horrible outrages
And malicious behavior!"
      Then again Laertes answered:
"If you are indeed my son Odysseus, give me
Some proof, clear and convincing."
      And resourceful Odysseus:
"First take a look at this scar, the result of a wound
Which I received on Parnassus from the sharp white tusk
Of a boar. You sent me on that trip yourself, you
And my lady mother, to visit her father Autolycus
And receive the gifts which he, on a visit to us,
Had sincerely promised to give me. But come, I'll tell you
The very trees in this well-planted orchard that you
Once gave me when I was a child, following you
All over the farm and asking a thousand questions.
We passed through these identical trees and you told me
The names of them all and talked to me about them.
And you gave me some trees of my own—thirteen pear,
Ten apple, and forty fig, and you told me the names
Of various vines and gave me fifty rows
In the vineyard here, upon which the clusters hang heavy
At different times throughout the season, as the weather
Of Zeus weighs them down from above."
      As he too remembered
The days Odysseus so surely described, his father
Grew weak in the knees and his old heart faint. He threw
Both arms about his dear son, and the noble Odysseus,
Patient and strong, held him close till his spirit revived.
When he had collected himself again, the old King

Spoke thus:

"O Father Zeus, surely you gods
Are still there on lofty Olympus, if truly the wooers
Have paid for their wickedness and folly. But now in my heart
I've a terrible fear that all the men in Ithaca
Will descend on us here and send out for help to cities
Throughout Cephallenia."

To which his capable son:
"Cheer up, and try not to worry about it. Let us go
To the house back there by the orchard, where I sent Telemachus,
The cowman, and swineherd to fix us a meal in a hurry."

When they reached the attractive and comfortable house,
they found
Telemachus, the cowman, and swineherd carving an abundance
Of meat and mixing the sparkling wine. Then,
While the old Sicilian bathed great-hearted Laertes,
Rubbed him richly with oil, and helped him into
A fine cloak, Athena approached and greatly improved
The physique of the people's shepherd, so that he seemed taller
And better built than before. When he came from the bath
Like an immortal god, his son could hardly believe
What he saw, and his words came winged with wonder:

"Surely,
My father, one of the gods everlasting has made you
Seem taller and better looking than ever."

Then Laertes
Answered with spirit, saying: "I only wish,
O Father Zeus, Athena, and Apollo, that I
Was still the man I was when I, as King
Of the Cephallenians, took the fort of firm-founded Nericus
On the mainland cape, and so might have stood by your side
With armor about my shoulders in our house yesterday
And battled the wooers. You would have joyed to see

403

The number of knees that buckled on my account!"
        While they were talking, the others finished the carving,
And now they sat down in the chairs, both reclining and straight,
And started to help themselves, when the aged Dolius
Came in with his sons, weary from working. Their mother,
The old Sicilian woman, had gone out and called them,
She who saw to their raising and took good care
Of their father, now that old age had hold of him.
When they saw Odysseus and knew who he was, they stopped
In their tracks, stunned with amazement. Then Odysseus spoke
With kind and gentle wit:
        "Come on, old man,
Sit down to your dinner—and the rest of you, don't look
So surprised. We've been waiting here a long time, eager
To eat, but expecting you every moment."
        At this,
Dolius covered the distance between them with both
Of his arms outstretched, took the hand of Odysseus
And kissed him on the wrist, then spoke to him
These winged words: "Beloved master, you have
Come back to us, who wanted to see you so much
But never thought that we would. Now the gods themselves
Have brought you—so greetings and the gladdest of
                welcomes, and may
Those same gods give happiness to you. But tell me frankly,
For I'd like to find out: does wise Penelope know
That you've really returned, or shall we send her the news?"
        And the able Odysseus replied: "She knows already,
Old friend. No need to bother yourself about that."
        He spoke, and Dolius sat down on a polished low seat.
And now his sons surrounded great Odysseus
And welcomed him warmly with words and hearty handshakes.
Then they took their seats by Dolius their father.
        While those at the farm were busy eating, quickly

The messenger Rumor went all over town, telling
The terrible news of death and fate for the wooers.
The people all seemed to hear it at once, and they came
On the run from all directions, murmuring and moaning,
To the house of Odysseus. Then each of them bore out
And buried his dead, and those from other cities
They put aboard swift ships, that seamen might carry
Them home. Then sadly they went in a body to the place
Of assembly. Once there and suitably seated, Eupeithes
Stood up to speak, for grief unending bore down
On his heart, grief for his son Antinous, the first man
To die at the hands of brave Odysseus. Weeping,
He addressed the assembly:
      "Surely, my friends, this man
Has caused the Achaeans no end of monstrous trouble.
He sailed away with many fine men in his ships
And proceeded to lose forever both ships and men.
Returning he murders the pick of the Cephallenians!
But quick, before he can flee to Pylos or sacred
Elis, the Epeans' domain, let us go in pursuit,
Or we'll never be able to live with ourselves again!
If we don't take vengeance on those who have murdered our sons
And brothers, even our children's children will hear
Our story with shame. To me, at least, life
Would no longer be sweet. I'd sooner die now and take
My place with the dead. But quick, let's go! We'll be
Altogether too late, if they get across the wide water."
      At these tearful words, all the Achaeans felt pity.
Then Medon and the sacred bard approached the assembly.
They had just waked up and left the house of Odysseus,
And now the Ithacans wondered to see them stand
In their midst. Then thoughtful Medon spoke to them thus:
      "Hear me, O Ithacans, and believe me when I say
That Odysseus did what he did with divine assistance.

I myself saw an immortal, exactly resembling
Mentor, stand close by the side of Odysseus. At times
He'd appear before him urging him on. Then again
He would storm through the hall throwing panic into the wooers
And heaping them up around him."

      He spoke, and they all
Turned pale with fear. Then the old hero Halitherses,
Son of Mastor, spoke. His vision alone
Included both past and future, and now with all
Good intentions he addressed the assembly: "Hear me, Ithacans,
And consider what I have to say. These things have happened,
My friends, because of your own irresponsible weakness.
For you wouldn't listen to me, nor to Mentor, shepherd
Of the people, and make your sons desist from wickedness
And folly. They did a terrible thing, wantonly
Wasting the wealth and insulting the wife of a King,
Who they said would never return. But now pay attention
To me and do as I tell you. Let none of us go
In pursuit, or many of you may bring still more
Unhappiness on yourselves!"

      At this, over half
The assembly leaped up with battle cries and rushed
For their weapons, while all the others stayed put. In sympathy
With Eupeithes, heedless of Halitherses, the avengers
Clad their bodies in gleaming bronze and mustered
Just outside of town on a wide open field. Eupeithes
Foolishly took command. He thought to avenge
The death of his son, but he himself was never
To come back alive, for on that very day
He overtook his fate.

      Now Athena spoke thus
To Zeus, the son of Cronos: "O our Father
And lord of lords, tell me what hidden purpose
You now have in mind. Is it your will that evil

War and horrible uproar of battle should arise
Between them, or will you join them in friendship again?"
      To this appeal, cloud-gathering Zeus replied:
"My child, why ask me of these things? Was it not
All your own idea for Odysseus to come
And properly punish the wooers? You do as you please,
But here's what I think is right. Since noble Odysseus
Has settled accounts with the wooers, let the rest of his people
Swear an oath in good faith and solemnize their word
With sacrifice, that he may be their King as long as
He lives, and we will cause them all to forget
And forgive the slaying of sons and brothers. Then,
As before, let them love one another and live mid peace
And plenty."
      He spoke, and Athena, who needed no urging,
Flew into action, as down she went darting from the peaks
Of Olympus.
      When those at the farm had finished their meal
Of food delicious as honey, enduring Odysseus
Spoke to them thus: "Somebody go out and see
How close they are."
      So one of Dolius' sons
Got up. When he reached the threshold he saw the whole
          company
Bearing down on the house, and his words flew back to Odysseus
Winged with excitement: "Here they are now, right on us!
Quick, everybody, get ready to fight!"
      They sprang
To their feet and put on their armor. Odysseus and his men
Were four, the sons of Dolius six, and the two
Gray-headed old men, Laertes and Dolius, put on
Their armor too, soldiers by force of need.
When all were clad in the gleaming bronze, they opened
The doors and went out, with Odysseus leading the way.

    Then Athena, daughter of Zeus, with the form and voice
Of Mentor, approached, and the noble, long-suffering Odysseus
Rejoiced to see her and at once spoke thus to the dear son
Beside him: "Telemachus, now in the heat of battle
Where the best men are tested, you'll learn how not to disgrace
The house of your fathers, who have at all times been best
In valor and manly prowess all over the world."
    To which his thoughtful son: "In my present mood,
Dear father, I warrant I'll bring no disgrace, as you put it,
Upon your house!"
    He spoke, and Laertes exulted,
Saying: "What a day, O precious gods,
This is for me! How joyful can a man be?
Here are my son and grandson trying their best
To outdo each other in valor and manly achievement!"
    Then the blue-eyed goddess Athena stood by the old King
And spoke to him thus: "O Arceisius' son, by far
The best friend I have, pray now to the blue-eyed maid
And Father Zeus, then quick as you can draw back
Your long-shadowing spear and let it fly!"
    So saying,
Pallas Athena inspired the aged Laertes
With strength for a mighty effort. He made his prayer
To the daughter of almighty Zeus, then quickly drew back
His long-shadowing spear and hurled it. It pierced Eupeithes
Through the bronze cheek-piece of his helmet. The point
        of the spear
Cut through with ease, and he crashed to the ground with a thud
And a clanging of armor. Then Odysseus fell on the front rank
Of fighters along with his gallant son, and they beat them
Back with swords and two-pointed spears. And now
Not one of their foes would ever have gone back alive
If Athena, daughter of Zeus who bears the aegis,

Had not cried out and stopped the battle:
    "Enough!
You Ithacans. Cease your miserable fighting and go
Your separate ways without further shedding of blood."
    At the sound of her voice, pale fear gripped all of them **hard.**
They threw down their weapons and headed for town, all eager
To go on living. But the stalwart, courageous Odysseus
Uttered a terrible cry, and gathering himself
For a charge he plunged upon them like a high-flying eagle,
At exactly the moment when Cronos' son hurled down
A flaming bolt of thunder that landed directly
In front of the mighty Father's bright-eyed daughter.
Then Athena, her blue eyes blazing, spoke thus to Odysseus:
    "Son of Laertes, Zeus-born, resourceful man,
Hold back! and end the brawling of war, disastrous
To all, before you offend far-thundering Zeus."
    She spoke, and the heart of Odysseus was glad to obey.
Then Pallas Athena, daughter of aegis-bearing Zeus,
She who appeared like Mentor in form and voice,
Made a sacred and lasting covenant of peace between them.

409

INDEX

The following index shows syllabic accent for most of the proper names in this book and gives selected page numbers for their occurrence.

415